STRUCTURED LUCK

Contents

	List of Illustrations	ix
	About the Author	xi
	Acknowledgments	xiii
	Introduction: Lucky Winners	1
Chapter 1	The Diversity Immigrant Visa Program and Structured Luck	13
Chapter 2	A Context of Desperation: "Why Does Everyone Want to Go Abroad?"	37
Chapter 3	"Come, Let Us Play the Lottery!"	55
Chapter 4	Diversity Visa Entrepreneurs in Ghana and Unintended Consequences	75
Chapter 5	Disrupted Undergraduates: A Created Category of Diversity Immigrants	116
Chapter 6	"We Are Talking About American Citizenship"	141
Chapter 7	Conclusion: Making Sense of the Lucky Win	158
	Methodological Appendix	177
	Notes	183
	References	209
	Index	223

https://doi.org/10.7758/gibz4552.2298

Illustrations

Figure 1.1	Predicted Differences in Ln Income by Admission Category between Time 1 and Time 2	36
Table I.1	Forms of Migrapolicy Interventions	8
Table 1.1	Diversity Immigrant Visa Program	26
Table 5.1	Disrupted Undergrads' Education and Work Experiences	124
Table A.1	How Diversity Immigrants Fare in the U.S. Labor Market: Mixed-Effects Linear Models Predicting Ln Income in the United States	178
Table A.2	Post-Hoc Differential Analysis by Class of Admission	180
Table A.3	Selected Impactful Experiences of Study Respondents	181
Photo 4.1	Street Tent near the University of Ghana–Legon Medical Campus, Accra, 2017	82
Photo 4.2	Street Tent near the Accra Mall, 2017	82
Photo 4.3	Street Tent in Circle, a Major Public Transportation Hub, Accra, Ghana, 2017	83

Photo 4.4	The Circle Street Tent and the Intracity, Intercity, and International Motor Park, Accra, Ghana, 2017	83
Photo 4.5	Street Tent near Government House, Accra, Ghana, 2017	84
Photo 4.6	Front View of Flyer Distributed by a Travel Agency, Accra, Ghana, 2017	112
Photo 4.7	Back View of Flyer Distributed by a Travel Agency, Accra, Ghana, 2017	113

About the Author

ONOSO IMOAGENE is associate professor of social research and public policy at New York University, Abu Dhabi.

Acknowledgments

THERE ARE MANY people and institutions I must thank for helping me finish this book. I wrote most of the first draft of this book while a visiting scholar at Russell Sage Foundation in the academic year 2019–2020. I must extend my sincere appreciation to the foundation for its support. I thank RSF staff and scholars for creating a stimulating intellectual environment where I developed my arguments, focused on writing, ate delicious food, and shared laughs and conversation with my fellow RSF scholars.

I must thank the leadership of New York University–Abu Dhabi in 2018—Mariet Westerman, Fabio Piano, and Herve Cres—for agreeing to cosponsor my first year at the university to be a visiting scholar at RSF. I thank the program head of Social Research and Public Policy at that time, David Cook-Martin, for taking the request to leadership and for his comments during a talk on the project that ended up shaping several arguments in the book.

I frequently tell people that I embrace the review process; even though challenging, it makes my work stronger. One of my colleagues recently described feedback from reviewers as "gifts," which is such a beautiful way to view reviewers' comments, which can sometimes be difficult to read. My colleague's perspective helped renew my resolve to be more sanguine during the revision process of this book, which in turn accelerated its completion. In helping me shape this book to what it is now, I would like to thank the three anonymous RSF reviewers for their detailed and wonderful feedback. I would also like to thank my mentor, Mary C. Waters, for reading the entire manuscript and helping me find my way through the deluge of comments. I thank my friend Van Tran for his feedback, especially on my quantitative analyses of the New Immigrant Survey included in the book. I thank members of my book club, Hewan Girma and Chinyere Osuji, who read very early drafts of the book. I thank Janet Mansfield for the insightful comments she gave me on my book over several lunches in the basement. And I send a big thank-you to Amy Tsin,

Sofya Aptekar, and Monica McDermott, fellow RSF visiting scholars, for reading and giving me great feedback on several chapters.

I thank Suzanne Nichols, Russell Sage Foundation's director of publications, for her keen summaries of what needed to be done and her patience, as it took me much longer than I expected to finish the book. I thank Tamara Nopper and Nina Shope, two extremely skilled editors, who helped me sharpen what I wanted to say. I thank my friend George Edozie, a renowned Nigerian painter whose painting, *The Last Consignment to Lampedusa*, graces the cover of this book.

I must extend my deepest gratitude to all the individuals in the United States, Nigeria, and Ghana who spoke to me for this book. I thank them for being willing to take the time and being so honest and forthcoming about their experiences. This book would not have been possible without you all.

Finally, I thank my family; of particular note, my sister Anikphe, just as with my first book, read and reread multiple drafts of this book. Thank you so much for your unwavering support and invaluable feedback. I thank my husband, Isaac, for his steadfast support. He has been my constant support through the challenges of Covid-19, a relocation to Abu Dhabi, and several life challenges. Thank you.

Introduction | Lucky Winners

THE DIVERSITY IMMIGRANT Visa Program (DV Program) is a lottery that awards winners from underrepresented countries the chance to apply for legal permanent resident status in the United States.[1] The program serves as one of the main migration pathways for Africans entering the country, yet despite its long history and increasing popularity in developing countries, there are few studies on the experiences of African diversity immigrants.[2] In an interview with Jeanine Pirro of *Fox News*, President Donald Trump in 2018 accused the program of randomly selecting low-quality immigrants to allow into the United States.[3] His remarks focused a spotlight on some of the problematic misunderstandings and misrepresentations of the lottery system.

"Lotteries" purport to give everyone an equal chance of winning, but despite its supposed "random" design, the DV Program in fact selects well-educated African immigrants to fill U.S. labor needs, diversify its immigrant streams, and become Americans. Diversity visa immigrants, regardless of country of origin, actually boast a higher rate of college degree attainment than native-born Americans.[4] In fact, African diversity immigrants outperform Americans dramatically: 61.5 percent of them hold at least a bachelor's degree, compared to 35 percent of Americans.[5] Yet these highly skilled, highly educated, highly selected immigrants are often underutilized, their full potential denied in ways that harm not only themselves but their adopted homeland. If diversity visa winners are lucky, is it possible that they themselves are the real prize, and one that the United States is squandering?

What we will learn from the firsthand accounts of the Ghanaian and Nigerian diversity immigrants interviewed for this book, and from quantitative analysis of how diversity immigrants fare in the U.S. labor market compared to other legal immigrants, is that while the United States has done well so far with this program, it can do better. We could ease the incorporation of diversity immigrants into U.S. society and minimize the program's unintended negative consequences. Current formulations that the nation is in crisis due to unchecked immigration, especially along the U.S.-Mexico border, cannot be used to silence this call for change.

WHY THE DV PROGRAM MATTERS

If we consider that the DV Program has contributed only 5 percent of the approximately one million legal immigrants admitted to the United States each year since 2000, it might seem that studying the program and its participants is not worthy of scholarly attention. But if we change the lens with which we look at the program by understanding that the visa lottery admits a diverse group of people who establish themselves within the United States and sponsor their family members, then the importance of the program becomes clear. The lottery shapes U.S. immigration flows not just within its own admittance category but also within the family-based category, which is the largest group of legal immigrants admitted each year, comprising between 60 and 70 percent of the total immigrant pool. Additionally, the fact that a significant portion of African immigrants enter the United States via the program makes the lottery worthy of study.

Since the DV Program went into full effect during the 1994–1995 fiscal year, approximately 700,000 Africans, including 390,000 sub-Saharan Africans, have entered the United States via the visa lottery. It has become a main driver for the growth of the African population in the United States. The Africans who have immigrated via the lottery have proceeded to sponsor relatives via the family reunification system, thus expanding the size of the African population within the United States from just 80,000 individuals in 1970 to 2.6 million in 2021 (or from 0.8 percent to 5.7 percent of the total immigrant population).[6] Narrowing the focus to the sub-Saharan (Black) African immigrant population, the number of Black Africans grew from a small population of 130,000 in 1980 to 2.09 million in 2018.[7] Between 1990 and 2000, diversity visas accounted for 47 percent of the rise in African migration to the United States. In the twenty-first century to date, they account for one-third of that increase.[8]

Despite the program's more than two-decade-long history, little is known about the impact of the lottery on winners, their families, and their countries of origin. U.S. migration scholars have been criticized for focusing only on what happens to immigrants within the United States and not extending their gaze beyond its borders.[9] There are exceptions to this pattern in the several excellent studies that have focused on the transnational impact of U.S. immigration laws on individuals seeking to enter the United States and on their communities, but these studies have focused largely on undocumented immigrants or migrants from Mexico and other countries in Latin America.[10] Similarly, much of the scholarship regarding the link between immigration policy and integration focuses on how U.S. immigration and criminal laws combine with enforcement to enact "legal violence," referring to the harmful ways in which U.S. law "can potentially obstruct and derail" the integration of undocumented immigrants into the United States.[11] The concept has proven useful in helping to "capture the experiences of other immigrants in unresolved legal statuses today."[12]

In many ways, the greater attention paid to undocumented immigrants is understandable, as legal status is increasingly a source of stratification—that is, immigrants with legal status are elevated to higher rungs of the stratification ladder than undocumented immigrants.[13] Documented immigrants have greater access to resources and legal protections,[14] and legal status plays a crucial role in shaping an immigrant's eligibility for housing, education, and employment.[15] Overall, the situation of legal immigrants seems far less dire in comparison to the plight of the undocumented, and that may account for the imbalance in research.

However, the focus on immigration violations, criminal laws and enforcement, Latino immigrants, and undocumented immigrants within the United States has created a gap in our knowledge of the impact of U.S. immigration policies that facilitate *legal* migration. How do such policies affect immigrants who are *not* undocumented, less skilled, or undereducated?[16] How do such policies affect immigrants who originate from communities *outside* Latin America? What is the impact of such programs *prior* to migration—when immigrants still reside in their country of origin?

Structured Luck addresses these questions within the arena of Black and African migration, with a particular focus on West African emigration. It explores the impact of the DV Program on immigrants, nonmigrants, and communities from Nigeria and Ghana. Until 2014, when Nigeria became ineligible for the diversity visa when it lost its status as an underrepresented nation, Nigerians and Ghanaians were the top applicants submitting valid entries, being selected in the lottery, and receiving diversity immigrant visas. In fiscal year 2013, Nigerians and Ghanaians together accounted for 28 percent of the 7.9 million valid lottery entries received.[17] *Structured Luck* examines the lottery's role in patterning emigration from both countries and in creating wide-ranging downstream effects for immigrants and their communities. In doing so, it fills problematic gaps in current migration research.

This book also refocuses the lens through which we view the visa lottery. Debates about the DV Program and African migration usually focus on two key issues. First, the program contributes to the loss in African sending countries of human resources and exacerbates a "brain drain" of highly skilled professionals, hindering the development of those countries.[18]

Second, although supporters argue that the program allows a more racially diverse group of immigrants, including Africans, to settle in the United States,[19] some critics claim that the increase in diversity necessitates a trade-off in immigrant quality.[20] The latter argument contradicts the concern about a brain drain by devaluing diversity immigrants. It also arises primarily from a misconception (or misrepresentation) of the visa lottery as an arbitrary system delivering randomly selected immigrants to the United States. Although both debates draw attention to important issues, they remain at the macro level and fall short of discussing the DV Program's impacts on diversity immigrants at the micro level—which is to say, the human level. I am attempting to rectify that omission.

HOPES AND DREAMS

The journey of a diversity visa immigrant begins with hope. That spark may be lit in countless ways:

- Walking to university lectures with a friend, Peter, a student in Ghana, who has no immediate thoughts of emigrating, is hailed by a stranger at a table to come "play" the U.S. visa lottery for "free."[21]

- An uncle who is living the "good life" in the United States wants to help his niece. He tells Shormeh, a nurse in Ghana, about the visa lottery and pesters her to apply. He even goes the extra mile of using his niece's passport picture to register her online for the program, thinking that, if he can't offer Shormeh money, at least he can give her this, the next best—or perhaps even better—thing.

- A coterie of white-collar workers lament the substandard pay and dismal prospects for career advancement at the office while sharing stories of people they know who are enjoying life in America. Inspired, they fill out diversity visa forms while offering prayers to the deities they believe in. They say to themselves, "What do we have to lose? We might win!" They believe that they are making their own luck by registering.

Despite the pervasive (and purposeful) aura of fortune surrounding the visa lottery, this book argues that the DV Program is entirely a process of "structured luck," from who gets to register for the lottery to how people hear about it and who chooses to participate, to the design and administration of the program's bureaucracy and the steps required to apply for the lottery and then for the immigrant visa. On the surface, the phrase "structured luck" might read as oxymoronic. As I will detail, however, the semblance of luck and of "being lucky" is part of how the DV Program is both promoted and received when, in fact, an organized and structured process governs every step of the way.

By studying the effects of the DV Program, I reveal in *Structured Luck* key mezzo- and micro-level impacts of the lottery, most of which have gone unexamined in research or have been ignored in the recent debates surrounding the program. The book answers the questions about why people migrate, addresses the aforementioned brain drain, and moves beyond those discussions to offer empirical insights gleaned from my primary research study—a set of in-depth interviews with Nigerian and Ghanaian diversity immigrants and my ethnographic observations in Accra, Ghana.

My respondents' stories reveal the successes and failures of the DV Program. For lottery winners, the program is a tool of upward mobility, most of them having succeeded in improving their lives and the lives of their family members. At the same time, their stories reveal how the lottery's design, implementation, and consequences result in substantial human capital interruption, significant exploitation within origin countries, and persistent suboptimization of immigrants' potential in the United States.[22] I coin the term "migrapolicy interventions" to label and name such consequences, arguing that several forms of migrapolicy interventions affect diversity immigrants' integration into the United States.

REDIRECTED AND DISRUPTED LIVES

My concept of "migrapolicy interventions" describes the effects of an economically advantaged country's immigration policy, experienced through its design and administration, on immigrants and in immigrant-sending countries. The concept seeks to capture both the intended and unintended consequences that immigration policy has for legal immigrants and their countries of origin—effects that can interrupt the natural order of some events, create stumbling blocks that have to be overcome by immigrants, and create new infrastructures and actors in the migration industry. This book details several forms of migrapolicy interventions that result from the structure and administration of the U.S. DV Program and that influence or interfere in the lives of diversity immigrants, their family members, and their countries of origin.

The migrapolicy interventions discussed in this book are mostly transnational (occurring in an immigrant's country of origin and in the United States); take positive, negative, or neutral forms; and occur at the micro and mezzo levels.[23] Positive forms of migrapolicy interventions facilitate socioeconomic assimilation and social well-being. Negative forms of migrapolicy interventions arise from the contradictory or unforeseen consequences that create difficulties or delay, or that derail legal immigrants' incorporation. Neutral migrapolicy interventions have a limited impact and do not cause permanent harm.

By adopting a transnational lens, we can analyze how immigration policies spread and impact nonmigrants. In West Africa, a veritable migration industry (MI) has emerged to advertise, facilitate, and monetize the DV Program. One of the mezzo-level migrapolicy interventions this book identifies is the emergence of visa entrepreneurs.[24] These entrepreneurs are fleet-footed, displaying organizational innovation as they transform or mutate their services to monetize receiving countries' immigration policies and cater to clients but also sometimes engaging in practices that compromise the well-being of migrants and their relatives.

For lottery "winners," several negative forms of migrapolicy interventions occur at the micro level. The most consequential intervention is the interruption of human capital attainment (education and skills acquisition) prior to migration. This has long-term consequences for diversity immigrants' educational and socioeconomic success in the United States. Another negative intervention is the impaired generation and activation of an immigrant's social network. The analysis performed in this book demonstrates that, despite their high education and skill levels, diversity immigrants are more likely to have limited or no social ties. In their early years in the United States, they earn less than immigrants in other admission categories but recover to attain earnings parity.

For families, negative forms of migrapolicy interventions include the creation of temporary kinship ties and transnational families, the termination of kinship bonds, and an increased vulnerability to love or marriage impostors. These interventions occur on both the micro and mezzo levels, as they affect more than just the individual immigrant.

THE POWER OF "HAVING PAPERS"

By far the most positive migrapolicy intervention is the grant of lawful permanent resident (LPR) status to diversity immigrants when they enter the United States and the pathway to citizenship achievable after the fifth year of their stay. There are significant flow-on effects from "having papers" that members of families—both families of procreation and of orientation—enjoy. (A family of procreation is the family created through marriage, and a family of orientation is the family an individual is born into or raised in.) These benefits range from better educational opportunities for diversity immigrants' children to the chance to migrate and become U.S. citizens via the family preference system for diversity immigrants' parents and siblings and their families.

The diversity immigrants interviewed for this book felt fortunate to have such opportunities. They expressed feelings of belonging to the United States, becoming what I call "affective Americans": Americans by emotion, especially gratitude. They were happy that their migration "win" had benefited their families. A more critical view of the macro processes that establish and sustain the cycle of migration correctly points out the imbalance between core countries and peripheral ones, highlighting the structures that have created and maintained the unequal relationship. But within this system, immigrants from struggling countries expressed contentment, thankfulness, and basic satisfaction, feelings that often stemmed from a frame of reference that assessed the situation in the United States as, if not fulfilling their dreams, being better than where they would have been back in their country of origin.

Such feelings of gratitude must be acknowledged if we are to better understand how migration cultures and the higher status ascribed to immigrants (especially in the Global North) help sustain immigration flows. Even as diversity immigrants work to make sense of their migration experience, reflecting on how their expectations and dreams match or do not match current realities, they rarely express regret for migrating. These positive sentiments filter home in the form of social and emotional remittances, and as they circulate they create cultures of migration by engendering in many others the desire to emigrate.

However, these positive consequences and feelings of gratitude must be discussed alongside the legitimate flaws within a system that holds real lives in the balance. The experiences of Ghanaian and Nigerian diversity immigrants indicate that we must pay more attention to the downstream effects of immigration policy. We must understand how these policies are reshaping the patterns of migration, the lives of immigrants before and after they arrive in their host country, and the people and countries they leave behind.

Table I.1 summarizes the different forms of migrapolicy interventions that are identified in this book and discussed in depth in several of the book's empirical chapters.

IN THEIR OWN WORDS

To explore the downstream effects of the DV Program on immigrants and their families, I conducted in-depth interviews between March 2016 and April 2019 with seventy-four diversity immigrants in the United States. The respondent pool comprised thirty-nine Ghanaians and thirty-five Nigerians, as well as twenty-one of their family members and seventeen of their peers in Ghana and Nigeria. Conducting the interviews myself,

Table I.1 Forms of Migrapolicy Interventions

Level		Positive Forms	Scope
Micro/immigrant	Documented immigration ("having papers")	Becoming a legal immigrant with a pathway to citizenship, a benefit obtained after winning the visa lottery and successfully completing the application process	Transnational
Micro/immigrant	American identity	As "affective Americans," feeling a sense of gratitude that the U.S. visa lottery advertises, encourages, and grants legal entry to new immigrants, even those from developing countries in the Global South	In host country (the United States)
Mezzo/family	Family win	Family members benefiting from remittances and the opportunity to obtain U.S. citizenship	Transnational
Mezzo/visa entrepreneurs	Migration facilitators	Operating as an MI actor who helps thousands register for the opportunity to migrate to the United States and who earns money by coaching migrants and applying for, preparing, and obtaining their documents	In immigrant-sending countries

Level	Negative Forms	Scope
Micro/immigrant	Negative impact on educational and socio-economic attainment	Interruption of human capital accumulation (education and skills) when lottery win delays schooling or training	Transnational (but initiated in immigrant-sending countries)
Micro/immigrant	Failed or strained social networks	Impacts on the generation of social capital	Transnational
Micro/immigrant Mezzo/family	Creation of transnational families	Family separation when some relatives do not use the diversity visa by emigrating within the window of one to one-and-a-half years	Transnational
Micro/immigrant Mezzo/family	Marital and familial instability	Divorce and broken relationships with children	Transnational
Mezzo/visa entrepreneurs	Debt burden	Possible exploitation by visa entrepreneurs, including charging lottery winners exorbitant fees to continue the process of getting the visa; entanglement of family members and community when visa recipient asks for help coming up with the money to pay fees	Transnational (though initiated in immigrant-sending countries, the impacts can carry over to the receiving country)

Source: Author's compilation.

I spoke with most study participants over the phone; some welcomed me into their homes in Pennsylvania and New Jersey. I interviewed participants from the first wave of diversity immigrants in 1995 and others who arrived later but had been in the country for at least three years.[25]

I knew thirty of the study participants. I have known them for a long time, some for decades, either as close friends or close acquaintances. I met many when they were single, and I was involved in their lives when they got married, had children, buried parents, changed jobs, bought houses, and, for a few, returned to Nigeria or Ghana. All of them graciously agreed to be formally interviewed for this study and were very open with me about their experiences as diversity immigrants and as individuals trying to support family members back home. The other forty-four participants were strangers to me at the start of this study but were equally forthcoming because of my status as a Nigerian immigrant. Many have since become friends.

I combined interviews with ethnographic observations in Accra, Ghana, during the 2017 diversity visa registration period. In addition to my observations of various street-tent registration sites, I spoke to migration industry actors who offered registration services to Ghanaians for a fee. I interviewed the owners of two diversity visa lottery businesses and eight members of their staffs. I also conducted short informal interviews with over twenty Ghanaians who were utilizing these visa entrepreneurs' services. Altogether, this book is based on in-depth interviews with 122 respondents based in the United States, Nigeria, and Ghana.

A TRANSNATIONAL JOURNEY

Structured Luck takes readers on a transnational journey in order to explore the societal, personal, and political implications of the U.S. Diversity Immigrant Visa Program.

Chapter 1 presents the history of the DV Program, situates *Structured Luck* in the larger field of literature about immigration policy and immigrant incorporation, and lays out the book's novel theoretical contributions. The chapter utilizes a longitudinal national survey of legal immigrants to examine how diversity immigrants fare compared to immigrants who enter the country via the three other major classes of legal admission: refugee status or asylum, employer sponsorship, and family preference.

Chapter 2 discusses the historical and contemporary causes of the deteriorating economic and political conditions in Ghana and Nigeria that have created a context of desperation that fuels dreams of exit among many Nigerians and Ghanaians. The chapter discusses how legacies of colonialism still affect both nations today. It also provides brief sociodemographic profiles of Nigerians and Ghanaians in the United States.

Chapter 3 discusses how potential migrants learn about the DV Program and why they choose to "play the lottery" and continue the process until they get their diversity visas. The chapter explores an important aspect of the program's structured luck by which winners are selected only from the educated classes, further entrenching the class divisions in immigrant-sending countries.

Chapter 4 discusses how visa entrepreneurs create a market for their services via cultural economies by selling expertise, professionalization, and connections. The chapter examines why immigrants work with and relate to diversity visa entrepreneurs and how the requirements of the DV Program, and thus by extension the U.S. government, have helped lay the groundwork for such actors to thrive.

Chapter 5 deals with the experiences of "disrupted undergrads": Ghanaian and Nigerian diversity immigrants who were on track to obtain university degrees but were derailed by winning the U.S. visa lottery. This chapter focuses on the interruption of human capital accumulation, one of the most negative consequences of migrapolicy interventions, and elaborates on the concept of structured luck by showing how the program's bureaucracy works in tandem with the activities of visa entrepreneurs to target high school and college students to play the visa lottery because they fit the educational profile required by the program.

Chapter 6 discusses the positive migrapolicy interventions that result from documented immigration, or "having papers," including increased status and emotional remittances that diversity immigrants enjoy in their U.S. communities and in their countries of origin. The chapter discusses how the program's class dynamics reveal the highly designed nature of the lottery process. By further delving into interviewees' responses, it explores how diversity immigrants understand their experiences and make sense of their trajectories in the United States in light of their pre-migration expectations.

In the conclusion, I revisit the concepts of structured luck and migrapolicy interventions while exploring positive aspects of the lottery program that make it a tool of upward social mobility. I discuss the importance of my examination of the DV Program to U.S. immigration policy and its contribution to furthering our understanding of African emigration, African populations, and African immigrant experiences.

LET'S WIN MORE

We think of diversity immigrants as lucky, and they think of themselves as fortunate too. This book reveals that, despite the rosy terminology, there are two sides to the coin of winning. By focusing on both the positive and negative migrapolicy interventions experienced by diversity immigrants, *Structured Luck* seeks to emphasize the impact of policy on human lives. It moves beyond macro-level debates to foreground the figure who should always be at the center of the discussion: the immigrant. The book also emphasizes what is often erased—the disorientation, trauma, broken dreams, struggles, resilience, accomplishments, and determination of immigrants who settle in an unfamiliar country where they must create home and comfort anew.

Ensuring that some diversity immigrants receive the "golden ticket" of a green card neither makes all things well with them nor excuses us as a society from doing more to improve their chances of achieving their dreams.[26] It is not idealistic to believe that the goal of migration policy should be to achieve a win-win for all key stakeholders: the immigrant, the immigrant's family, the United States, and the immigrant's country of origin. When an immigrant does not achieve their full potential, or when their dreams are derailed, it is not only the immigrant who suffers. Their host country loses something too, as do their families and country of origin.

Although the DV Program gives West African diversity immigrants an enviable opportunity to migrate as lawful permanent residents with a pathway to U.S. citizenship, the program could still be improved. The DV Program is to be commended for affirmatively encouraging people from all over the world—of every race, ethnicity, religion, age, and gender—to apply for a chance to migrate legally to the United States and pursue their dreams. We should also remember, however, that the United States gains benefits from this program, and that these benefits come with certain obligations. The program helps the United States accumulate soft power, sell an image of itself as a magnanimous and welcoming destination for immigrants,[27] and acquire a steady and motivated stream of educated immigrants who help meet the nation's labor needs.

Structured Luck argues that such benefits ought to come with responsibilities and, at the very least, with a commitment to minimize the unintended negative consequences of the DV Program. U.S. politicians and policymakers have clearly expressed their interest in attracting more skilled migrants, but this stance becomes incoherent when they actively undermine the goals of the DV Program and neglect the skilled immigrants it has already brought in. Policymakers must be mindful of unintended consequences and craft policies that balance the interests of all stakeholders. And ultimately, citizens must reflect about immigration and engage in public conversations about it in order to build the political will needed to inspire change and turn a win-lose "game" into a win-win for all involved—immigrants and their families, the host country, and the immigrants' country of origin.

Chapter 1 | The Diversity Immigrant Visa Program and Structured Luck

OWING TO THE educational requirements of the DV Program, diversity immigrants are human capital immigrants.[1] The diversity visa is granted only to individuals with at least a high school diploma or its equivalent— twelve years of primary and secondary school study and a passing grade on the required graduation exams. The requirement can be met by work experience if an individual has an occupation that demands a specified level of preparation and training.[2] Human capital is defined by how much education and training a person possesses. Highly educated human capital immigrants hold professional jobs in medicine, computer science, engineering, and the like. They tend to assimilate quickly and reliably achieve parity with their ethnic counterparts and often with their native-born White counterparts as well.[3] They tend not to live in ethnic enclaves, as they can choose where to live and often select more integrated, higher-income residential neighborhoods in cities and suburbs.[4] As legal human capital immigrants, diversity immigrants find themselves elevated to a "preferred" status among the population of foreign-born occupants of the United States.[5]

Somewhat ironically, there has been limited study of diversity immigrants to date (thus disadvantaging the advantaged), owing in part to their legal status, their preferential treatment, and their relative success. According to sociologists Richard Alba and Victor Nee:

> Human capital immigrants have been less a focus of research than traditional labor migrants in part because they tend to assimilate economically and culturally within a relatively short time after their arrival. Those educated abroad, after a period of downward adjustment, appear to shift into jobs commensurate with their education, as they acquire local work experience and facility with the English language.[6]

However, Alba and Nee's assessment fails to capture a huge part of the story for human capital immigrants, who face persistent suboptimization and deferred, or even derailed, dreams. We must consider how the very policy that recruits such immigrants might hinder and slow their assimilation or impact their experiences in the United States. Alba and Nee's assurance that human capital immigrants "appear to shift into jobs commensurate with their education" needs unpacking so that we can understand the challenges that immigrants face as they attempt to do this, learn what strategies they use, recognize what the process looks like, and determine how fully it succeeds. In investigating these questions, *Structured Luck* fills some of the gaps in our understanding of human capital immigrants' experiences in the United States and adds to what we know about the link between immigration policy and immigrant integration.

PART 1: RULE MAKERS

A History of the Diversity Immigrant Visa Program

The origins of the diversity visa are profoundly ironic. The DV Program emerged from a call to increase "cultural diversity" by bringing more White immigrants (especially Irish migrants) to the United States, yet it has nonetheless become a significant driver of African migration.

The program was initially a response to unintended consequences of the Immigration and Nationality Act of 1965 (commonly known as the Hart-Celler Act). Because the act replaced the national quota system with a preference system based on family reunification, policymakers and members of Congress did not expect substantial increases in the number of immigrants or fundamental changes in the ethnic and racial makeup of the immigrant stream.[7] But by the 1980s, in the aftermath of eliminating the national quota system, most legal immigrants were coming from Asian and Latin American countries to reunite with family members.

Abolishing national quotas opened the United States to migration from all over the world. Declining economic conditions pushed Asian and Latin American nationals to migrate overseas, and many chose the United States as their destination because they felt they could earn higher wages there and send more money back home to their families. U.S. refugee policy also helped to increase the number of immigrants from Latin America and Asia, as the U.S. government used the policy as part of its arsenal to fight communism during the Cold War (and in the aftermath of the U.S. wars fought in Korea and Vietnam).

Via presidential parole power, US presidents sometimes bypassed Congress and settled migrants outside of established preference categories and quotas established by the 1965 Hart-Celler Act. Between 1975 and mid-1980, presidential parole allowed about 690,000 Cubans and 360,000 refugees from Southeast Asia to resettle in the United States.[8] The passage of the Immigration Reform and Control Act of 1986 (IRCA), which granted amnesty to undocumented immigrants who had been in the United States before 1981, accelerated the process of family reunification. Together, those developments changed the ethnic makeup of U.S. immigration as Asian and Latin American nationals came to dominate migration flows.

In response, a group of young Irish immigrants formed the Irish Immigration Reform Movement (IIRM) in 1987 to lobby for a permanent law that would make visas available to Irish immigrants outside of the family preference system and offer legal status to Irish immigrants already residing in the United States.[9] The IIRM advocated on behalf of a group of Irish citizens who had traveled to the United States in the 1980s because of an economic downturn in Ireland. They overstayed their visas and became undocumented immigrants. Most could not regularize their stay via IRCA because they had arrived in the United States after the policy's cutoff date for amnesty. The leaders of IIRM, Sean Benson and Sean Minihane, stated that they wanted more immigrant visas to be awarded to countries "adversely affected by the 1965 law."[10] That language referred to thirty-six countries that were predominantly in Europe.

IIRM and other Irish-American lobbies traded on Ireland's history with the United States, explicitly arguing for special treatment for the Irish. But they veiled their self-interest in the language of cultural diversity, which was a key goal of U.S. immigration reform in the 1980s. They argued that admitting more Irish and European immigrants would lead to greater immigrant diversity while preserving a proven and successful model of immigrant assimilation. They claimed that doing so would also prevent any particular ethnic or national group from dominating U.S. immigration and would uphold the U.S. identity as a nation of immigrants.[11] Their pitch proved persuasive and brought on board several influential policymakers, including Senator Charles Schumer (D-NY), Senator Edward Kennedy (D-MA), Senator Alan Simpson (R-WI), Congressman Brian Donnelly (D-MA), and Speaker of the House Thomas P. O'Neill.[12] Most were of Irish ancestry.

Donnelly, who described himself as an "Irish kid from Dorchester," sponsored several lottery programs, all named after him, that favored the Irish.[13] These programs were followed by the Berman program. Congressman Howard Berman (D-CA) represented a district in California that was heavily populated by Asians and Latinos, and so he did not have undocumented Irish constituents to advocate for. He felt that the United States should not be so partial in addressing only the concerns of the Irish and other Europeans. As a result, his program made ten thousand visas available to independent migrants from underrepresented countries, defined by the U.S. government as countries whose citizens received less than five thousand immigrant visas, which was 25 percent of the maximum immigrant visas available in 1988. Under this formulation, 162 countries were eligible. The Berman program was a test run that would show how well the U.S. government could run a worldwide lottery program. But the Irish lobby was unhappy: even though the Berman program was widely advertised in Irish communities, only 362 Irish received visas. The majority of visas were received by citizens of Bangladesh, Pakistan, Egypt, and Peru.[14]

The pro-European lobby and IIRM went back to work. The Diversity Immigrant Visa Program was created in 1990 in response to their lobbying efforts.[15] It went into full effect in fiscal year 1995, with a three-year (1992–1994) transition period that delivered on the demands made by the pro-European lobby. The transition program, named after Congressman Bruce Morrison (D-CT), made forty thousand immigrant visas available per year to nationals of countries adversely affected by the 1965 Immigration Act. A special provision in the transition program reserved 40 percent of those visas for "the foreign state the natives of which received the greatest number of visas under section 314 of the Immigration Reform and Control Act," also known as the Donnelly visa program (or NP-5). Since Ireland had won most of the Donnelly visas, Irish nationals received at least forty-eight thousand of the transition visas.[16]

As it currently stands, the DV Program gives independent immigrants—individuals who have no family ties or employment offers in the United States—as well as individuals from countries that have not traditionally been sending countries an opportunity to become lawful permanent residents. The program employs a formula that allocates most of the immigrant visas to the regions that send the fewest immigrants to the United States—Europe, Africa, and Oceania—and the formula is linked to each region's population.[17] A smaller allocation was awarded to Asia and Latin America since they already received nearly 87 percent of preference admissions at the time the program was enacted.[18] Beginning in 1995, fifty-five thousand annual visas were awarded under the diversity program, but the number decreased to fifty thousand in 1999, with no country receiving more than 7 percent of the visas. That created a cap of thirty-five hundred diversity visas per nation.[19] According to the program's rules, nationals of countries that receive more than fifty thousand immigrant visas in any preceding five-year period become ineligible because their citizens are no longer considered underrepresented in the United States.[20]

As the original bill made its way through Congress, lawmakers decided that awarding points for education level and English fluency (as Canada does) would be too expensive and burdensome to administer, as qualifications would need to be verified and could lead to fraud.[21] Instead, Congress settled on an educational requirement and a lottery. Designing the program as a lottery, for convenience and cost savings, set in motion a process of structured luck that has governed the program ever since.

"Shithole Countries"

The DV Program gained attention in 2018 when reports leaked that President Donald Trump had railed against the visa lottery, asking, "Why are we having all these people from shithole countries come here?"[22] President Trump's remark came in an Oval Office meeting with several U.S. senators on January 11, 2018, to discuss the contours of a bipartisan immigration bill that would cut the DV Program's yearly allotment of fifty thousand immigrant visas by half and, as advocated by the Congressional Black Caucus (CBC), reserve the diversity visas for underrepresented African countries and countries with temporary protected status (TPS), including Haiti.[23] Trump was unhappy with this proposal, asking, "Why do we need more Haitians? Take them out."[24] In the same meeting, he asked why Americans could not get more immigrants from Norway. The leaked comments drew a worldwide response. President Trump later denied making the comments, only admitting to using "tough" language during the meeting.[25]

Condemnations of President Trump's language were swift and vehement: the African Union, the fifty-five-member umbrella body of African nations, said it was "frankly alarmed."[26] The Botswanan government released a press statement proclaiming, "We view the utterances by the current American President as highly irresponsible, reprehensible and racist."[27] Critics agreed with the sentiment expressed by the Botswanan government, accusing Trump of saying the silent part out loud: that most immigration restrictionists in the United States did not want immigrants from certain countries—those that were predominantly Black, Latino, Middle Eastern, or Asian—but were happy to receive immigrants from countries viewed as providing "good," White, "traditional" immigrants, like the Scandinavian countries and western European countries.

This was not the first time President Trump had complained about the DV Program. One key objection he had with this program and similar ones was that the indirect effect of U.S. family preference systems would allow "chain migration." Immigrants from "shithole" countries would sponsor their low-skilled relatives, causing mass migration to the United States from nations he deemed undesirable. But Trump lobbed attacks against the DV Program for another reason as well. On many occasions, particularly at the rallies he organized, the president, when accusing the United States of not being smart, would launch broadsides against the diversity program for not getting the "best people." In an interview with Jeanine Pirro of *Fox News* on February 24, 2018, Trump stated:

> We need something to do with chain migration and something to do with visa lottery. I mean, we actually have lottery systems where you go to countries and they do lotteries for who comes into the United States. Now, you know they are not going to have their best people in the lottery, because they're not going to put their best people in a lottery. They don't want to have their good people to leave. We want people based on merit. Not based on the fact they are thrown into a bin and many of those people are not the people you want in the country, believe me.[28]

I highlight President Trump's misleading remarks because, as the face and head of the U.S. government, he denigrated the DV Program in comments that were heard by millions of Americans. His words amplified similar views held by people in key administration roles in homeland security and the citizenship and immigration agencies (many of whom were his appointees) as well as in Congress. Such officials shape U.S. immigration policy, and such commentary can shape American opinions.

The debate surrounding the DV Program says much about the fight over how to define "who is an American." Support for the program has eroded on Capitol Hill as fewer and fewer immigrants arrive from countries that enjoy a long immigration history with the United States—such as Italy, Ireland, Britain, and Germany—and more arrive from African countries. The lack of enthusiasm in some quarters of U.S. society for this development can be read as resistance to the fact that the program is not bringing people from majority-White, European countries. And yet this is a misconception: on average, 30 percent of the visas are awarded to Europeans, 15 percent to Asians, and 40 percent to Africans.[29] It must be noted that the Europeans coming to the United States under this program are not from the "traditional" European countries that have long relationships with the United States but from the newer European countries that emerged from the defunct Soviet Union bloc—countries such as Uzbekistan, Azerbaijan, and Kazakhstan.

A recent change instituted for fiscal year 2021 that requires program entrants to provide the number of an unexpired international passport at the time of application for the lottery—a seemingly colorblind administrative change to prevent fraudulent entrance that, in fact, aligned with the Trump administration's efforts to curb both legal and illegal immigration—reduced the number of African applications to less than half of what they were in fiscal year 2020, when the total number of applications from African countries was 11.32 million. With the change the following year, the total number of applications from African countries was 4.9 million.[30] The African region was the hardest hit by this change; Africa's total number of applications dropped by 57 percent, Asia's by 34 percent, Europe's by 45 percent, North America's (consisting only of the Bahamas) by 39 percent, Oceania's by 29 percent, and those from South and Central America and the Caribbean by 40 percent.[31] The time and expense involved in getting an international passport works to reinforce selectivity in the diversity visa process. Many citizens do not have international passports unless they need them for international travel; such a need places these passport holders near or at the top of their country's class structure. This rule change exemplifies how African immigration to the United States has been increasingly limited, imperiled, and begrudged by U.S. policymakers and politicians like former president Donald Trump.

The DV Program is not rapidly changing the racial and ethnic composition of the United States. The program accounts for only fifty thousand of the one million immigrant visas granted, on average, each year. And even that number is overshadowed by the more than forty-two million people, on average, who enter the United States annually. They include people who cross the U.S.-Mexico border without papers, those who overstay their nonimmigrant visas, and those who transition from nonimmigrant visas to legal permanent resident status.[32]

Not Norway: A Brief History of African and Caribbean Migration

The Diversity Immigrant Visa Program is important to Africa because it fosters new streams of immigration from the continent to the United States. Unfortunately for President Trump and others who hold sentiments similar to his, citizens of economically advantaged countries like Norway do not play the U.S. visa lottery in large numbers, as most citizens of these countries have minimal reason to migrate to the United States.[33] But the program is reaching its objective of diversifying the immigrant streams to the United States, as an almost equal number of diversity visas are awarded to citizens of African countries as are awarded to citizens from European countries, with the majority of European visas awarded to citizens of Russia and less-privileged European countries such as Uzbekistan,

Azerbaijan, Turkey, Moldova, and Belarus, to name a few. Under constantly revised regional calculations, about 40 percent or more of the visas awarded each year go to Africans and another 30 percent or more go to Europeans.[34]

Apart from Africans' forced migration to the United States through the transatlantic slave trade, voluntary migration of Africans to the United States has been highly restricted throughout most of its history. A 1790 law limited naturalization—the process by which a migrant attains U.S. citizenship—to free White persons. This restriction was subsequently embedded in the Immigration Act of 1924 (Johnson-Reed Act), which barred the admission of "aliens" who were ineligible for citizenship—meaning all non-Whites—and severely limited the visas available to African and Caribbean countries, as the quotas were based on 1890 admissions data.

Even though the 1965 Immigration Act (Hart-Celler Act) ended the national-origin quotas that had previously limited African immigration, the lack of Africans in the United States at the time of the law's passage kept opportunities for Africans to migrate negligible until passage of the 1980 Refugee Act and 1986 IRCA. Prior to 1980, the only significant stream of voluntary African migration to the United States was Cape Verdean migration to New England. The Refugee Act admitted refugees and started streams of migration from Liberia, Sudan, Ethiopia, Eritrea, Somalia, and the Democratic Republic of Congo. The Temporary Protected Status (TPS) Act, which was included in several immigration bills in the 1990s, benefited certain Africans who were temporarily in the United States and unable to return to their countries. Through IRCA, 300,000 Africans became permanent residents.[35] All of these acts increased African migration but did so starting from a historically low level rooted in the initial discrimination against Black immigrants.

Black Caribbeans also had minimal opportunities to migrate to the United States during the period when country quotas were in effect, as few of them were living in the United States at the time of the 1890 census on which the country quotas were based. But there were more Black Caribbeans in the United States at that time compared to Africans. The groundwork for mass migration from the Caribbean Islands was laid in the early 1900s by the cultivation of bananas as a cash crop, which created transportation systems that brought tourists to Caribbean islands and established routes to move Caribbeans to the United States. Migration from the islands also increased after Caribbeans, who had been recruited to build the Panama Canal and become accustomed to higher wages, began migrating to the United States in search of jobs with higher wages.[36] Few Caribbean immigrants arrived in the United States during the second migration wave, between 1924 and 1967. During that period, the Caribbean colonies were grouped with their respective "mother countries," and so, for example, citizens of British Caribbean colonies could enter the United States as British subjects. However, Britain had a large country quota of 34,007 individuals, which went unfilled. Officials at the U.S. consulates in migrants' home countries, which had been newly established under the Johnson-Reed Act, discriminated against Caribbean applicants, refusing them entry visas. As a result, most Caribbeans who chose to migrate during this time opted to resettle in Britain instead.[37] In 1924, 10,000 Afro-Caribbeans migrated to the United States. This number fell to 308 in 1925 and settled at an annual average of 617 from 1924 to 1932.[38]

Since 1967, when contemporary migration began, the population of Caribbeans in the United States has increased dramatically, fueled by economic hardships in their countries of origin and by a 1962 British immigration law that eliminated the visa waiver for citizens of non-majority-White British Commonwealth countries. The IRCA law and changes in U.S. refugee policy, which increased the flow of refugees from Haiti, also helped increase the number of Caribbean immigrants in the United States. The IRCA law allowed 100,000 undocumented immigrants from English-speaking Caribbean countries to become legal permanent residents.[39] During the third wave of migration, many Caribbeans who could not enter the United States via the family preference system entered with visas reserved for people with certain skills that could receive certification from the U.S. Department of Labor. It was easy to obtain certification for two occupations—nursing and domestic service. As a result, contemporary Caribbean migration to the United States was dominated by nurses and domestic workers and skewed majority-female.[40]

From the 1960s through the 1980s, most Black immigrants came from the Caribbean, but since the 1990s, the majority (over 60 percent) have come from Africa.[41] Because of their significantly larger migration numbers, certain Caribbean countries, including Jamaica, were not seen as under-represented when the Diversity Immigrant Visa Program was created, and thus their citizens could not use this pathway to enter the United States.

Even though the DV Program has become an important channel for African migration to the United States, there are still insufficient means by which Black immigrants can enter the United States. Black immigrants (Caribbeans and Africans) comprise about 15 percent of the annual growth in lawful permanent residents (which is, on average, one million a year). However, they represent only 5 percent of the forty million non-immigrants (students and temporary visa holders) who enter the United States each year, 7 percent of unauthorized immigrants, and less than 4 percent of professional-class visa holders.[42] Europeans constitute a similar percentage of LPRs (14 percent), while dominating the non-immigrant group at

40 percent and comprising 29 percent of professional-class visa holders.[43] Latinos and Asians each receive about one-third of the permanent resident visas awarded each year, Asians are 29 percent of the professional class of workers, and Latinos dominate among unauthorized immigrants at 77 percent.[44] What these figures tell us is that while all other racial groups have multiple opportunities to enter the United States—as immigrants, non-immigrants, or nonmigrant workers—Africans have minimal avenues beyond the legal permanent resident route, of which the diversity visa is a foundational part that enables further African migration via family-based migration.

The "Best People"

Following the Trump administration's hostility to the DV Program, the 2021 Citizenship Act, written and introduced by the Biden administration, stands out as a promising and surprising change, as it calls for an increase in diversity visas, from fifty thousand to eighty thousand. Previous comprehensive immigration bills that were drafted, deliberated upon, or voted on proposed terminating or severely curtailing the DV Program. One such bill, proposed in 2013 and 2014 during the Obama administration, died in the U.S. Congress because Speaker John Boehner (R-OH) refused to put it on the floor for a vote. However, the legislative record reflects the fact that critics of the diversity lottery had succeeded in convincing many lawmakers that the program was not worth retaining. All of these immigration bills, even the one proposed in 2021, have sought to move the U.S. immigration system to one based more on skills-based visas, as that is seen as a better way to meet the economic interests of the United States.

While we can trouble the idea of "the best immigrants" by questioning the focus on skills and formal education that undergirds the discourse of merit, the claim that the diversity visa does not bring in "the best" is simply not true. According to the New Immigrant Survey (NIS), a nationally representative sample of legal immigrants in the United States, 50 percent of all diversity immigrants have at least a bachelor's degree (32 percent with a bachelor's degree and 18 percent with a graduate degree).[45] Africans overperform in this category: 61.5 percent of African diversity immigrants and 62.5 percent of Nigerians and Ghanaians possess at least a bachelor's degree.[46] Those rates are higher than the U.S. national average of 35 percent.[47]

How is it that a program based on a lottery has become exclusionary? How has it developed into a system that selects the best-educated immigrants from the least-educated countries, especially in Africa? This "surprising" result is in fact a structured element of the selectivity built into the program, and it has nothing to do with luck or chance. In truth, the lottery program "structures luck" through its educational requirement. In the early years of the program, tailors, painters, and mechanics were deemed eligible to get diversity visas, but no longer. Individuals who are not formally educated, those who lack a high-quality education, and the unskilled and the semiskilled need not bother to apply; even if they do apply and win the visa lottery, they will be deemed ineligible to continue the application process. In other words, the United States has upskilled the Diversity Visa Program.[48] Such limitations guarantee that those who ultimately secure a U.S. visa are selected only from the educated or skilled classes in each eligible country.

Indeed, the requirements of the diversity visa shape the educational profiles of sub-Saharan African immigrants. When compared to the national college averages and literacy rates of many developing countries, the United States is certainly getting "the best" individuals from these countries in terms of educational attainment. For example, in Nigeria, only 7 percent of the population possesses at least a bachelor's degree, and that is the highest percentage among all West African countries. Yet 62 percent of Nigerians in the United States have at least a bachelor's degree.[49]

With its intense selectivity, the diversity visa should in fact qualify as a highly skilled immigrant program in line with stated U.S. interests. Unfortunately, despite the fact that the DV Program brings in well-educated immigrants, particularly from African countries, the only remaining defenders of the program in Congress are members of the Congressional Black Caucus, who acknowledge that the program gives independent immigrants from Africa an opportunity to migrate to the United States. (Frustrating as this is, it is somewhat heartening to consider that the CBC's support indicates that a broadening coalition of Black people are being included within the shared group identity of "the Black community" within the United States.) There is also broad support for the program among advocacy groups and labor unions.

Still, most Americans are likely to be unaware of the actual high quality of the immigrants recruited by the DV Program. The obscuring of that reality is one of many erasures implicitly and explicitly enacted by the program's structure, administration, and promotion as a "lucky win."

PART 2: WINNERS AND LOSERS

The Language of Structured Luck

The term "lottery" accurately applies only to the first phase of the DV process, into which anyone can enter; only qualified people are allowed, however, to proceed following a win. Registrants compete for a coveted "prize"—the opportunity to apply for a diversity visa that offers permanent legal residency in the United States and a pathway to citizenship. The actual visa application process that follows requires the submission and verification of numerous credentials, a health check, a police check, an interview with U.S. consular officers, and payment of fees. Only after successfully completing all these steps does a diversity immigrant truly "win" entry to the United States (a move that they must be able to self-fund).

Still, since the process begins with a lottery, selectees are seen as lucky. They have won something that applicants have an extremely low probability of attaining, and they have done so through a process that was beyond their control.[50] The language surrounding the program emphasizes notions of "playing" and "luck." It further asserts the values of "winning" and "who wins." It is strange to talk of a government program and an immigration policy in such terms.[51] But the impacts of that language on both the lottery selectees and the U.S. government are not coincidental.

For the U.S. government, this language reflects a purposeful withdrawal of responsibility for the people who win the lottery and later enter the United States. When we think of lottery winners—especially people who win jackpot (cash) lotteries—we are not particularly worried about their subsequent well-being and often view them as extremely fortunate just for winning.[52] The diversity visa is promoted as a gift bestowed upon lucky immigrants. Winning is a feature of their luck. So even though we, as a society, might want them to succeed, few people really give much thought to them after they "win." The language itself enables a kind of sink-or-swim view of their changed prospects.

The language of the lottery program affects the people who apply by denying the serious consequences of registering for a life-changing opportunity. Presenting this opportunity as "play," it encourages a "what do I have to lose" posture. The language purposely downplays the potential risks of making a spur-of-the-moment decision, encourages mass participation, and reinforces a widespread fantasy of life in the United States as the ultimate "prize."[53] Ultimately, the persistent notion of winning projects a future free of all complicating factors and obscures the massive disruptions that lottery selection entails.

Experiencing the Diversity Immigrant Visa Program

The lottery registration period opens in October and closes in November every year. The results are released online in May of the following year. Now that the program is online, individuals receive a unique confirmation number when they register, which they use to check their status once the results are released.

There is complete silence for about six months after one applies. Registrants who do not win are not contacted by the U.S. government; they must go to the results webpage, where most, after entering their confirmation number, will read a brief message that their lottery entry was not selected. Winners are not notified either; they must check the results to find out about their win.

The entire lottery process usually takes about two years from the time one applies to when one arrives in the United States. Applications are due two years prior to the fiscal year in which visas will be issued. For the 2022 Diversity Immigrant Visa Program (DV-2022), the registration period to enter the lottery opened on October 7, 2020, and closed on November 10, 2020. The winning results were released online on May 8, 2021. Selectees who decided to apply for the diversity visa could start processing their applications from the start of the 2022 fiscal year, which began on October 1 2021, and ended on September 30, 2022. To be a successful winner of the diversity visa for fiscal year 2022, the winner and their derivatives (spouses and unmarried children under age twenty-one) had to obtain their visas by the end of that fiscal year (for a step-by-step overview, see table 1.1).

On average, between 100,000 and 150,000 applicants win the lottery each year. Winners of the lottery are encouraged to submit their immigrant visa and alien registration application without delay because the program awards only 50,000 visas in each fiscal year. Even a highly skilled professional who successfully completes the process will not be awarded an immigrant visa once the cap of 50,000 is reached. In that unfortunate event, the opportunity is lost, and the individual has to register again. Not completing the visa application before the fiscal year deadline or before the cap is reached are two paths to disqualification. Lottery winners also can be disqualified for failing to meet the educational or work experience requirements, for failing their health screening, or for misrepresentation or fraud. A person who wins an immigrant visa from the program has to enter the United States within six months of the visa's issuance.

Having little to no time to prepare to become an immigrant is a function of the program's design and part of what it means to be a diversity immigrant. When people play a lottery, even if they hope that they will win, they are realistic—they know that their chances of winning are very slim. Every diversity visa application period, any one individual is competing with, on average, fifteen million other applicants. Hope and faith are very different from knowing something for sure. On the other end of the spectrum, some applicants forget that they ever registered for the lottery and may learn of their selection only after being chased down by a tenacious visa entrepreneur (see chapter 4). In that event, the time they have to complete the remaining steps in the process is radically shortened.

Table 1.1 Diversity Immigrant Visa Program

Step 1 *Submit an Entry*	Step 2 *Selection of Applicants*	Step 3 *If You Are Selected*	Step 4 *Confirm Your Qualifications*	Step 5 *Submit Your Immigrant Visa and Alien Registration Application*
Entry must be submitted electronically online. Registration opens sometime between October and November every fiscal year. Since 2020, applicants need a valid international passport to apply. Keep the unique confirmation number you are assigned. There is no cost to register.	The selection of applicants is random. On or about May 7, results are announced on the Entrant Check (E-DV) webpage. You know that you have been selected when you see that your unique confirmation number has been verified. Notification is only through the E-DV webpage.[a]	Visa lottery winners complete an online DS-260 application to schedule an interview. It is best to fill out this application immediately. Selection does not guarantee a visa.	The principal visa applicant is required to have a high school education or two years of qualifying work experience as defined by U.S. law. Visa lottery winners should not continue the process if they do not meet the education or work qualifications.	The principal applicant and all family members must complete form DS-260. If family circumstances have changed, add new family members at this stage (for example, a different spouse or additional children).

Source: Adapted from U.S. Department of State, Bureau of Consular Affairs, "Diversity Visa Program," https://travel.state.gov/content/travel/en/us-visas/immigrate/diversity-visa-program-entry/diversity-visa-submit-entry1.html.

Note: Since 2003, when the diversity visa application went online, individuals have been required to submit a single valid entry. Individuals who submit more than one entry are disqualified. The United States uses sophisticated recognition software to identify duplicate entries.

[a] A tool on the DV website allows individuals who have lost their confirmation number to retrieve it by entering the email address used to register and certain personal information.

Diversity Immigrant Visa Program   27

Step 6 *Submit Supporting Documents*	Step 7 *Interview*	Step 8 *Prepare for the Interview*	Step 9 *Applicant Interview*	Step 10 *After the Interview*
After the Kentucky Consular Center (KCC) has reviewed your application, you must submit your supporting documents online. Required documents: birth certificates, police certificates, photocopy of valid passport, biographical data page. If applicable, also submit court and prison records, and military records.	After the KCC reviews your completed DS-260, an interview is scheduled and the time and date communicated to you via email. The interview location is the U.S. embassy chosen by the principal applicant on the DS-260 form.	Schedule and complete a medical examination only at a hospital or clinic on the U.S. embassy or consulate list of approved sites. Gather all required documentation and bring originals and copies to the interview. Submit evidence of the required education or work experience. If applicable, submit the following U.S. documentation: marriage certificate, marriage termination documentation, custody documentation. Pay a fee of $330.	The principal visa applicant and, if applicable, the spouse and all qualified unmarried children must attend the interview.	Your visa application is either approved or denied. Because visas usually expire after six months from the date of issuance, you must travel within six months after that date. Ensure that all children have vaccination records. Pay the U.S. Citizenship and Immigration Services (USCIS) fee of $220.

Winning is only the beginning of the DV journey. Selectees must subsequently embark upon the visa application process, run the gauntlet of requirements, and satisfy the U.S. government's criteria to be deemed worthy of the visa. During this leg of the journey, applicants must prove that they meet the education requirement; pay the diversity visa fee, which has been set at $330 since 2012 but was $819 in 2010 and 2011[54]; chase down and acquire all needed documents, such as certificates of exam results, birth certificates, police reports, and international passports; pass a medical exam; complete their screening interview; find the money to pay for airplane tickets (one ticket for single individuals, multiple tickets for an entire family); and then, upon entering the United States, pay a $220 green card processing fee. Married couples must do all of this as well as provide a satisfactory U.S. sponsor and prove during an interview with a suspicious U.S. consular officer that their marriage is real. The diversity visa applicant must complete all these steps within twelve to fifteen months after being notified that they have won the lottery. They must literally rush to do all this while going to work (if they are employed), selling off their assets, disengaging from their lives in their country, and otherwise meeting the challenges of their daily lives.

There is not much time for deliberation. The structured randomness of selection and the shock of winning, exacerbated by the twelve- to eighteen-month window they are given to complete the process and enter the United States, puts winners under tremendous pressure, which inevitably affects their decision as to whether or not to migrate. The true window of time in which they must make a final decision is six months: it opens after their diversity visa is approved and closes when their visa for entry to the United States expires six months later.[55]

Following the screening interview with a U.S. consular officer, there is a period of uncertainty that ends only once the visa is approved. Thus, successful applicants have insufficient time to thoroughly weigh the pros and cons of migrating to the United States. They are pressured by family members to take the opportunity because they see winning the U.S. visa lottery as a family win; I explore this view in greater depth in chapter 3. Admittedly, the poor economic conditions in developing countries in the Global South create what I call a "context of desperation" that makes virtually all diversity immigrants from these countries willing to jump at the chance, as I discuss further in chapter 2.

As currently designed, the DV Program offers no extensions and no rollovers. If diversity immigrants cannot afford to pay the visa processing fees for all their family members when they apply and buy airplane tickets for their family members by the time their visas expire, their family members lose the opportunity. The principal visa applicant will have to wait to become either a lawful permanent resident or a U.S. citizen to file for permission to bring over family members left behind. It is usually faster to wait until one becomes a citizen to sponsor immediate family members (spouses and children) for their own immigrant visas. But gaining citizenship takes years. In this way, the design of the DV Program separates families and creates transnational families.

For other diversity visa winners, the compressed time line and a lack of funds make them vulnerable to offers to sell a spot on their winning application so they can pay for the process, for which total costs, including airfare, can reach close to $3,000 per individual. Winners of the U.S. lottery who are in college are likely, unless they are close to graduating at the time of their win, to leave school and thus migrate without completing college. This abrupt end to their education has long-term consequences for their education and employment experiences in the United States (see chapter 5).[56]

Economic Incorporation of U.S. Immigrants

One way in which scholars answer the question of how immigrants fare in the United States is by examining their earnings and occupational mobility in the U.S. labor market. These indicators demonstrate how well immigrants can support themselves and their families, their prospects for economic prosperity, and how well their skills and educational qualifications are recognized and transferable to U.S. society. Economic assimilation is said to occur when immigrants earn as much as their native-born counterparts and work in mainstream U.S. society.[57]

When the seminal work on U.S. immigrant earnings, using U.S. census data, was published by economist Barry Chiswick in 1978, it showed that foreign-born White men earned less than U.S. native-born White men with comparable educational levels, suggesting that immigrants' skills and experience were undervalued in the U.S. labor market.[58] Chiswick also found, however, that even though foreign-born White men's earnings were lower for the first ten to fifteen years after migration, they subsequently started earning more than native-born White men. He found a "similar earnings crossover" of fifteen years among foreign-born Mexican men and native-born men of Mexican ancestry.[59] Chiswick attributed immigrants' higher earnings to "self-selection in favor of high ability and [high motivation]," noting that these workers were willing to self-finance further education to improve their skills.[60] His findings also suggested that the rise in immigrant wages after ten to fifteen years was partly a result of increased time spent in the United States and perhaps also the result of obtaining some U.S. education.

Since U.S. census data is cross-sectional and offers only a onetime snapshot of the people surveyed, other scholars wondered whether immigrants' earnings took such a long time to converge with those of U.S.-born natives because of a trend toward lower-quality immigrants entering the United States. Or could it be that, if only "successful" immigrants remained in the United States, those present after years had elapsed would necessarily look "better" when compared to a group of recent arrivals from which the unsuccessful had not yet weeded themselves out?

In 1985, economist George Borjas, elaborating on Barry Chiswick's findings with his own analysis, found that the lengthy time it took for immigrants' earnings to converge with the earnings of U.S. natives was due to a trend of lower-quality (less-educated) immigrants entering the United States.[61] He saw this decline in quality as linked to a shift in the source of immigrants from western Europe to less-advantaged developing countries in the Global South. Borjas argued that the particularly low level of formal schooling among Mexicans and Central American labor migrants would lower their likelihood of attaining economic assimilation compared to earlier waves of immigrants. Other studies have since found this not to be true.[62] Rather, it seems that immigrants earn less on arrival because their skills are less transferable in the U.S. labor market. In general, as they acquire experience in the U.S. workforce, immigrants achieve economic parity over time with U.S.-born members of the same ethnic group.[63]

Several individual-level characteristics have been found to be strong determinants of immigrants' earnings in the U.S. labor market. Increasing levels of education generally lead to higher wages; however, *where* an immigrant obtained an education—whether in a foreign country or in the United States—is important.[64] But there is no consensus on whether acquiring some U.S. education has a positive impact on immigrants' earnings in the U.S. labor market.[65] Years of U.S. work experience are positively correlated with wages. The ability to speak English well is positively correlated with earnings. Gender and age also matter, as they are correlated with educational attainment and relevant work experience.

Studies have shown significant differences in immigrants' economic incorporation in regard to race and ethnicity.[66] Race and ethnicity affect immigrant economic outcomes in two ways. First, studies from the field of economic assimilation have established that returns from foreign education are highest for education received in countries that are as economically advanced as the United States and whose official language is English. The highest returns from foreign education, comparable to education received in the United States, are found in Canada and the United Kingdom.[67] Using this conceptual framework, immigrants who acquired their education in non-English-speaking countries or in less-developed countries, such as some

African countries, would earn less than U.S. natives and their immigrant counterparts with comparable educational levels from advanced countries in Europe and Canada. Some studies find that it is beneficial for immigrants to retrain or gain some education in the United States, as it can increase returns to the educational level they have already achieved abroad.[68]

Second, each immigrant group and its members face different structural and contextual factors. Three factors influence the context of reception for each immigrant group: whether government policies toward the group are hostile, passive, or welcoming; the degree of discrimination the group faces in the labor market; and the size and composition of the ethnic community, which affect the degree of support (social capital) available to immigrants.[69] Within this conceptual framework, U.S. immigrants who are seen as White—and thus do not encounter racial barriers to their presence and devaluation of their foreign schooling—tend to do well in the U.S. labor market. In contrast, members of immigrant groups that have negative experiences along these three dimensions of the context of reception earn lower wages in the U.S. labor market.

Research on immigrants' socioeconomic assimilation concludes that immigrants follow a U-shaped labor market assimilation model in the United States. This model suggests that immigrants will experience some downgrading upon arrival but will begin to rise to achieve economic parity with their U.S.-born ethnic counterparts as they acquire U.S. work experience, additional education, the professional credentials necessary for ascension, and increased English fluency, especially for those whose native language is not English.[70]

Labor Market Trajectories of Legal Immigrants by Class of Admission

To fully assess diversity immigrants' path to economic incorporation, we must consider the effect that class of admission has upon different populations of legal migrants. To do so, I performed an analysis of longitudinal data from the New Immigrant Survey that I will discuss toward the end of the chapter. The NIS asks immigrants about the last job they had before migrating and about their first, subsequent, and current jobs after their arrival in the United States. Those answers allow scholars to ascertain legal immigrants' labor market trajectories.

Because the survey follows new legal immigrants drawn from the four classes of admission—family-based, employer sponsorship, diversity visa, and refugee status or asylum—it also allows scholars to investigate how the admission categories that facilitate legal immigration affect immigrants' incorporation into the United States. I report on two studies by sociologist

Ilana Akresh that attempt to explore the impact of class of admission by focusing on occupational mobility, which can be used in conjunction with immigrant earnings to understand immigrants' socioeconomic assimilation and their expected labor market trajectories.

Akresh's study using NIS pilot data shows that 50 percent of U.S. immigrants experienced occupational downgrading when their final job before migrating is compared to the job they held in the United States.[71] She defines occupational downgrading as an immigrant's U.S. occupation being of a lower index level, calculated as the average education of individuals in these positions, than their last occupation abroad. When compared to immigrants sponsored by an employer, immigrants from all other categories were more likely to experience downward occupational mobility.[72] Her study found that occupational downgrading varies by region: more than three-fourths of the highest-skilled immigrants from Latin America and the Caribbean ended up in lower-skilled jobs than they had held before they migrated. Among the highest-skilled immigrants from Latin America and the Caribbean, 35 percent ended up in the lowest-skilled jobs in the United States, compared to only 7 percent of comparable European immigrants and 18 percent of Asian immigrants. These numbers suggest that Black and Latino immigrants experience racial barriers to upward occupational mobility in the U.S. labor market, partly because that market values an education acquired in Latin America or the Caribbean less than an education acquired in Europe, Australia, or Canada.

According to Akresh's other study, conceptually, certain categories of admission are thought to predict different outcomes in the U.S. labor market.[73] Employer-sponsored immigrants are expected to have a distinct advantage over immigrants in all other categories because they tend to have been in the United States longer and to have jobs. Because there is competition for these highly educated immigrants' skills, they can find employment that offers them wages and remuneration equivalent to what is earned by U.S.-born natives with similar skills and educational profiles.[74] Among all other immigrant categories, refugees and asylees are expected to do least well in the labor market because they have been forcibly displaced from their lives abroad and tend to arrive with lower levels of human, financial, and social capital. Family-based immigrants and diversity immigrants are expected to fall in the middle. Family-based immigrants tend to not be as highly educated as employment-based immigrants because sponsorship by relatives who are American citizens or legal permanent residents is not as selective a process as employee sponsorship. They also tend to have less-transferable skills. Finally, because they must meet the DV Program's education and skills requirements, diversity immigrants are expected, according to Akresh, to "fare more like economic [employer-sponsored] immigrants than like family immigrants or refugees."[75]

Using the first wave of the larger NIS to test occupational mobility, Akresh found that, except for female diversity immigrants, men and women in all categories of admission exhibited the U-shaped pattern of labor market assimilation, though the degree of downgrading and recovery varied. Female diversity immigrants experienced similar downgrading with their first job in the United States, but unlike both men and women in the other groups, they did not experience a subsequent improvement from their first to their current job.[76] Instead, they experienced continued occupational downgrading. As expected, the U-shape was shallowest for employer-sponsored immigrants, while refugees experienced the deepest plunge but also the steepest recovery. Diversity immigrants and family-based immigrants fell between employer-sponsored immigrants and refugees, the latter having the second-shallowest downward plunge compared to employer-sponsored immigrants. The findings of this study were an early flag that diversity immigrants' actual occupational mobility was not as predicted. My own analysis—which uses two waves of longitudinal NIS data, whereas Akresh's study used only the first wave of the NIS— confirms and extends this finding of lower-than-expected socioeconomic attainment.

In addition to a period of labor market adjustment, many immigrants face the pervasive problem of underemployment, also known as "brain waste," "skill underutilization," or "suboptimization." Brain waste occurs when college-educated immigrants end up either unemployed or holding jobs that require no more than a high school diploma.[77] The proportion of more highly educated immigrants to the United States has been increasing in the last two decades. Half of recent immigrants to the United States have at least a bachelor's degree.[78] Twenty-one percent of college-educated immigrants (about two million) are either unemployed or working in a job that requires no more than a high school diploma. Many work in less-skilled jobs as retail salespersons, nannies, or home health aides.[79] We all know of or have heard about immigrants who trained as engineers or doctors or teachers, only to find themselves employed in the United States as taxi drivers or home health aides, many via temp agencies that offer no health insurance or retirement benefits. The same factors identified as determining immigrants' earnings in the U.S. labor market are correlated with brain waste.[80]

Searching for Clues: How Diversity Immigrants Fare Vis-à-Vis Other Legal Immigrants

As I spoke to diversity immigrants from Ghana and Nigeria about their experiences, it became clear that, for many, life in the United States had not turned out as they were told it would or as they had dreamed. Many of the challenges they faced were tied to winning the diversity visa lottery. Their narratives about their lives in the United States made me question why their experiences did not conform to the economic incorporation pattern expected of diversity immigrants. Why did they not easily assimilate socioeconomically? After all, they arrived in the United States as lawful permanent residents. They did not have to negotiate the legal violence inflicted on the undocumented in the United States. Their stories of difficulties and challenges allowed me to conceptualize the various forms of migrapolicy interventions enacted by the DV Program. I decided to complement my examination with an analysis of the two waves of the New Immigrant Survey in order to compare diversity immigrants' earnings with those of other legal immigrants. I wanted to know if an analysis of a nationally representative sample of diversity immigrants would point to the presence of a different set of challenges experienced by this immigrant group.

The analysis offered several surprising findings in light of the model of labor market performance predicted for diversity immigrants, though after my conversations with study participants, I found them less unsurprising. The first is that diversity immigrants earned significantly less than all other immigrants at the beginning of their time in the United States, both within the pooled sample and within every region of origin except Latin America and the Caribbean. Mixed-effects OLS models and the post-hoc differential analysis (see tables A.1 and A.2 in the methodological appendix) showed that diversity immigrants in the pooled sample earned on average *70 percent less* than their peers with employer-sponsored visas and *61 percent less* than their counterparts who arrived as refugees. These results held even after education, age, and years of work experience were controlled. Diversity immigrants from sub-Saharan Africa earned about 83 percent less than employer-sponsored immigrants and about 67 percent less than refugees from the same region.

Contrary to what the extant literature predicts, diversity immigrants' earnings did not fall in the middle between the earnings of employer-sponsored immigrants and refugees, and they did not rank second to employer-sponsored immigrants. In fact, they fared worse than refugees in their early years in the United States. This finding was surprising, since refugees and asylees are said to migrate with significantly lower levels of human, financial, and social capital compared to other immigrants and are expected to do the least well of all legal immigrants in the U.S. labor market.

But there is good news: even though diversity immigrants measured significantly worse than their peers at time 1 (June 2003 to June 2004), their earnings significantly improved over time.[81] By time 2 (June 2007 to

December 2009), the average income of diversity immigrants had attained parity and was even higher than the average income for refugees, but it remained less than the average income for family-based and employer-sponsored immigrants.[82] My analyses of NIS data make clear that the stories of the challenges faced by the West African diversity immigrants in this book were not particular to them, people in their communities, or migrants from the nations of Nigeria and Ghana. It is a story that could be told by immigrants from around the world who are using this class of admission to enter the United States.[83] Figure 1.1 is a pictorial presentation of the analysis.

Even though diversity immigrants recovered quickly, it is important to ask why these differences exist. Research on immigrant incorporation clearly tells us that strong social networks help tremendously in adjusting to life in America.[84] Immigrants coming to the United States via the migration channels of family preference, asylum or refugee status, and employer sponsorship have significant support networks and resources that ease their incorporation into American society. Those coming under family-based admission have relatives who provide room, board, and informational networks that ease their transition. Those coming via employment sponsorship have jobs and access to company resources, and they are often knowledgeable about the United States or have lived there prior to obtaining their LPR status. Refugees receive both pecuniary and nonpecuniary assistance from the U.S. government, private organizations, and individuals. That assistance provides refugees with immediate access to social support networks and bridging ties that connect their own small ethnic networks to larger mainstream social networks, which tend to be racially, ethnically, and socially diverse (in terms of class). Such support allows refugees to acquire cultural and social capital that helps them navigate the American system; gain institutional knowledge; and find apartments, schools for their children, and jobs.[85]

Diversity immigrants are on the other end of the spectrum when it comes to support structures and the receipt of assistance. Some have considerable resources and strong support networks, especially if they are highly educated human capital immigrants, if they have family members already in the United States, or if they won the visa lottery while already in the United States. But since the U.S. diversity program was designed to give independent immigrants an opportunity to legally migrate to the United States, many are not so fortunate. Some diversity immigrants do not find coethnics in the towns and cities where they settle. Thus, the ethnic community, an important resource in helping immigrants' incorporation into the United States, is not part of many diversity immigrants' experience.[86]

Figure 1.1 Predicted Differences in Ln Income by Admission Category between Time 1 and Time 2

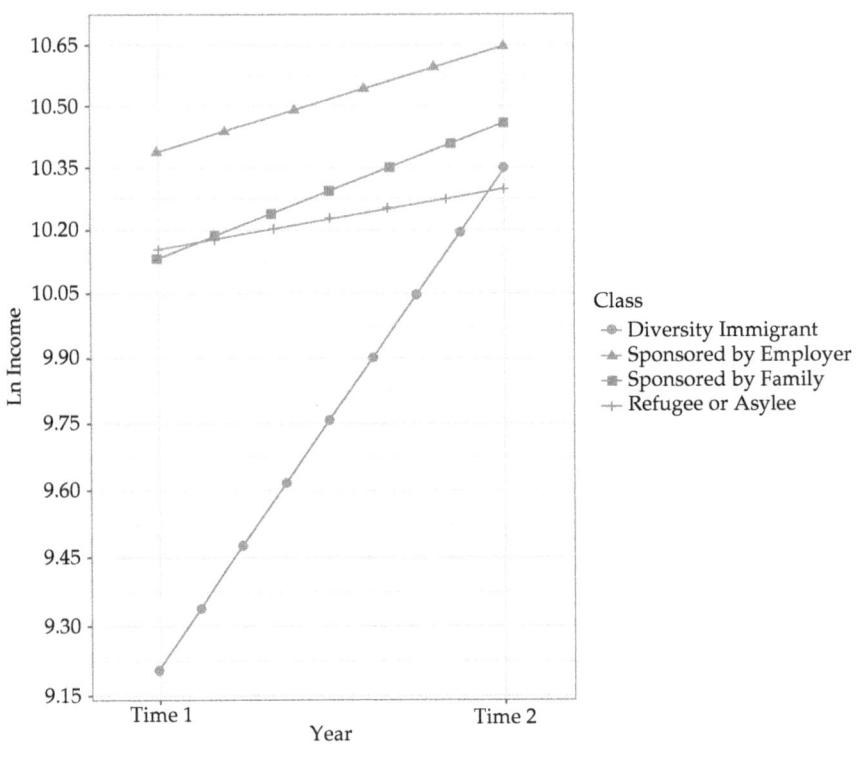

Source: Author's analysis of New Immigrant Survey data, 2003–2009.

Lacking networks and connections, the experiences of diversity immigrants are diametrically opposed to those of family-based immigrants. Members of the latter group are selected for having networks and connections to people already settled in the United States. Analysis of the NIS data reveals the proximity of earnings for family-sponsored immigrants and employer-sponsored immigrants. This is yet another finding pointing to how important social networks are in helping immigrants integrate into U.S. society. And it raises questions about the continued calls for more "skill-based" immigration, since family-based immigrants fare about as well as those who enter through skills qualification.[87]

Chapter 2 | A Context of Desperation: "Why Does Everyone Want to Go Abroad?"

LIFE IS HARD for many people in Nigeria and Ghana, owing to a lack of well-paying jobs. While Ghana is doing better than Nigeria, the provision of basic social services and infrastructure is inadequate in both countries: roads are bad, electricity blackouts are common, and pipe-borne water is a luxury enjoyed by very few. (Only the wealthy can manage to sink private boreholes; most Nigerians fetch water from streams and wells.) Hospitals are so lacking in equipment and staff that patients are often asked to bring their own blood donors and buy essential equipment like syringes, IV fluid drips, and bandages. Rising inflation makes it difficult for many to eat enough (nutritious) food and buy necessary commodities. While the wealthy can cushion themselves from some of these inconveniences, everyone is affected by ethnic conflicts, poor security, a corrupt government, officials who must be bribed to do their jobs, and weak institutions that leave all at the mercy of callous actors.

I grew up in a middle-class home in Nigeria in the 1980s. My parents were teachers, and we were not flush with cash. I remember hearing the word *austerity* everywhere in the 1980s, right after Nigeria implemented the Structural Adjustment Program (SAP) policies in exchange for loans from the International Monetary Fund (IMF). The word *austerity* was always on my mother's lips—every time she went to the market and prices had skyrocketed, every time common items became scarce, every time the naira lost value, and in her conversations with my father and others. To hear *austerity* constantly repeated was surprising, because I remember my father frequently showing a Nigerian documentary in which Nigeria's head of state, General Yakubu Gowon, stated in 1973 that "money is not our [Nigeria's] problem but how to spend it." By the 1980s, it had become "our problem." At home, we used one can of evaporated milk for several days, each of us ladling out one to two spoons per cup of beverage. There was no electricity to power our fridge, so we put the can in water to help it last a few days—after peeling off tiny strips of the wrapping and placing them over the holes on top of the can to prevent ants from crawling in. We were fortunate. At least my parents could afford milk. Most could not. Bowlegs and K-legs (knock-knees) on children were a common sight owing to the lack of balanced diets and sufficient vitamin D and calcium to support growing bones. It was during this time period that the great wave of African migration to the United States and Europe began. But things are worse now.

In Nigeria and Ghana, people are constantly being surprised to discover that there is no rock bottom—that things keep getting worse. In my interviews, Ghanaian and Nigerian diversity immigrants described what I call a "context of desperation" that made them want to emigrate. The U.S. visa lottery was a wonderful chance to get out of Nigeria and Ghana. Immigration scholars often discuss the context of reception that immigrants face in the host country and how it affects their integration; however, we must also talk about the context of exit, which can either push people out of their country of origin or make them decide to stay. Economically advantaged countries are net-migration states precisely because most of their citizens feel no need to leave. On the contrary, many diversity immigrants experience the context of desperation described by my interviewees. The deteriorating economic situation that pushes Nigerians to emigrate made Sakiru Adebayo, a Nigerian blogger in South Africa, declare that "the Nigerian dream is to leave Nigeria."[1] A new Nigerian slang term has emerged: "Japa syndrome" describes the mass exodus of Nigerians who are *japa*-ing overseas. *Japa* is a Yoruba word that means "to travel abroad to seek greener pastures." A Ghanaian professor of African studies at the University of Ghana at Legon expressed the same idea when he told me, "All [that] the young people are thinking about is leaving Ghana."

Indeed, not everyone seeks to go abroad because of hardship. Some people simply want to experience life in another country. Some, including those privileged few who have decent, high-paying jobs in their home country, such as medical doctors, want the opportunity to use cutting-edge technology in their jobs or aspire to work at top-of-the-line facilities. Many immigrants want to join their families, attend school, or improve their children's opportunities for the future. These motivations are similar among people from all countries who choose to emigrate. But the sheer number of Nigerians and Ghanaians who aspire to migrate abroad starkly indicates the challenging and deteriorating economic and political conditions in their countries.

In 2017, the Pew Research Center's Global Attitudes Survey reported that 75 percent of Ghanaians and 74 percent of Nigerians would be willing to live in another country if they had the means to do so. Out of the six African countries included in the survey, Ghana and Nigeria reported the highest levels of this sentiment; the remaining four were Kenya at 54 percent, South Africa at 51 percent, Senegal at 46 percent, and Tanzania at 43 percent.[2] Forty-two percent of Ghanaians and 38 percent of Nigerians said that they had plans to move to another country sometime in the next five years.[3]

The 2017 Global Attitudes Survey was the last to include Ghanaians among its respondents. The same survey conducted by Pew a year later, in 2018, showed that the number of Nigerians who said they planned to migrate to another country in the next five years had risen to 45 percent, which was by far the highest share among the twelve countries surveyed across four continents.[4] It would not be surprising, and is in fact likely, that a similar upward shift in this sentiment occurred in Ghana, given that it is one of the top applicant-sending countries for the Diversity Immigrant Visa Program and that, in 2017, more than 6 percent of the population registered for the visa lottery.[5]

According to the 2018 Pew survey, a significant number of Nigerians were actively planning their emigration, as 34 percent of them had saved or borrowed money in preparation for travel. Fifty-five percent had gathered information about moving to another country, and 30 percent had applied for the necessary government documents, such as a passport or a visa.[6] In terms of destinations, 28 percent of the respondents chose the United States, 19 percent Europe, 19 percent the Middle East, and 9 percent Africa; 24 percent selected "other countries."[7] The 2018 Afrobarometer survey of Ghana found that 39 percent of respondents chose the United States and 30 percent chose Europe as their destination choice.[8]

In the 2018 Pew survey, Nigerian respondents were asked why they wanted to emigrate. Ninety-two percent cited a desire to find better educational opportunities, 85 percent said to find better job opportunities, 72 percent cited reuniting with family members currently living in another country, and 69 percent said they wanted to escape from Nigeria.[9] Only 39 percent of Nigerians were satisfied with democracy in Nigeria; 60 percent were dissatisfied. Seventy-two percent of Nigerians believed that Nigerian politicians were corrupt, and 57 percent felt that elections were unlikely to bring about significant change, revealing low levels of trust and faith that the system could work for all Nigerians.[10] Fifty-four percent of Nigerians described the economy as bad, though this was an improvement from the 71 percent holding this opinion in 2016.[11] These statistics support the notion that poverty, economic hardship, and failed political leadership have created dreams of exit, or what anthropologist Charles Piot calls "fantasies of exile," in which many people long for and look for ways to escape and to migrate abroad.[12] Echoing this sentiment, a Ghanaian diversity immigrant, Abena, told me, "Coming from Africa, everybody wants to come to the United States. Anything that will bring you here, yes!"

In accordance with the push-pull theory of why people move, African migration to the West is propelled by poor economic and sociopolitical environments in home countries, such as low pay, lack of jobs, underemployment, poverty, political instability, ethnic conflicts, and environmental crises. The numbers from the Pew Global Attitudes Survey support this theory. Such conditions heighten the attraction of migrating to advanced countries in the Global North in search of higher wages, improved job satisfaction, freedom from violence and persecution, educational opportunities, and reunification with family members.[13] That Nigerians and Ghanaians cite a combination of *all* these factors distinguishes them from less-dysfunctional immigrant-sending countries. The elevated percentages of citizens hoping to emigrate from both countries further distinguishes them among all African nations surveyed.

World systems theory elaborates on the dynamic from an illuminating and slightly different angle: it posits that the global capitalist system disadvantages African and other nations on the economic periphery.[14] Peripheral countries lack a level playing field for marketing finished goods, and their agricultural products face steep competition in the world market against subsidized agricultural products from the West. Because the majority of their revenues come from commodities, their economies are vulnerable to price volatility in the markets. Unequal economic relationships between developed and developing countries have caused the latter to suffer from political instability, high levels of poverty, and insufficient government investment in critical infrastructure, public education, and health. African citizens have come to see the U.S. DV Program as a route to social mobility, and this is why they play the U.S. visa lottery and why they experience such joy when they win.

CONTEMPORARY NIGERIA

Located in West Africa, the Federal Republic of Nigeria is about double the size of the state of California. The country is bordered on the west by the republics of Benin and Niger, on the east by Cameroon, on the north by Niger and Chad, and on the south by the Gulf of Guinea. Nigeria is the most populous nation in Africa and the seventh-most-populous nation in the world. In 2021, it was home to an estimated 211 million people, which constituted 15 percent of the total African population.[15] There are

250 ethnic groups in the country, the three largest being the Hausa/Fulani (36 percent), Yorubas (15.6 percent), and Ibos (15.2 percent). Together they comprise 67 percent of the total Nigerian population.[16] There are 510 indigenous languages spoken in Nigeria, but English is the nation's official language—a bequest from its British colonial roots.[17]

Nigeria's ethnic divisions correlate with regional partitions. Northerners are predominantly Hausa and Fulani, while southerners and easterners are predominantly Ibo, Yoruba, Edo, Ijaw, and Itsekiri. The northern groups are predominantly Muslim, while the ethnic groups in the south are predominantly Christian. The southern groups are significantly more educated than the Hausas and Fulanis; as a result, the southern part of Nigeria has significantly higher educational levels than the northern regions. The national literacy rate, as reported by the 2006 Nigerian census, was 67 percent.[18] The adult literacy rate among Nigerians in the north was 35 percent, while the adult literacy rate in the south and southeast was more than twice that at 74 percent.[19] This educational gap affects who chooses to emigrate. Nigerian immigrants in advanced, democratic, Western countries are predominantly southerners and easterners from the most-educated regions of Nigeria.

Nigeria was once described as "the giant of Africa," a descriptor that technically still applies since the country continues to have the largest economy in Africa several decades into the twenty-first century. However, Nigeria today, with an economy that has made minimal progress toward development, would be better described as a "sleeping giant." At the time of its independence from Great Britain in 1960, Nigeria had attained the same level of development as South Korea.[20] Sixty-one years later, Nigeria's GDP per capita (PPP) was $5,459, while the Republic of Korea's PPP was nine times that at $46,918.[21] A strong sense of hope and national identity existed among Nigerians after independence. It was expected that since Nigeria was blessed with many resources, including crude oil and natural gas, it would become an economic powerhouse that served its people well. That expectation has not been met.

Rather, Nigeria has stumbled to become one of the poorest nations in the world, ranking at the bottom on corruption and standard-of-living indices. The reasons for this poor state of affairs are myriad, starting with the legacies of eras of slavery, colonialism, and intervention from the West and extending to poor leadership, weak institutional capacity, neoliberal economic reforms, ethnic conflicts, rapid population growth, and political instabilities resulting in military coups and contested elections.

A founding problem is that the Nigerian nation-state is a colonial imposition onto a diverse number of precolonial political systems, including centralized kingdoms and decentralized ethnopolitical groups. The imposition culminated in 1914, when Britain amalgamated the northern and southern Nigerian protectorates into the nation of Nigeria. These protectorates grouped together peoples dissimilar in ethnic membership, religious beliefs, cultural practices, political systems, and political cultures.[22] Although Britain was perceived as pursuing a policy that prepared its larger and resource-rich colonies like Ghana and Nigeria for life after independence, this was not really true.[23] The British ruled during colonial times in ways that intensified ethnic rivalries and ethnic consciousness.[24] Far from resolving seething tensions, the British exacerbated them, and they were only too relieved to bequeath responsibility to the new Nigerian leaders. As the journalist and historian on Africa Basil Davidson put it, the British transfer of power was a transfer of crisis, and nationalists inherited a crisis of social disintegration.[25] Immediately after independence, nationalist movements based on ethnic mobilizations began to flare up and entrench divisions. Different regions wanted to secede. The Nigerian Civil War from 1967 to 1970 began when the Ibos in eastern Nigeria attempted to secede to create the independent nation-state of Biafra.

In response to the failure of post-independence and civilian leaders to deliver economic development and improve the standard of living of the masses, Nigeria was governed by a series of military rulers from January 15, 1970, when the civil war ended, to May 29, 1999, when the country returned to civilian rule under the government of General Olusegun Obasanjo. A civilian government remained in place for four and a half years, from 1979 to 1983, under the leadership of Alhaji Shehu Shagari. But Shagari's government was toppled by a military coup that brought General Muhammadu Buhari to power and ushered in a fifteen-year span of military rule that also encompassed the tenures of General Ibrahim Babangida (from 1985 to 1993) and General Sani Abacha (from 1993 to 1998).

Despite the fact that these coups occurred in response to Nigeria's economic decline, military rule and the concentration of state power in the hands of the few did not bring about economic revival. Rather, the decline worsened, and corruption became endemic and woven into the national fabric. Every military regime was guilty of silencing the voices of dissidents and violating the human rights of the citizens. Nigeria transitioned to the democratically elected government of General Olusegun Obasanjo in 1999 and has successfully maintained democratically elected governments since then. But Nigeria's economic challenges remain.

The grave post-independence mistake made by African leaders, including Nigerian leaders, was trying to do too much in too short a time. Post-independence leaders, modeling their vision of development on Western systems, decided that statism would deliver the economic development necessary to reduce poverty, increase national wealth, and elevate the standard of living. Statism is an approach in which the government is the main actor driving industrialization and delivering rapid development. Because African leaders were funding almost all development projects from the national purse, they soon ran out of money, creating a fiscal crisis that required external bailouts. Beginning in the 1980s, in exchange for loans needed to maintain their governments, African countries were pushed to adopt strict austerity measures that drastically cut state budgets, trimmed public-sector workforces, and privatized government enterprises and corporations by selling them off to private actors. They had to allow exchange rates to respond to the forces of demand and supply and devalue their currency, give unfettered rein to the forces of the market to control the economy, remove tariffs, and open up domestic markets to foreign importers.[26] The IMF and the World Bank promised that these austerity reforms, which were shaped by a neoliberal ideology that sought to retrench the government's social and economic expenditures, would deliver economic growth and development. They did not.

Instead, the economies and social contracts with citizens in the countries that instituted the SAP reforms, including Nigeria and Ghana, were decimated.[27] SAP reforms did not attract the foreign direct investment they were supposed to deliver. In fact, many foreign companies ended their investment in Nigerian enterprises during the late 1980s and early 1990s; as a result, the country's efforts to diversify its revenue sources, which was supposed to be one deliverable of the reforms, were stymied. Oil and gas still account for 80 percent of Nigeria's total national revenue, only a slight improvement from when both accounted for over 90 percent of total revenue.[28] Additionally,

> the SAP also caused serious hardships for Nigerian citizens and failed to achieve many of its anticipated results. Unemployment levels increased markedly under the SAP, for a variety of reasons. While the rising cost of imports encouraged local sourcing by industry, it also caused much Nigerian industry to operate at below-capacity production levels. External sources of raw materials became more expensive, which meant that companies purchased less and, consequently, produced fewer finished goods. As a result, profits often decreased, leading to a reduction in wages and/or staff. Government and public service departments cut staff and reduced salaries as part of the austerity measures designed to reduce government expenditure. Devaluation of the currency brought with it rapid inflation and a decrease in the purchasing power of the average Nigerian. The naira, which had stood at N1 = $1 in 1985, fell to N4.21 to the dollar in 1988, N7.48 in 1989, and N22 by 1994. The inflation rate stood at between 40 and 70 percent from about 1988 to 1995, and per capita income declined from an estimated $778 in 1985

to just $105 in 1989, making it difficult for people to afford basic necessities such as food, clothing, electricity, health care, education, and anything else that cost money.[29]

In December 2022, the official exchange rate was N480 = $1, but it was N750 = $1 on the black market, which is where most people purchase foreign currency. In October 2023, the exchange rate was N1210 = $1.

The reduction in government spending on social welfare and job creation led to rising unemployment rates, as many government workers lost their jobs and fewer new jobs were created, resulting in lower standards of living. Educational institutions, being insufficiently funded, declined in quality and could not meet the demands of a rapidly growing population. Insufficient funding also sent other social services and utilities into a downward spiral. Since then, Nigeria does not generate enough electricity to meet its needs, resulting in frequent blackouts, and many areas are not even connected to the grid. Lack of reliable electricity supply affects the ability of Nigerian businesses and industries to operate reliably, further hobbling Nigeria's economic diversity and job creation.

The second catastrophic error resulting from statism was establishing price controls to supposedly make selected goods affordable. Price controls created a scarcity economy and thriving black market, which contributed to the culture of corruption and bribery that prevails to this day.[30] In Nigeria, the mistakes of the 1960s have not been unlearned. Subsidization of petroleum products is undermining the economy, as the government uses a significant percentage of its earned revenue to subsidize fuel—monies that could be reallocated to build needed infrastructure and fund health and education. Between 2015 and 2020, Nigeria spent $5.5 billion on its petrol subsidy policy; in 2021, that figure rose to $9.8 billion. In the first quarter of 2022, Nigeria paid out $6.2 billion in petrol subsidies, leading to a projection that it would spend $15.7 billion in total petrol subsidies in 2022.[31] That amount would exceed the total expenditure of all thirty-six states of the federation. Past governments attempted to eliminate the subsidy, the result of which would have been Nigerians paying prices set by the price of crude oil on the world market. These attempts were all met with widespread popular resistance in the form of labor strikes, riots, and national unrest. When President Bola Tinubu came into power in May 2023, his government ended fuel subsidies in their first week in office. From the subsidized price of N130 per liter, petrol has risen to N500 per liter and keeps rising. In July 2023, it was N580 per liter. This increase has caused great suffering for Nigerians. In 2022, with rising inflation rates mainly driven by higher energy and food prices, Nigeria had the eighth-highest inflation rate in sub-Saharan Africa and the twenty-fifth-highest in the world.[32]

Rising fuel prices would not help ease inflation. But Nigerians hope that the federal government will use the money saved to improve the lives of citizens.

Colonialism bequeathed economic challenges to ex-colonies. As Nigerian historians Toyin Falola and Matthew Heaton note:

> British colonial rule also affected the Nigerian economy. The colonial economic model focused on expanding Nigeria's import-export markets through increased cash crop and mineral production, thereby creating an extractive economy based on the export of raw materials and the import of finished goods and luxury items. The British also instituted a cash economy based on the UK currency and forced Nigerians into wage labor, transforming in a few short years the processes of agricultural production and capital accumulation that had developed among Nigerian communities over centuries. This was done primarily as a means to redirect economic activity towards external markets and thereby make the colonial endeavor self-sustaining for the colonial government and profitable for British and European business.[33]

The British failed to establish infrastructures for Nigeria to produce finished goods to sell on the world market, and subsequent governments have also failed to do so. Because of this failure, Nigeria has not developed forward-and-backward linkages in its economy that would diversify its revenue streams and create sufficient jobs for its population. The U.S. bailout of the automobile industry during the Great Recession of 2008 illustrates the important role that backward-and-forward linkages play in ensuring robust economic growth and the creation of sufficient jobs in a domestic economy. When President Barack Obama gave huge loans to the car companies in Detroit, Michigan—a step that was decried as a bailout in many parts of the country—he argued that letting those companies fail would create a domino effect that would decimate thousands of companies and millions of U.S. jobs, since industries and businesses involved in supplying goods to the car companies would also fail.

Post-independence, most African countries have been unable to break out of the colonial economic model, and their economies remain subordinated to supplying the needs of more-developed world powers, including China, the United States, and the nations of Europe. Because they lack diversified local industries, African countries, including Nigeria and Ghana, are unable to provide enough jobs for their populace. Drilling for oil does not provide as many jobs as would industries that use the oil to power manufacturing that produces myriad finished products. Their country's lack of industrial diversity compels citizens to migrate in order to achieve economic mobility and secure livelihoods on which they can maintain their families. Their lack of diversity also ensures that these countries cannot achieve robust economic growth to fund necessary infrastructure projects, such as constant electricity, clean pipe-borne water, good roads, adequate health care and education, and sufficient and well-trained security and police forces to guarantee the security of persons and property.

Today Nigeria can be described as a poverty-stricken nation. In 2021, Nigeria ranked 162nd and 172nd, respectively, measuring GDP per capita (in U.S. dollars) ($2,085) and GDP per capita, PPP (in current international dollars) ($5,429).[34] Over 40 percent of the population lives below the country's poverty line of $2 per day.[35] For more than a decade, Nigeria's unemployment rate has hovered around 28 percent; in 2020, it hit 33 percent.[36] Rapid population growth has proved to be a major stumbling block, as it puts even greater strain on the government's ability to provide the populace with sufficient fixed and social infrastructure and challenges its capacity to create jobs that will gainfully employ the nation's youths. In 2000, Nigeria's population was 122.3 million. In 2021, its population reached 211 million.[37] Sixty-two percent of the population was younger than twenty-four years old.[38]

Poverty is a potent fertilizer for unrest, and not surprisingly, ethnic and religious conflicts are rampant in Nigeria. New groups and nationalist movements keep the nation in turmoil. Since the 1980s, there have been countless clashes between Christian and Muslim populations, particularly in northern Nigeria. Peoples of the Niger Delta resent that their region continues to be underdeveloped even as the government extracts oil and gas from their lands and pollutes their fishing waters and arable territory. In response, militant gangs destroy property and kidnap foreign employees of multinational oil companies. The Movement for the Actualization of the Sovereign State of Biafra (MASSOB), a modern Biafran nationalist movement, continues to fight for secession in eastern Nigeria. Meanwhile, a huge problem has emerged in the last decade. In northern Nigeria, in response to desertification and loss of grazing lands for cattle, Fulani herdsmen have begun to move southward, using violence and killings to displace people along the way.

Boko Haram, a group operating in northern Nigeria that has been deemed a terrorist group, seeks to overthrow Western education and establish an Islamic state governed by sharia law. The group carries out bombings and killings that target innocent people, especially Christians in places of worship. In April 2014, Boko Haram's kidnapping of 276 (mostly Christian) girls from the Government Girls Secondary School in Chibok, Borno State, received worldwide attention. The inability of the Nigerian government to secure the release of over 100 still-missing girls taken from Chibok and to stop the violence of Fulani herdsmen exposes the country's weak institutional capacity and the government's failure to protect its citizens. Ideally, the government would quell such unrest through more equitable distribution of resources and policies to improve the standard of living and reduce poverty. Its inability to do so has contributed to the growing disdain that many Nigerians feel for their government and its leaders. The continuing cycles of violence destroy lives and property, hobble economic development, heighten political tensions, encourage ethnic balkanization, foster distrust of government, and weaken national identity.[39]

In addition to ethnic and regional unrest, the country is subject to frequent civil unrest. Despite being one of the top petroleum-producing nations in the world, Nigeria has failed to improve the lives of the masses via its oil wealth. Often, public-sector workers, such as civil servants, university professors, and teachers, are not paid for months. Labor strikes are common. It is not uncommon for students in federal and state universities to lose years of academic study because of these strikes. In 2022, students lost ten months after the academic staff union called a strike.

As an ex-colony of Britain, Nigeria modeled its educational system on the British system, and English remains the language of instruction in Nigerian schools. The population's fluency in English produces educated individuals whose qualifications are well matched to meet the needs of employers in the U.S. labor market. In Nigeria, however, university graduates find themselves unable to secure well-paying jobs. The country's rapid population growth, in combination with most of its population being under the age of eighteen, has led to huge demand for university spots. With the proliferation of private universities to meet that need, Nigeria is producing thousands of tertiary-institution graduates who cannot find jobs in Nigeria but who have enough information and can find the funds to migrate and try their luck overseas.

The large youth population has become a politically active, protest-oriented demographic. In 2020, Nigerian youths led nationwide protests against police brutality, the unwarranted killings of Nigerian citizens, and rampant corruption by Nigeria's police and security forces. Protesters called out the Special Anti-Robbery Squad (SARS) police unit as the most egregious offender. The #EndSARS protests demanded that the Nigerian government disband the SARS unit. Youths took to the streets in large numbers not only to protest police brutality but also to air their frustrations at being unable to find gainful employment. Even as the Nigerian government agreed to disband the SARS unit, the protests were forcibly quelled by army and police forces, with significant loss of life and property. This nationwide protest was a culmination of young Nigerians' frustration with their leaders and dissatisfaction with a country that educates them but cannot put them to work. Meanwhile, the exodus of Nigerian students continues, much as it has since the 1960s, as many leave Nigeria to obtain educational qualifications in the West and now, increasingly, in China and other Asian countries.

A similar exodus is occurring among the populace as a whole, professionals and nonprofessionals alike, in response to the continuously deteriorating economy and constant political turmoil, which began in the 1970s, worsened in the 1980s, and became critical after 2012. Attracted by the opportunity for self-advancement, better jobs, security (both economic and personal), and better educational and life opportunities for their children, Nigerians are emigrating to Europe, the United States, Canada, several Arab states, and many other countries. The diaspora is widely dispersed. Globally, there is a significant Nigerian presence in nearly every country. In recognition of their global dispersal, Nigerians are commonly described as "the Jews of Africa."

A "brain drain" has developed from the out-migration of highly skilled professionals—chief among them doctors, nurses, teachers, engineers, and IT professionals. The loss of talent is worsening Nigeria's economic challenges and decimating the country's health care system, which is in a precarious position.[40] The well-off use private clinics and travel overseas for treatment; in fact, the nation's leaders travel overseas for medical care. Ex-president Buhari, who left office in May 2023, spent months in England receiving treatment for an undisclosed illness. Those without sufficient means are not so lucky. Nigeria has a low life expectancy at birth of 61.3 years, which ranks 217th out of 227 nations and states, and an infant mortality rate of 56.68 per 1,000 births, which is the fourteenth-worst outcome in the world.[41]

Nigerians in the United States

Given Nigeria's large population and its high levels of emigration, the U.S. government's extremely restrictive and selective screening criteria have produced a Nigerian migrant population that ranks among the most-educated immigrant groups in the United States. According to the 2021 American Community Survey, only 3.2 percent of the Nigerian population over the age of twenty-five had less than a high school diploma; 24.2 percent had some college or an associate's degree; and 62.4 percent had a bachelor's degree or higher, which exceeds rates in the United States, where a bachelor's degree or higher is held by 35 percent of the population, 38.9 percent of Whites, 24.9 percent of Blacks, 56.4 percent of Asians, and 19.7 percent of Hispanics. English fluency among the Nigerian population in the United States is extremely high: 57.3 percent speak English only, 42.7 percent speak

English and other languages, and only 6.3 percent speak English less than very well.

Nigerians are the largest national group from Africa in the United States. According to the ACS, there are 681,650 Nigerians in the United States, 333,353 of whom were born here. Nigerians comprise 19 percent of all first-generation Black Africans in the United States, a significant share given that forty-eight countries make up sub-Saharan (Black) Africa. However, their share has fallen in recent decades: in 1980, Nigerians comprised 37 percent of the Black African population in the United States, and in 1990 they comprised 30 percent. Most foreign-born Nigerians who are currently living in the United States arrived after 2010 (54 percent); 23 percent arrived between 2000 and 2009, and 23 percent arrived before 2000.[42]

Most U.S.-based Nigerians are professionals: 53.1 percent work in management, business, science, and engineering occupations; a plurality (35.5 percent) are concentrated in the educational and health care industry; 12.9 percent have professional, scientific, and management jobs; and the third-largest concentration, at 10.6 percent, work in retail trade. Seventy-six percent of Nigerians are in the labor force, compared with 63 percent of U.S. workers. A tiny proportion, 5.8 percent, are self-employed.

In 2021, the median household income for Nigerians living in the United States was $71,465, compared to the African American median household income of $46,774, the White median household income of $74,932, and the American median household income of $69,717.[43] Almost 25 percent of Nigerian U.S. households made over $100,000 a year, compared to 10.6 percent of African American households. More than 5 percent of Nigerian households earned over $200,000 a year, compared to 1.3 percent of African Americans.[44] Despite having a higher median household income than the U.S. average, Nigerians' homeownership rate, at 40 percent, is lower than it is for White people and on par with African American homeownership rates.[45]

Most Nigerians in the United States live in urban areas, predominantly in New York City; the Maryland, Washington, D.C., and Virginia area; and Texas.[46] In New York, and more generally, Nigerians are found in extremely diverse neighborhoods that are home to significant numbers of African Americans and to other immigrants, especially Caribbean and other African immigrants.[47]

CONTEMPORARY GHANA

With a population of thirty-one million, according to its 2021 census, Ghana is the second-most-populous nation in West Africa, behind Nigeria. It is the thirteenth-most-populous nation in Africa and ranks forty-seventh worldwide. In terms of land area, Ghana is slightly smaller than the state of Oregon. It is bordered by Togo to the east, Burkina Faso to the north, Côte d'Ivoire to the west, and the Atlantic Ocean to the south. The countries of Benin and Togo, ex-colonies of France, separate Ghana from Nigeria. Like Nigeria, Ghana was colonized by the British and thus has a similar history of colonial administration and designates English as the national language.

During the colonial era, Britain ruled the colonies of the Gold Coast and Asante (the Ashanti) as well as the protectorate of the Northern Territories. After World War I, when German territories were repossessed under the mandate of the League of Nations, Britain administered the western part of former German Togoland. In 1956, British Togoland chose to become part of the Gold Coast under the leadership of Kwame Nkrumah, and these four territories became the nation-state of Ghana, which obtained its independence from Britain in 1957.

Ghana is ethnically diverse, with approximately seventy-five ethnic groups and seventy-three indigenous languages.[48] The five largest ethnic groups, in terms of population, are the Akan (which includes the Akwapim Twi, Asante, Baule, Fante, and Guang) at 47.5 percent, the Mole-Dagbani at 16.6 percent, the Ewe at 13.9 percent, the Ga-Dangme at 7.4 percent, and the Gurma at 5.7 percent. The country suffers from episodic ethnic tensions, especially in the northern region.

Like Nigeria, Ghana's post-independence leader, Kwame Nkrumah, adopted statism to deliver economic development, with similar results. The approach failed and led to a debt crisis, establishing a cycle of economic challenges that persist to the present day. Ghana was overly dependent on a monocrop—cocoa—for the majority of its national revenue. The problem with monocrop and monomineral economies is that they are extremely vulnerable to price volatility and commodity price decreases in the world market. After independence, Ghana drew up a seven-year plan to achieve agricultural and industrial expansion and modernization, but it could not implement the plan because an extreme drop in cocoa prices led to a lack of funding. By 1965, the price of cocoa, which comprised more than 80 percent of the country's total revenue, had fallen to £87.10 per ton, substantially lower than the £200 per ton that had been projected in the budget. As was the case in Nigeria, statism faltered because the government tried to be the main actor to deliver industrialization instead of creating an environment that encouraged the private sector to lead the charge.[49]

The failures of statism bedeviled Kwame Nkrumah, a passionate advocate for pan-Africanism, which to him meant a unified Africa liberated from European colonial rule and founded on a recognition of common interests. Nkrumah was overthrown in 1966 while he was visiting Beijing, China; the coup d'état was led by the National Liberation Council under the chairmanship of Lieutenant General Joseph A. Ankrah. Ghana, like Nigeria, went through a period of military rule, but it successfully transitioned to democratically elected governments in 1992. The most notable military ruler in Ghana was First Lieutenant Jerry Rawlings, who came to power in 1981. In 1992, after eleven years of military rule, Rawlings exchanged his military uniform for civilian clothes and, as head of the National Democratic Congress (NDC), was elected president.

By the 1980s, the shortfalls of statism led Ghana's government to try to generate revenue by raising taxes. The government established import controls, which led to shortages; the government responded by establishing price controls, which in turn created black markets and widespread corruption. As in Nigeria, the high expenditures associated with a government-driven economic development approach created a debt crisis that required loans from foreign bodies. As a result of these missteps, the economy fell into dire straits. In exchange for loans, Ghana instituted the IMF/World Bank–funded Economic Recovery Programme (ERP) in 1983. While the reforms resulted in progress in some areas, particularly in improving agricultural production, Ghana struggled to extend beyond a tiny group of elites the seemingly good (or great) economic growth rates and other fiscal indices to all of its citizens.

For the masses, strong economic performance becomes relevant when it translates into plentiful, high-quality, well-paying jobs. While fueling Ghana's economic growth rates, the discovery of oil and the commencement of its commercial production in 2011 continued the country along a path similar to Nigeria's—dependence on export earnings from a few primary commodities.[50] Since Ghana's growth was concentrated in the extractive sector, which is not labor-intensive, few jobs were created. The manufacturing and agricultural sectors, which are labor-intensive and do create needed jobs, experienced weak growth. With the decline in these two sectors—particularly in manufacturing, which is negatively impacted by the importation of goods from China and elsewhere—strong growth rates, which are often touted as indicators of good economic health, are not leading to a widely felt economic transformation.

Ghana's employment rate has lagged behind its economic growth. A study by the Ghana Statistical Service put the unemployment rate in Ghana at 13.4 percent in 2021, when 1.74 million people ages fifteen and older were unemployed—out of a total working population of 13 million.[51] Only about one-third of the jobs in Ghana can be classified as "gainful" or "productive" employment, and seven out of every ten jobs fall into the "vulnerable" employment sector. "Vulnerable employment" is defined as precarious, informal work arrangements, with no access to benefits or social protection programs. Over 88 percent of the jobs in Ghana are in the informal sector, employment in the formal sector having declined since the 1980s owing to the loss of government jobs caused by ERP reforms.

The working poverty rate in Ghana stands at over 20 percent, which means that at least one in every five working persons lives in a household identified as poor.[52] The majority of Ghanaians continue to lack access to adequate health services, educational facilities, and housing. Life expectancy is 64.94 years, and infant mortality stands at 30.8 per 1,000 live births.

The key takeaway from all these statistics is that, in Ghana, although people are working, few hold decent jobs that fully meet their needs and support their families. The greater majority of employed Ghanaians are working in jobs that do not pay well and that keep them close to or in poverty.

As with Nigeria, a broad-based and reliable public revenue stream must be established via effective taxation of its citizens. Such revenue could fund and close the constant budget deficits that necessitate foreign and domestic borrowing—which, in turn, keeps both nations dependent on economically advantaged countries and leads to gross underfunding of public infrastructure, health services, education, and welfare programs.

Basic education—twelve years of formal education from primary to secondary school—is free in Ghana. There are long-standing and reputable government universities and technical colleges, but the rapid population growth and the relative youth of the populace have strained the ability of educational facilities at all levels to meet educational demand. The median age of Ghanaians is 21.5 years; 39 percent of the population is under the age of eighteen, and nearly two-thirds of the population is younger than thirty. Ghana's literacy rate is 79 percent. Just as in Nigeria, because the official language is English and educated Ghanaians are trained in a Western education system, thousands of Ghanaians are equipped with skills that should be valued by employers in the United States and other economically advantaged countries.

Ghanaians in the United States

According to the 2021 American Community Survey, there are 203,327 Ghanaians in the United States, of which 79,644 are native-born. Most foreign-born Ghanaians came into the United States after 2000; 28.1 percent arrived before 2000, 29.2 percent arrived between 2000 and 2009, and 42.7 percent arrived after 2010. Given Ghana's colonial history with Great Britain, 39.2 percent of Ghanaians in the United States speak only English, 60.8 percent speak English and other languages, and only 11.5 percent speak English less than very well.

Although not as highly educated as Nigerians, Ghanaians are a well-educated population. According to the ACS, only 5.2 percent of the population over the age of twenty-five have less than a high school diploma, 50.9 percent have a bachelor's degree or higher, and 23.8 percent have some college or an associate's degree. The percentage of Ghanaians with a bachelor's degree or higher is greater than the U.S. national average of 35 percent, the White average of 38.9 percent, the Black average of 24.9 percent, the Asian average of 56.4 percent, and the Hispanic average of 19.7 percent. Seventy-eight percent of Ghanaians are in the labor force, and their unemployment rate is 8.8 percent. A plurality of Ghanaians are in professional occupations, with 46.6 percent in management, business, science, and engineering occupations and 24.5 percent in service occupations. In terms of the industries, 43.7 percent work in educational and health care industries, 11.5 percent in the retail trade, and 8.7 percent in professional, scientific, and management industries. The median household income is $72,089, compared to the African American median household income of $46,774, White median household income of $74,932, and American median household income of $69,717.[53] Ghanaians' homeownership rate of 33.3 percent is lower than the U.S. average and that of African Americans.

Most Ghanaians in the United States live in urban areas, the top three being New York City; the Virginia and Washington, D.C. area; and New Jersey. Ghanaian immigrants are most concentrated in Worcester, Massachusetts, even though they are a minuscule percentage of the city's population at 0.5 percent.[54] In New York, Ghanaians are found in extremely diverse neighborhoods with significant numbers of immigrants.

FIXING THINGS BACK HOME

When we consider why Ghana and Nigeria became net-emigration states after achieving independence from Britain, the similarities between the two nations and their histories cannot be ignored. One thing that economists, observers, and scholars who study these countries agree upon is that conditions could improve if a few core issues were addressed: diversifying their economies, reducing their dependence on revenue from raw materials and commodities, and increasing revenue through effective taxation policy and administration (particularly in regard to the informal economy). The additional revenue could fund needed basic infrastructure projects such as paving roads, updating transportation systems, generating and distributing electricity, upgrading sanitation, providing clean water, improving health care, and ensuring adequate educational facilities. Institutional capacity must be increased to carry out necessary government tasks and to monitor and punish violations, corruption, and unaccountability at all levels of the government and civil society.

Rather than undertaking the lengthy, though necessary, process of sorting out their own political configurations and developing the governmental systems that would have best suited them, precolonial African societies had the European nation-state system imposed upon them. As a result, countries like Nigeria and Ghana face a difficult challenge in building a strong sense of national pride, identification, and patriotism. As I discussed in my first book, *Beyond Expectations*, a sense of national identity becomes more salient for citizens living within the diaspora, whereas ethnic identification holds greater sway for people living within their country of origin. Purposive action must be taken to instill a strong national identity among both groups.

A failure to address legitimate claims of distributive economic injustice weakens citizens' social contract with the nation, as well as national identification. And it engenders disdain toward those leaders who are failing to ensure prosperity and opportunity for all citizens. Young people in Nigeria and Ghana are coming of age with dismal prospects for finding gainful employment. Their governments are failing them. If these problems are not addressed, thousands of young people will keep emigrating in order to achieve upward social mobility and help support their family members.

Some of my respondents were aware that migration was draining their countries. Aba, a thirty-nine-year-old medical doctor from Ghana, agreed that the Diversity Immigrant Visa Program is a good thing but said, "Coming to think of it too, it's like it's hurting Ghana more, it's draining Ghana, because of late, I see a trend: it looks like they are only giving it to educated people, the people that have certain forms of education or professions. Most of the people that are getting it are the people who have gone to the universities, they are professionals." Other respondents were unapologetic about the brain drain. Saheed, a thirty-eight-year-old engineer from Nigeria, angrily exclaimed in his interview, "I don't care, why should I? If the government had not failed us, being so corrupt and doing nothing for the people, we would not be clamoring to come here. Back home people are suffering. [University] graduates cannot find jobs. Stop it with that [brain drain] nonsense, I say." Kike, a thirty-eight-year-old Nigerian, concurred, if less angrily: "Why should we stay in the country? There is nothing, no future for us in Nigeria. If you can go abroad, jump at it."

Chapter 3 | "Come, Let Us Play the Lottery!"

"Come, let us play the lottery! What harm can it do? What do we have to lose? You never know, we might win!" These were Stacy's words to Monica when encouraging her to fill out the U.S. visa lottery form that a colleague had brought to their office. Monica worked as a teller in a small loan company in Accra, Ghana. Each workday, she walked the streets of Accra's markets, collecting loan payments from market women. She described her job as "very hot and sweaty" because she was under the scorching tropical sun all day, enjoying only a few moments in the shade. Even though she was in a "dead-end job," Monica "was reluctant" to fill out the form because she had not won the lottery in previous years. She went along with her officemate and applied, but she was the last to "drop her form in the mail, on the last day in fact." As she dropped off her form, Monica prayed to God, saying, "Let Your will be done."

I asked Monica what conversations she'd had about the lottery and why she played it. She replied, "It is just what we heard; everybody wants to travel and, maybe, better their lives or something, especially because of what was going on in the country, a Third World country. If you had the opportunity to go out, you took it." The DV Program offered that opportunity. She was motivated by "seeing people who have gone out and they come out better, and they are doing okay. So when we got the chance, and they said, 'They are doing this one; they will give you free, you don't have to pay for it.' Everybody likes what is free. So, we decided to just try it, and it did work out." Monica was the only one in her office to win the diversity visa lottery that year.

Why do people register for the visa lottery? And if selected, what makes them choose to become diversity immigrants? This chapter focuses on how Nigerian and Ghanaian diversity immigrants learned about the DV Program, why they decided to play the lottery, and, when selected, why they decided to emigrate to the United States. It also discusses how, before migration, the DV program brightens social class divisions in immigrants' country of origin. Later chapters deal with the results and consequences of their decisions.

LEARNING ABOUT THE LOTTERY

In communities across Ghana and Nigeria, almost everyone knows someone who has won the U.S. diversity visa lottery. The winner might be a close relative, such as a brother, sister, or parent; a close acquaintance, such as a friend, classmate, or workmate; or a distant connection, such as a friend of a friend or a schoolmate who was a few years ahead.

I was hanging out in the office of my friend, a lecturer at the University of Ghana at Legon, the top-ranked university in Ghana, when his teaching assistant, Silas, told me that there were "only six degrees of separation" between Ghanaians and lottery winners, as "everyone in Ghana knows someone who won the diversity visa." Silas was referencing the Hollywood movie *Six Degrees of Separation*, directed by John Guare, which builds on Guare's notion that "everyone on Earth is theoretically separated from everyone else by only six people."[1] When people learn that someone in their social network, no matter how near or far, has won the diversity visa, it becomes real. They realize that the program is not a scam or a fantastical urban legend. "Success stories" spread until the lottery becomes a fever, an event that sweeps through families, universities, colleges, churches, mosques, worksites, internet cafés, and social networks. Francis, who was a teacher in Ghana, learned about the DV Program after his "friend's brother had won it." Parents hear about the program from friends at work or in ethnic associations and pass along the information to their children.

Many individuals find out about the program from family members who are immigrants in the United States and other countries. As Silas shared, "I get texts on my WhatsApp secondary-school alumni group telling me about the program. I just got a Facebook message from my friend in Denmark telling me to apply." Family members in the United States, who know they cannot apply for immigrant visas for extended family members, see the program as an opportunity to help those back home by sharing information about the registration period and how to complete the lottery form. Friends do the same. Notification messages about the start of the program's enrollment period are regularly exchanged on social media. Places of worship and ethnic associations send out messages about the program to members on their social media platforms, particularly WhatsApp. The scope and reach of "word of mouth" has been greatly amplified by the advent and spread of smartphones with internet connectivity, which enables an individual to send a message about the U.S. immigrant visa lottery to all of their contacts with a simple tap of the screen. Telecommunication companies have made smartphones and data for internet connectivity accessible to every kind of person—high-income, low-income, educated, less-educated, rural, and urban. Despite their failing electricity grids and decaying infrastructure, many African countries have advanced telecommunication systems.

Diversity visa entrepreneurs play a major role in spreading news about the lottery and helping people register for it. They pay to run jingles on public radio, and they erect street tents at busy population hubs. Even staff members at internet cafés, which are ubiquitous in both rural and urban spaces in Africa, offer to help clients apply for the visa lottery.

"PLAYING" THE VISA LOTTERY

Most people decide to enter the visa lottery in three stages. The first stage is registering for the lottery itself. The DV Program was paper-based until 2003, at which time it moved online. When the lottery was paper-based, registrants just needed to write some identifying information on a blank sheet of paper and mail it to the Kentucky Consular Center (KCC). The only information required from lottery entrants was full legal name, date of birth, address, marital status, the name of one's spouse (if married), and a list of all children (if a parent). After providing a two-by-two-inch, recent passport photograph of themselves and of each family member on their application, the applicant then signed the form. A signature served as the primary security measure: during their screening interview at the U.S. embassy's consular office, winners were asked to sign their names multiple times. These signatures were compared to the signature on the original application form, and if they matched, the lottery winner could continue the process. If the signatures did not match, the lottery winner was deemed ineligible and disqualified from moving forward. Since then, the United States has introduced stricter security measures.

The program moved online in 2003 for DV-2005 so that the U.S. government could use photo identification software to catch people who were submitting multiple lottery applications. Currently, people registering for the lottery use an online form that requires them to provide their name, gender, birth date, city and country of birth, country of eligibility, the number of a valid international passport, their passport photograph, mailing address, country of current residence, phone number (optional), and an email address.[2] Requiring a passport number at this stage of the process— a requirement first implemented with DV-2021—is an additional attempt to eliminate identity theft and fraud. It ensures that the person applying for the lottery is the same person applying for the visa ten months down the line.

The second stage of the decision-making process begins after winners decide to proceed with the visa application. At this point, they must submit a mountain of documents to prove their eligibility. They must present certificates establishing that they have successfully met the education or work requirements. They must undergo a health screening at one of the hospitals or clinics that appear on an approved list published by the U.S. Embassy, and they must receive a certification of good health. To satisfy the requirement that they not have a criminal record, they usually need to provide an official police report from their country's police force. Married lottery winners must present marriage certificates and divorce or death certificates for any prior marriages. Additionally, married couples must find a person in good standing in the United States to serve as their sponsor. The U.S. government makes it very clear that sponsors are financially responsible for the new immigrant(s) and requires that anyone who is stalwart enough to agree to the role sign affidavits of support and share their tax documents to prove their financial wherewithal to make that decision. This stage of the process requires a lot of effort and a fair amount of money.

The third stage in the decision-making process is choosing whether to become a diversity immigrant. This decision must be made rather quickly, as the diversity immigrant has just six months after receiving their visa to enter the United States. After that, the visa expires.

WHY PLAY?

Many diversity immigrants apply to the lottery because friends and family persuade them to register. Rotimi, a thirty-nine-year-old Nigerian diversity immigrant, said, "A friend of mine talked me into it. He was like, 'People are winning it,' and I should try."[3] Skeptical, Rotimi told his friend, "'I don't think it's true; it's a scam.' On the last day, he still came to me with the same thing, quarreling that we must play it. Then I said okay, and luckily, I won, but he did not win." However, the same year that Rotimi migrated to the United States, his friend moved to London to earn a master's degree and has since been able to bring his wife and children to England to join him.

Office sites and work colleagues often push people to register for the visa lottery. Such was the case with Monica. She filled out the form and dropped it in the mail because her friend Stacy persuaded her to do so. Monica agreed because everyone in her office was applying. Some offices make registering for the lottery an annual event. When the lottery was paper-based, everyone in the office would fill in a form and mail it. In Africa, playing the diversity lottery is similar to collective company- or department-wide activities like the office pools of U.S. coworkers who collectively enter money lotteries like Powerball and Mega Millions.

Sometimes a person's family members and friends will apply to the lottery for them. Shormeh's uncle—who was actually not her uncle but rather her mother's cousin—told her about the program and then went a step further and registered her for it. Her uncle had migrated to the United States in the 1980s. He had enlisted in the U.S. military and was stationed in Germany when he registered her for the visa lottery. He called her, asking her to send him her passport photograph. Years later, thirty-nine-year-old Shormeh laughed as she remembered sending the picture just to stop her uncle from bothering her. At the time, she was finishing her degree in nursing in Ghana. Her uncle told her:

> "Shormeh, I know you like studying. Growing up, you are one of my kids who will always be studying. You like science, you like math, and I think if you come to the U.S. here, they have a lot of opportunities. You can go to school, further your education, you can get a very high degree in education, in the science field or whatever you want. You can even become a doctor if you want."

Shormeh did in fact end up becoming a doctor in America.

Abena, a forty-four-year-old Ghanaian diversity immigrant, had a friend in New York who registered her for the program. As Abena recounted, her friend "heard about it, and then everybody was talking about it, and then she called me and asked me to send her [a] picture of mine and a passport photo and that she will do it for me, and I did it, and I won."

Some respondents were persuaded to apply because they dreamed of traveling overseas, seeing the world, or going to America. The DV Program offered an opportunity, a chance to realize their dreams. Efe, a thirty-five-year-old Nigerian, was hounded to apply. "I really applied because this friend of mine put pressure on me. That was really the major reason." But later in the interview, Efe shared that when she was a child she dreamed about living in America.

> I had always wanted to come to the United States, I guess, to study, and I guess at the back of my mind, to live. I never really, like, had a plan about how everything was going to work out, but my mother told me that when I was little, I used to tell her that when I am big, I was going to live in America, and I will buy her a big house, and she will, like, beg me that will I let her come and stay with me, and I will tell her that if she is nice, then I will let her stay with me. So, you know, somewhere at the back of my mind, it was just something I had wanted to do.

Given her long-standing but unformed dream to go to school in the United States, Efe responded to her friend's pressure and applied.

Most applicants register for the visa lottery because they believe that their lives will be better in the United States. As a young revenue collector working for a utility company, Thomas was struggling when he ran into Ghanaians who resided in the United States and were visiting Ghana. They told him about the diversity visa and how wonderful life was in America. A few of them encouraged him to apply because they were trying to cover their embarrassment for not having enough money to pay their bills while they were in Ghana.

> Some people, when you visit their houses, don't have money to pay. So, for you not to disconnect their service, they try to woo you with these stories. The way they managed to become who they are and things like that. So I really got a lot of goods [knowledge about America] from these people because they encourage you. They say, "Oh, you are a young person, you can do it. Oh, I wish I can easily give you a visa to go. But this is only thing that you can do—the lotto visa is on right now. Try to keep applying for it."

Thomas got an "official" U.S. visa lottery form (though he could have applied on a plain white sheet of paper) from one of the clients who was trying to save face by dishing stories about life in America. "Some of them even had the form, and then, they will give you the form and give you directions to follow. . . . 'This is what you are to do, it is not anything difficult, you just put your name on so so and so and then, keep trying.' That was how it is."

Thomas longed to leave Ghana to "see other parts of the world" and was seduced by images of life in the United States. The Ghanaians living in the United States whom he met while collecting revenue "put a lot of zest into me." He wanted what they had.

> They have good cars, some of them have beautiful houses, some of them put up shops right outside their compound [built onto the perimeter wall of the house]. Some of them even end up showing you the shops or businesses they have outside town. Some of them ended up being very close friends. They start teaching you business and other stuff like that. Some of them own schools, private schools. Some of them have different houses, put up in different places, that they rent out to individuals. Some of them have hotels, and then they have their own residences in reputable areas in Ghana.

When he compared the affluent lives enjoyed by the Ghanaian U.S. residents he met with his own lifestyle, the contrast became almost unbearable for Thomas. "They always dress very simple, but they look very clean and nice. You ask yourself . . . those days, I used to walk under the sun to collect money; I will sweat, and my clothes will be drenched like it was raining before I happened to reach their gate. And in your mind, you think you do not have to be doing this." As they kept talking to him about America and the DV Program, Thomas asked himself, "'Oh? When am I going to get the opportunity to be like these people?' These are the things that actually pushed me. I had to do something." He registered for the visa lottery and won.

CHOOSING TO BECOME A DIVERSITY IMMIGRANT

After their successful selection, applicants enter the next two stages of the decision-making process and determine whether or not to pursue immigration. The decisions that Ghanaian and Nigerian lottery winners make can only be understood within their national contexts, particularly within the context of desperation. According to macro- and microeconomic international migration theories, people emigrate because a cost-benefit analysis convinces them that, even after deducting the costs of the journey, emigration would maximize the returns from their human capital (education and skills).[4] Theories of the new economics of labor migration posit that migration is a decision made by families, who nominate a member of the household to migrate as insurance against market failures in the home country.[5] And indeed, many African immigrants view their move to the United States as an opportunity to maximize their income and help their families.[6]

Lottery winners' reasons for deciding to pursue the diversity visa can be slotted into three main categories: life will be better in the United States, the visa is permanent, and migration will benefit the family.

Life Will Be Better in the United States

For some winners who are trying to decide whether to proceed with the visa process, thoughts of a better life in the United States become a permanent fixture in their minds. They imagine being able to "make it" in "the land of opportunities," especially compared to life in Nigeria or Ghana. A consensus view among my study participants was that there were no jobs at home. About half of Nigerians in the under-thirty-five age group were either underemployed or unemployed.[7] In Ghana, the youth underemployment rate was 50 percent in 2020.[8]

Shadrach, a thirty-six-year-old IT specialist from Nigeria, was so happy when he learned that he had been selected in the lottery. "I screamed," he recalled. His comparison of Nigeria to the United States rendered a scathing judgment on Nigeria and its leaders:

> The opportunity is not there [in Nigeria]. There is no need of going to school; when you finish, you are just stuck again. No opportunities. The country is like you have well-educated people everywhere but there is no job for them. People even with a bachelor's, master's degree, they are all in the street. Even first-class [summa cum laude] graduates or whatever, they can't find a job. The government is not creating any jobs; they are producing nothing. They are solely dependent on oil, and now the oil is already failed. There is nothing; people are just out there, graduating from college, nothing to offer them. So everybody was trying to leave and find something better.

Maame, a forty-five-year-old Ghanaian, said,

> After my [one-year] national service, I was worried about how to get a job. In Ghana, most of the jobs are gotten through who you know. If your mum knows a top person in a company, then you can get a job. If your dad knows such a person, then you can get a job, that kind of thing. I was very worried. So when I won the lottery, I was like, "When I come to the U.S., I'm going to work."

Maame's comments reflected her belief that the United States would be better than Ghana and that she could find a job there without having to "know someone."

In an extremely depressed employment market, having connections is very important when it comes to getting a job. In West Africa, if you do not have such connections, or "leg"—the colloquial term for such connections being deployed on your behalf—you are unlikely to get a good, high-paying job or be able to set up a business that obtains profitable commercial or government contracts.

Albert, a thirty-seven-year-old Ghanaian, was unable to get a good job after he graduated from college.

> I grew up in the village. My parents were poor. After I finished university in Kumasi [the second-largest city in Ghana], I tried to find a job in Kumasi, and then came to Accra [the capital and largest city in Ghana] and could not find a good job. I did not know anybody. The only job I got was selling insurance on commission, which did not pay me up to $50 a month. How was I to eat?

Most of my money was used for transport, hustling to get clients. And I had a finance degree.

College graduates who have trouble finding jobs often end up hustling with side businesses to make ends meet. Many of these self-employed persons who promote themselves as successful business owners are, in actuality, suffering. Many struggle to pay rent and eat two square meals a day without financial assistance from people in their social networks. Moses, a forty-two-year-old Nigerian, could not find a job after graduating with a business administration degree from a reputable federal university. He ended up opening a wholesale business selling toiletries and other body-grooming products. His small shop in a market in Lagos was making about $5,000 a year (in U.S. dollars) in profit, but governmental changes to Nigeria's importation policies destroyed his business.

> There was no business. Obasanjo's [government] put some strict policy on importation. So I could no longer get goods from the people I imported from. At that time, they banned some toothpastes, and these were part of the ones that sold more. They wanted us to buy and sell goods made in Nigeria, like the ones Lever Brothers made in Nigeria, which is okay. But with that, sometimes I could not even make 20,000 naira [$150 at that time] in a month, in profit. So I was like, no, it is time for me to pack my load.

Prior to the collapse of his business, Moses had little interest in leaving Nigeria. He felt he was faring as well as those in the United States. "I had some friends in the United States then, and when they came back to visit, I took care of them. I fed, housed, and transported them around. I did not like them buying me stuff, and they were surprised." From his research after he won the visa, he knew "that while the United States was a wonderful, good country, at the same time, we all know we have to pay bills, you have to work hard. You have to be careful of what you do; people easily get into trouble." Moses's friends had warned him that it was not all rosy in the United States. Black people faced discrimination and needed to be careful when interacting with the police. His friends complained to him: "'It is not easy. It is not easy.' When we are back home, some people believe that they pick money in the United States, but I knew better. But the opportunity here [in the United States] is better than Nigeria, I must tell you that."

The Ghanaian and Nigerian diversity immigrants I interviewed did not spend much time thinking about U.S. race relations or about how racial tensions might affect them as Black people because, as residents of Black nations, their race was not their most salient identity. Back in Ghana and Nigeria, ethnicity and religion are the more salient identities; race moves to the forefront only upon emigration to majority-White societies. The diversity immigrants in this study got a lot of their information about African Americans from U.S. mass media and American movies and comedy shows. As I discussed in my first book, *Beyond Expectations*, many African immigrants had adopted negative stereotypes of Black people from what they had heard in U.S. mass media. Ghanaian and Nigerian diversity immigrants reported a wide range of experiences with African Americans following their arrival: some reported good relationships with African Americans, and others said that they had been discriminated against by African Americans at work.

Oyinkan, a friend of a diversity immigrant, had struggled to find a good job in Nigeria since she graduated with a bachelor's degree in history. She had tried to earn money from a series of direct-to-retail health products and currently had a cosmetic and perfume business that was "struggling." She was "increasingly discouraged because people have no money to buy and those who buy my products are not paying." She cried as she spoke to me about the challenge of making enough money to support her family.

Non-college graduates had a worse time finding good jobs. Before winning the lottery, Abena was trying to pass her science subject in her A-levels in order to enter university.[9] She worked running errands for her grandfather's small watch repair company. Her wages were basically room and board, as her father gave her a tiny stipend of less than $20 a month. But even finding a job does not guarantee that one will earn enough money to cover the bills and support one's family. Ambrose, who was forty-one years old, had a teacher's training certificate and was a math and science teacher in a secondary school. He recalled being paid "just like $40 or something a month." At the time of our interview, he marveled at the low wages that college graduates earned in Ghana. "Even right now, people are there, and when they tell you the money they are making, it's like $29 or whatever a month." Adaobi, Efe's friend and peer at the time she left Nigeria, currently worked as a class teacher in a primary school in Lagos. She held a master's degree in business administration. Between the school's monthly pay of 100,000 naira ($320) and the 80,000 naira ($260) she earned from private tutoring on the side, Adaobi took home 180,000 naira ($580) a month.[10] Her combined sources of income barely paid her rent, transportation, and other living costs. In contrast, Efe, a thirty-five-year-old lawyer who came to the United States with a diversity visa in 2008, earned a good salary as a lawyer in Boston and, with the help of her parents, had bought a house.

Critical events often drive home the need to make a change. For Gbenga, a forty-two-year-old Nigerian, the birth of his first child marked the moment he decided enough was enough and that he needed to leave Nigeria. Prior to that,

> I never thought of traveling from Nigeria. I was like, oh, I'm okay here. But something happened to me in 2000 when I had my first baby, and after that, that's when I started thinking, hmm, I think I need to have a change! I didn't like the medical attention my wife got in Nigeria, and that was the turning point for me. Can you imagine going to a hospital for delivery at night; my wife was about to put to bed, and the [hospital] generator was not working. There was no light!! NEPA [the national electric power company] was not there anyway; generator was not there. They had to use candle to light the delivery room and deliver our baby. I said, no, I'm done with this! That was my turning point.

This incident and "wanting something good for [his] children" made Gbenga emigrate. "I started playing visa lottery for myself and for my wife every year," he said. He won it five years later and migrated to the United States with his wife and young son. He had been doing well in Nigeria but wanted a better life for his children. Compared to many other diversity migrants, Gbenga had a relatively smooth transition. "I've been working in the same information technology sector I left in Nigeria. It has been a very nice story for me. It's like we unplugged in Nigeria, we came to United States and plugged in, and light is on."

Many respondents believed that there would be better opportunities to "make it" in the United States based on things they'd seen and heard. Seeing how well his friend was doing was a key reason why Fred, a thirty-eight-year-old Ghanaian, excitedly decided to migrate to the United States while he was still in college in Ghana. "My thinking was, 'Wow! My friend stayed here [in the United States] for five years. He built a house, and when he came to Ghana to visit, he was driving a nice car. So, you've been [in the United States] like five years! . . . Then America is good. If I can also make it [to the United States], I think my life will be better,'" he said.

Shadrach heard from friends and classmates who knew people in the United States that, unlike in Nigeria, or at least unlike at his university, students were being recruited out of college by reputable companies. "We heard about opportunities whereby before you got out of school, you see companies coming to the school to give you a job." He was enraged that this did not happen in Nigeria, which he called a "shitty" country. What Shadrach was told before he left Nigeria was confirmed by his own personal experience: "Before I got out of college here [in the United States], by the time I was finishing, a company came to my school to pick me up to give me a job, which doesn't really happen in Nigeria like that."

Some interviewees knew that life in the United States wasn't as wonderful as others made it sound. They had more measured views about the opportunities available. For instance, Simi, a thirty-six-year-old Nigerian, and her husband knew that, because they happened to be migrating to the United States during what was being called the Great Recession, it might be difficult for them to find good jobs. "We were not going to leave everything. We were just going to go and see." Her husband had a good job, so he did not resign from it. "He took a vacation, saying, 'Let's just see what is going on.'" Simi was a college graduate in accounting. She did not have a job but was running a business selling hair attachments (weave-ins). "To us, it was not like a do-or-die affair. If it did not work out, we would come back."

The Visa Is Permanent

Winning the U.S. visa lottery is like a dream come true for most Nigerians and Ghanaians. One of the reasons it is so prized is that it is "permanent," as Christopher, a thirty-two-year-old Nigerian, exulted. While the success of remaining in the United States as an individual without papers is always contingent upon immigration enforcement, the diversity visa gives a migrant the right to legally reside permanently in the United States. It is not a temporary visa, like those categorized as non-immigrant admissions, such as the visitor's visa (B1/B2) or the student visa.[11] People admitted legally under non-immigrant admissions run the risk of "becoming illegal," or undocumented, if they stay longer than the permitted days without adjusting their status.[12]

It is extremely hard for a Black citizen of a sub-Saharan African country to obtain a visitor's visa to the United States because of the "push factors" mentioned earlier. African countries experience some of the highest refusal rates for U.S. non-immigrant visas. For many, just getting a temporary visa is the equivalent of getting an immigrant visa: it is a foot in the door. U.S. consular officers are aware of this and, as a result, reject many visa applications.[13] Only countries suspected of harboring terrorists hostile to the United States, such as Yemen, have higher refusal rates than African countries. In 2019, the non-immigrant visa refusal rate was 67 percent for Nigeria and 57 percent for Ghana, compared to non-immigrant refusal rates of 7 percent for Switzerland and 18 percent for China. In 2006, the B1/B2 refusal rate was 66 percent for Ghana and 54 percent for Nigeria. The refusal rates for both countries from 2006 to 2020, the years with publicly available data, were similarly high.[14] Almost all other African countries had refusal rates similar to or higher than Ghana's and Nigeria's during the same period.

While Africans do not easily get visas, Europeans rarely need one. Most European countries belong to the Visa Waiver Program (VWP), which allows European citizens to visit the United States without a visa if their stay does not exceed ninety days. The barriers against African immigrants in other admissions categories, along with their inability to access the VWP, are additional reasons why winning the diversity visa lottery is extremely prized.

The people I interviewed knew that even if they obtained a student visa to study in another country in the Global North, such as the United Kingdom, those visas would be impermanent. Nat, a forty-year-old Ghanaian, took this into consideration when deciding to apply for his diversity visa. He was on his way to England and in the process of getting a student visa. He had been admitted to a university in England, and his uncle who lived there had pledged to pay his fees and support him. But the father of the friend who had brought home lottery applications for his son and Nat to fill out told him, "Son, when you go to London and you finish your school, the possibility of you remaining there is very small. They can send you back to your country. But when you go to America, you are talking about being an American citizen." American citizenship, becoming a citizen of a land that, in Nat's words, "was like heaven"—that was the prize. "So, with all these pumping of ideas," he said, "one day, I told my wife, we have to do it." Nat's uncle in England was upset. He felt Nat was making a terrible mistake. But Nat chose the diversity visa and the United States because he would become a U.S. citizen, and he wanted his wife to come along with him. If he went to England as planned, he would have had to leave her behind because the student visa would have been only for him, the student. And it would terminate once he earned his degree or left the program for any reason.

Migration Will Benefit the Family

As Nat's story reveals, another benefit of becoming a diversity immigrant after winning the U.S. visa lottery is being able to bring along loved ones. That makes the diversity visa superior to non-immigrant admissions, such as temporary visitor or student visas to the United States or to any other rich country in the Global North.

A spouse and/or children listed on a lottery entry form also receive diversity visas if the principal applicant is selected. There are exceptions, such as if a divorce or legal separation has occurred between the time of submitting the lottery form and the time of applying for the visa. The U.S. government also allows individuals who won the lottery but were unmarried at the time of submission to add on a spouse or children if they got married or had children in the interim, but that decision is not always consequence-free.

Wives and children aren't the only family members who can benefit from a diversity visa won by a relative. Once established in the United States, diversity immigrants can file to bring over their extended family members.

Many families in Ghana and Nigeria appreciate having a "family Joseph"—this was the phrase used by Abeke, the sister of Lanre, a Nigerian diversity immigrant, who lived in Houston, Texas. She lived in Lagos, Nigeria. She said, "In my family, we think of our brother as the family Joseph." She was drawing an analogy between her brother's role in their family and that of the biblical character, Joseph, son of Jacob, who was sold into slavery in Egypt by his brothers. After serving time as a slave and as an incarcerated inmate, Joseph became second-in-command to Pharaoh, Egypt's monarch, and he was put in charge of preparing the nation to survive a severe seven-year famine. After Joseph's brothers traveled down to Egypt to buy food during the famine, they reunited with Joseph, who told them that God had sent him ahead to Egypt to ensure that his father, Jacob, and Jacob's eleven other sons and their families would be welcome in Egypt and would survive the terrible seven-year famine. Thus, the Israelites, made up of Jacob and his progeny, moved to Egypt for a period of four hundred years. Likewise, Abeke's brother Lanre planned to file applications so that all his siblings and their spouses and children could migrate to America. His ability to do so made him a figure of biblical stature to the rest of his family.

Brianna, a forty-nine-year-old Nigerian who migrated via the diversity visa in 1995, had been able to have her entire family to join her in the United States. "I was able to bring my son [born when she was in secondary school in Nigeria]. I was able to bring my mum here, then my dad. In 2016, I was able to bring my brothers and their wives and kids." At the time she filed for her brothers, they were unmarried, but because the process took about ten years, they were married and each of them had two girls by the time they obtained their immigrant visas to the United States. At the time of our interview, one of her brothers had just had a third baby in the United States, giving her five nieces and "an addition to the family." Her parents were now U.S. citizens. The whole family lived within a five-minute drive of each other in Chicago. Brianna was a champion to her family.[15] "Oh, my God! They call me the family champion. I told them to stop doing that." However, her mother persisted. "My mum says that I brought success to the family. I brought them to America. I am the one who opened the way, and I am the one leading them."

The opportunity for a diversity immigrant's relatives to migrate via the U.S. family preference system puts considerable pressure on winners to seize the opportunity if they win the lottery. Relatives see it as a family win when one of them gets a diversity visa. That means winners carry not just their own aspirations but the dreams of their family members on their shoulders.

Lottery winners who already have family in the United States often see that as additional incentive to proceed with the visa application. Family members can teach recent immigrants the lay of the land and help them settle. If they have the networks, they can help new immigrants find jobs and may be able to provide room and board for a while. They are also full of advice—some useful, some not. And they make an immigrant's journey less lonely. Mamle, a fifty-year-old Ghanaian, was "so happy" to move to the United States because she had heard all about "the good things in America" from her uncle. He had also warned Mamle and her husband that they would have to work hard once they arrived. The couple stayed with her uncle and his family for over six months. The uncle helped them find an apartment to rent, and his daughter helped Mamle with her English and her certified nursing assistant course.

When he arrived in the United States, Daniel, a forty-two-year-old Nigerian, stayed with his sister, who had been granted the diversity visa the year before. He lived with her for three years while he went to school, completing his course prerequisites before entering pharmacy school. Having family in the United States, especially family members with legal status who are willing to help and with whom one has good relations, can prove to be invaluable.

Another family factor in the decision-making process is children. For Debo, it was a personal risk to play the U.S. visa lottery because he was relatively successful in Nigeria. A university graduate, Debo, at age forty-five, was employed as a senior bank manager and enjoyed the trappings of an upper-middle-class life, living in a gated estate in an exclusive neighborhood in Lagos. He earned a high enough income to support his wife as a homemaker, and his children attended private school. He owned several cars and had a company car and driver to chauffeur him about town. His family employed several household staff. Nevertheless, Debo decided to leave Nigeria "for family reasons." He worried about the future his children would have in Nigeria. He wanted "to give the kids the opportunity to [go to] school abroad."

For decades, the ability to send one's children to universities in the West has been a status symbol, as the education received there is considered superior. Since the 2000s, in response to the surging demand for university spots that public universities, technical colleges, and polytechnics in both countries cannot meet, there has been rapid growth in the establishment of private universities in Nigeria and Ghana. Nigeria is home to only

199 accredited universities: forty-three are federal universities, forty-eight are state universities, twenty-three are colleges of education, thirty-six are polytechnics, and ninety-nine are private universities, of which twenty were just given licenses to open in February 2021. Ghana is home to ten public universities, ten polytechnics, forty-six public colleges of education, and eighty-one private universities and colleges.[16] There were only two private universities in Ghana in 1999.[17]

Many of these newly opened private universities are substandard, with insufficient facilities. Most offer a limited number of degree programs, compared to the larger federal and state universities. The schools find it difficult to hire qualified and experienced lecturers, and many lure full professors from federal universities by offering much higher salaries; as a consequence, a shortage of qualified lecturers has developed at both private and public universities. Private universities tend to offer admission to students who would not have earned admission to the federal and state universities. In both Nigeria and Ghana, the admissions criteria vary by institution, but a baseline of qualifications has been established by the national ministries of education. Students must have at least passing grades (ranging from A to C) in five subjects and scores on their university matriculation exams that meet the cutoff points set by the universities for their intended major. Although private universities are lower-ranked and less reputable than federal and state universities in both Nigeria and Ghana, they charge high tuition that only affluent citizens can afford. By contrast, federal and state universities are free or charge very low tuition and fees.

Although public universities are more reputable in both countries, especially in Nigeria, student learning is often disrupted by faculty and staff strikes as academic and administrative staff fight for salary increases and better funding from the government. These strikes have been called in reaction to changes brought about by the structural adjustment programs and privatization that has impacted the national investment in public education. In Nigeria, the most recent strike by academic faculty began in March 2020 and lasted ten months. Students in public universities lost a full academic session. Even during periods of calm, most people fear that more stoppages loom on the horizon, as strikes are frequent occurrences. A selling point of private universities is that their faculty and staff do not go on strike. Ironically, private universities thus benefit from the relative lack of public investment in higher education.

Given the problems with both public and private institutions, parents who can afford it or who have an opportunity to do so choose to send their children overseas for college. In both Nigeria and Ghana, government leaders send their children abroad for college, not only because such schooling is a status symbol, but also in tacit acknowledgment of the decline in their country's tertiary institutions. In 2016, the president of Nigeria, President Muhammadu Buhari, when asked why his children were in colleges overseas and not in Nigeria (five of his eight children went to school in Britain), said, "Because I can afford it."[18]

Individuals who attended university themselves and had witnessed the decline in tertiary education in their country wanted better opportunities for their children. Debo told me, "It was clear that we were not going to be able to get good education in Nigeria, and that was when we ignited the desire to relocate." His choice to move his family to the United States had paid off: his first daughter had graduated from college, and his second daughter was studying bioengineering at an Ivy League university.

In a similar vein, parents with young children hoped to give them a head start with a U.S. education. On the one hand, Desola, a thirty-seven-year-old Nigerian who had two young children when she won the U.S. visa lottery, was angry that her credentials from African institutions (a bachelor's degree in accounting) were looked down upon. Despite possessing academic credentials, many African immigrants have to retrain in the United States in order to get well-paying jobs. "Like us, now, when we came here, they still wanted to make us go back to school. Like my husband has an MSc and an MBA, and yet they still made him go back to school." On the other hand, Desola recognized the reality facing her and the opportunity that she could offer her children. "But if you study here . . . and that is the way I look at it with my kids . . . if they study here, they would not treat them as second-class citizens. They would not have to go to school again, as it would be seen that they have already gone to school and they will be accepted." Desola explained that the benefits of U.S. credentials are transnational. "Even if they go to Nigeria, their U.S. certificates will be accepted in Nigeria. They would not have to go to school again."

Finally, the desire to support one's family in Africa is a powerful enticement to pursue the visa lottery. The currency exchange rate is so disparate that remittances sent in the form of U.S. dollars and then converted into Nigerian naira or Ghanaian cedis can add up to huge sums that will go far in immigrants' country of origin. In July 2023, US$100 converted to 85,000 naira at an exchange rate of $1 to 850 naira. In October 2023, US$100 converted to 120,000 naira. The naira has depreciated over 100 percent in relation to the dollar in the past year and is expected to keep falling. One U.S. dollar converts to 10 Ghanaian cedis. The cedi has lost over 100 percent of its value compared to the U.S. dollar in the past two years. Before the Ghanaian cedi was redenominated in 2007, the exchange rate was US$1 to 9,500 Ghanaian cedis.

Even small sums of U.S. dollars sent home can transform the lives of receivers in poorer countries. The money puts good food on the table. Aging parents are supported in retirement. Rents and tuition are paid. Sick people receive medical care. Transnational dollars build houses and open businesses for parents, other relatives, and, at times, the immigrant sending the money (if they choose to establish themselves in both countries). Immigrants also send nonmonetary goods, such as clothes, back to their home country. Children prance around in expensive Nike sneakers courtesy of an overseas aunty, uncle, or parent.

Thus, even if the rest of the family does not emigrate, they still "win" in other ways when a family member gets a diversity visa. Koya, a thirty-nine-year-old Nigerian diversity visa winner, angered his family by not fully embracing his situation immediately. His brother severely warned him not to "waste this opportunity" by dithering. "Why are you still here nearly six months after getting the visa. What is wrong with you?" he angrily exclaimed when Koya traveled down to his village to tell his family that he had won the visa. He waited to do so until after he had wrapped up his life in Lagos. Relatives were not impressed with Koya's seemingly nonchalant attitude toward the precious gift he had received.

Eno, a twenty-six-year-old Nigerian, remembered immediately thinking that she would use the opportunity to support her family. She said, "I just kept thinking of my family, they are going to live without a lot of money. My dad is retired, he wasn't really getting money." Her mother was a primary school teacher. "So I felt like that [winning the visa lottery] was a breakthrough for us." Benjy, a twenty-six-year-old Ghanaian, grew up with two younger siblings in a household headed by his mother. He did not know his father. His mother, who did not finish high school, ran a small day care center in Accra. Benjy dropped out of college to help his mom raise his siblings. "I had to choose between coming to live here [in the United States], struggle to go to school [in Ghana], or going back and forth [between the United States and Ghana]. I could not do it. I knew I will get a job to help my mom; help her to reduce the burdens on her because I have two younger siblings." Benjy chose to pursue the diversity visa. He said that the lottery "was a chance, and I did not have enough money to sustain that plan" of going back and forth to Ghana to finish college.

Lydia, a twenty-eight-year-old Ghanaian, had no doubts about applying for and using her diversity visa. "All I was thinking about was money, money, money, because when you are in Africa, you think America is all about making money. I heard there were many opportunities here and you just have to take advantage of them. So I just had in mind that I was going to work hard, do everything I can to be successful, and then take care of my family back home."

AN OPPORTUNITY TOO GOOD TO MISS OUT ON

Ghanaian and Nigerian diversity immigrants remembered feeling sheer joy when they learned that they had won the U.S. visa lottery. Among their responses when they heard the news: "I was so happy." "I screamed." "I was very, very excited." "I knelt down with my head touching the floor, thanking God." "I gave away all my stuff; I could not wait." These responses reflect what Saara Koikkalainen and David Kyle call "cognitive migration," which they define as

> the phase of decision-making in which the experimental, always-on, imagination actively, though not always consciously, negotiates one's future social worlds, and hence emotional states, converging around a core destination. This mental time travel into a possible future in a different country constructs a narrative on how one's life is likely to proceed if one chooses to migrate, not in the abstract, but under specific conditions in specific destinations.[19]

Before they migrate, diversity immigrants travel to the United States in their minds and like what they visualize about their future lives. They have dreams (imaginings) of a better life, largely shaped by information given them by friends, family, and the mass media. And the situations in their home countries are certainly not good enough to give them pause about making the move.

I remember having a conversation with a colleague who told me it would be a great idea to have a subsample of Nigerians and Ghanaians who won the U.S. visa lottery, successfully completed the interview process, were given the diversity visa, and then chose not to migrate to the United States. I laughed and told my colleague, "I do not think I would find such people." I would be searching for a needle in a haystack. I knew I would find (and did find) Nigerians and Ghanaians who had won the diversity visa, entered the United States, and then decided to go back home after becoming U.S. citizens. My colleague told me of his friend who won the U.S. visa lottery, obtained his green card, and then decided to remain in Argentina. I told him that the state of things in Nigeria and Ghana did not afford diversity immigrants the opportunity to turn down a green card. It would be seen as rampant foolishness. Their families would not let them turn it down.

Study participants' socioeconomic and familial backgrounds affected their migration decisions in some ways and not in other ways. University graduates and nongraduates alike worried about the lack of employment and the unlikelihood of getting good jobs in their home country. A few diversity immigrants, like Debo and Gbenga, had good jobs in their home country but chose to leave for family reasons. Married, college-educated lottery winners often decided to use the diversity visa for their children's sake.[20] Diversity immigrants like Eno, Benjy, and Lydia knew that they would need to take care of their parents in retirement and thus had to take the opportunity.

On the whole, diversity immigrants have much in common with each other and with other immigrants. They want to "better themselves" in America, a sentiment shared by all of the study respondents, regardless of their educational background. Some have dreams of going back to school, but all wish to get good jobs, earn money, and acquire the trappings of a middle-class life. They want the house with the white picket fence or the newly constructed suburban home with tray ceilings, an outdoor lounge, and a patch of lawn. They want to progress from owning a used car bought at auction, from a dubious used-car salesman, or on Facebook Marketplace, to owning a recent, minimally used car, and finally to purchasing a brand-new car with comprehensive insurance coverage. They want to reach the future they imagined in their premigration dreams.

In reality, the three-part decision-making process to become a diversity immigrant can be understood as a simple choice and decision. The chance to improve personal and family circumstances leads people to become diversity immigrants. Each winner wants a better life, feels that they need better things, and believes that they can achieve more overseas, whether they are middle-class or working-class; a professional, a college graduate in a white-collar job, or a high school graduate; employed, unemployed, or self-employed; single or married; with children or childless. Together, declining economic and political fortunes in many sub-Saharan African countries and a positive image of the United States strengthen the notion that the program offers people a great chance for social mobility and a better life abroad. Although this image is tarnished in the minds of some immigrants, most Africans have a positive image of the United States. In the 2017 Pew Global Attitudes Survey, 69 percent of Nigerians had a favorable view of the United States, compared to 20 percent who had an unfavorable view. In Ghana, the rates were similar: 59 percent with a favorable view versus 20 percent with an unfavorable view. In fact, across the six African countries surveyed (Nigeria and Ghana plus Tanzania, Senegal, Kenya, and South Africa), 56 percent of Africans had a favorable view of the United States, compared to 26 percent who did not.[21]

For all these reasons, the DV Program represents an opportunity that, in the national contexts of Nigeria and Ghana—and, I would posit, other (and more) economically disadvantaged countries and regions of the world—simply cannot be turned down.

Chapter 4 | Diversity Visa Entrepreneurs in Ghana and Unintended Consequences

Visa entrepreneurs serve as a bridge between the DV Program and the West African immigrants the program seeks to attract. Their engagement begins before the first step of the application process even occurs, in that visa entrepreneurs advertise the program's existence to millions of people, many of whom would not have heard of it without their efforts. In many ways, the ad hoc industry can be considered an informal feature of the lottery itself.

When the diversity visa application process went online in 2003, the U.S. government created conditions on the ground that allowed for-profit visa entrepreneurs to expand and evolve their services. Agents are now able to offer help with registration to people who do not have internet access or who are not internet-savvy. Even as more people acquire phones that use data to access the internet, many individuals have only minimal skills in navigating the internet. Their fear of making mistakes on the application motivates them to seek out expert help, as I discuss in the next section. That has allowed visa entrepreneurs to flourish and maintain a foothold in the industry.

Although visa entrepreneurs are admittedly small-scale players in the migration industry (MI), they are a significant piece of the immigration landscape in West Africa.[1] Diversity visa entrepreneurs belong to a sector of the migration industry that is defined "as the ensemble of entrepreneurs, firms and services which, chiefly motivated by financial gain, facilitate international mobility, settlement, and adaptation, as well as communication and resource transfers of migrants and their families across borders."[2] Per this definition, the sector includes "money lenders, recruiters, transportation providers, and travel agents, legitimate and false paper pushers, smugglers, contractors, formal and informal remittance and courier service owners, lawyers and notaries offering legal and paralegal counseling and promoters of immigrant destinations."[3] What these individuals monetize is their knowledge of the process. The numerous services they offer include, for instance, recommending the best route to use to successfully enter the host country; showing clients how to successfully petition for asylum or for a visa; offering tips for passing an embassy interview; sharing ways to gain admission to an educational institution abroad; and providing assistance in getting a job. Some of these actors work on the legitimate side of the spectrum, such as nonstate actors who work under license or agreement with nation-state governments.[4] Others cross over to the illicit side by helping to circumvent legal barriers, as is the case with clandestine operations carried out separately and untaxed—such as human smuggling networks, trafficking rings, and transnational criminal groups.[5]

In the African context, the most heavily researched MI actors are those operating in the expanded borderlands of Europe and in migrant transit countries such as Libya and Mali (in West Africa) and Morocco (in North Africa).[6] In the news, the most common migration stories arising from Africa are those about human traffickers helping people cross illegally into Europe. In 2017, CNN screened an explosive video report on West African immigrants being captured and sold as slaves in Libya as they attempted to use human smugglers to get them into Europe.[7] Additionally, there have been numerous documentaries about irregular migration and the dangerous passage to Europe via the Spanish islands of Ceuta and Melilla, as shown on CNN, Sky News, Al Jazeera, BBC, and other TV networks.

However, the focus on illegal MI actors and the plentiful research into larger-scale, government-contracted labor recruiters has not been matched with equal attention to the small-scale, nongovernmental MI actors, such as visa entrepreneurs, who are facilitating patterns of legal migration. This chapter begins to address that omission by providing a deep dive into the practices of diversity visa entrepreneurs working in West Africa. Although they are sometimes just lone individuals running their businesses out of internet cafés, visa entrepreneurs play an outsized role in shaping the social organization and patterns of African migration to the United States and contributing to an aesthetics of migration that bolsters emigration. Studying this topic offers a priceless opportunity to explore how different actors in the theater of migration—immigrants, visa entrepreneurs, family members, and community members—understand and negotiate their own position in systems of global inequality. Examining the complex interconnections and social relations across different spheres provides insights into how individuals frame their actions, negotiate, respond to, and make migration systems work for them, even as countries in the Global North work to restrict migration from the Global South.

The chapter is divided into two parts. In part 1, I discuss the role of U.S. immigration policy in creating conditions that foster visa entrepreneurship and the ways in which the administration of the DV Program manufactures a continuing market for agents' services. I discuss how visa entrepreneurs create their market and customer base by selling expertise and putting an economic value on the know-how they deploy to help people navigate the internet, acquire a passport picture, and obtain required documents. In taking advantage of the program's design and administration to do business, visa entrepreneurs have become part of the process of structured luck surrounding the DV Program. In part 2, I discuss the migrapolicy interventions that are outgrowths of visa entrepreneurs' activities, illustrating how the specifics of the U.S. Diversity Visa Program facilitate exploitative practices around legal migration.

PART 1: STRUCTURING AFRICAN MIGRATION

The Cultural Economy Propping Up Diversity Visa Entrepreneurs

One way to understand why people offer a set of services or products and why others buy them is to consider the cultural economy propping up these activities. The central dimension of a cultural economy is that people's demands, needs, concerns, and fears give rise to businesses that together constitute the economy; in other words, markets and economies are not free-floating entities made up of businesses that pursue profit and prosperity independent of the people in the society.[8] Rather, businesses emerge at the micro level precisely to meet the needs that a given culture has produced, and together they create markets and economies. This forms the cultural economy. Visa entrepreneurs make no apologies for offering their services and making money from the DV Program. I spoke to the owner of one visa agency, who boasted, "Talking to some Ghanaians, they told me that the ten cedis we charge is so cheap. Too cheap for helping people register." Migration industry actors involved in the diversity visa lottery have commoditized their know-how, expertise, and connections, imbuing them with economic value.

People who decide to register for the DV Program fear several things, and two in particular: one, that they will submit invalid entries for the lottery, and two, that if they are lucky enough to be selected, they will make disqualifying mistakes somewhere in the process of filling out and submitting their immigration visa and alien registration form. At the registration stage, the online system will not accept a person's entry until the digital image meets the stated specifications. If selected, they must not hurt their chances by making minor errors when filling out the forms or being unable to present the required documents. They must prepare for and attend their screening interview (a crucial and nerve-wracking step in which they must convince the U.S. consular officer that they are deserving of the visa) without rousing suspicions. At every stage, applicants fear making mistakes, and for many, these fears can be mitigated only with the involvement of experts.

Such fears are animated by the context of desperation in which many diversity visa applicants find themselves (see chapter 2) and by seductive images of "the good life" overseas, which have fueled their dreams of migrating, if only they could find a way to do so. As a result, they are susceptible to the cultural and economic blandishments of visa entrepreneurs. Because these agents are culturally embedded in their country's society and understand how hard life is there for many, they are familiar with a market that places economic value on their practices and knowledge.[9] Visa entrepreneurs work to cultivate and build that market (and add customer bases) to feed their enterprises.

Meeting People in the Streets

I visited Ghana in October and November 2017 to observe the registration period for the DV-2019 cycle and talk to diversity visa entrepreneurs and their customers. I wanted to understand how the immigration policies of economically advantaged countries in the Global North impacted immigrant-sending countries in the Global South. When I discovered that some of the Ghanaian and Nigerian diversity immigrants I interviewed had encountered or used the services of visa entrepreneurs, my interest was further piqued.

I stayed in Dansoman, a middle- to low-income Accra neighborhood, with a couple whose sister I knew from my church in Philadelphia in the United States. My host—my friend's brother—came to pick me up from the airport, and I immediately began my investigations. "Have you heard about the U.S. diversity visa lottery?" I asked him. "Oh, yes!" he replied. "It is everywhere. On my way to work, I see the tents." *What tents?* I wondered.

"Circle," "Korle Bu," "37," "Medina," "Zongo Junction" — these were some of the places, my hosts and Accra residents told me, where I could find the street tents. "Go to the University of Ghana–Legon campus, you will find them there." I set out to observe these spots. For many days I traveled via public transportation on buses locally referred to as "tro-tros," partly because, unlike private taxis or rider apps, public transit stopped at the connection hubs where many of the tents were located. That was no coincidence, as such hubs reliably have high levels of pedestrian traffic. I discovered street tents advertising the DV Program and registration sites for the program. Registering for the lottery cost 10 to 15 Ghanaian cedis, the cost of a simple lunch meal, or approximately $3 to $4 per individual. I sat for hours watching various street tents do business.

Banners adorning the tents prominently featured the program name, along with the business name of the diversity visa entrepreneur. All the tents were red, white, and blue, with some featuring a U.S. flag or the Statue of Liberty (which stands near Ellis Island in New York). Some tents referred to the DV Program as the "American lottery" or the "visa lottery." That seemingly innocuous detail actually served a purpose: it sent the message that the lottery's "prize" was not money, but rather the possibility of moving to the United States. For many Africans, that would be a win equivalent to a cash jackpot, as most of them believe that they can and will make money in America. As some study participants shared, before they traveled to the United States, they believed in a vision of America not that far removed from the metaphorical "streets paved with gold" and the hyperbolic idea that "money lies on the streets" just waiting to be scooped up. In other words, they believed that the opportunities to make money in America were easy, plentiful, and omnipresent. Such colorful descriptions, relayed with rueful laughter now but reflecting earnestly held beliefs before they emigrated, speak to the image that so many Africans (and other immigrants) hold of America as the "land of opportunity"—the answer to blocked upward mobility in their home countries.

The businesses' banners proclaimed that a person could work, study, and reside legally in the United States. The mention of legality suggests that even diversity visa entrepreneurs, who live thousands of miles away from the United States, have heard about the trials of being an undocumented immigrant in America and know that the prized status of lawful permanent residency is a major selling point for the lottery. We could say that these advertising slogans on their banners were evidence of transnational migrations of U.S. conceptions of illegality and legality.

At the bottom of each banner was a chyron that advertised what some entrepreneurs touted as their "track record"—the number of their clients successfully selected in the visa lottery each year. Such advertising for these businesses reinforced the message that the DV Program was real—not a fantasy or a con—and that they could attest to its reality. They also promoted the idea that using their services to apply would increase an applicant's luck, but I found no evidence that it did.

The tents set up in high-traffic areas, such as the transportation hub in Circle, bustled with activity. The process reminded me of doctors' consultations: individuals entered tents, enclosed by strung banners, that provided the agents and customers with privacy. At busy sites, chairs were placed outside but behind the tent, to offer privacy for waiting customers.

Sometimes there were not enough chairs and customers stood, waiting patiently for their turn. Inside the tent, customers sat at tables, paid the fee, and filled out their forms. After they completed the paperwork, they moved to a corner of the tent and had their picture taken against a white background.

Some tents were in wretched condition, with old, dirty, torn, and ripped canvasses. Some were decent, however, and some had been wired for electricity, like the one in Circle. The tent in Circle had laptops and internet connectivity, facilitating the immediate submission of applications. In these better-equipped locations, registrants left with a piece of paper confirming that they had submitted a valid entry for the program. In some locations, customers had to come back to check if their application had been submitted. I spoke with several Ghanaians who trooped into these tents to register, and I interviewed a few workers.

I spoke with Alfred, the sole employee working in a street tent in Korle Bu. He was a graduate of secondary school (equivalent to high school) and had taken the job to keep busy. He had applied for the DV Program himself and was hopeful. Alfred viewed his job as helping his fellow Ghanaians gain "a chance to make something of themselves." He said, "On a good day we have about twenty people come in. On a bad day, one person." His tent had no electricity, so people simply completed the application form there and had their passport picture taken. At the end of the day, Alfred took the forms to the office to input them and get confirmation numbers. He told me that he asked applicants to come back to the tent in two days to receive confirmation numbers, but he confessed that his office was eight days behind in obtaining the confirmation numbers. I witnessed two clients being told to come back the following week to get their confirmation slips. Alfred later told me that their applications had yet to be submitted.

The people registering for the U.S. visa lottery were predominantly young men and women in their twenties and thirties. I saw only a few people in their fifties. I did not see a single gray-haired older person enter one of these street tents, an observation underscoring that diversity visa migration, on the whole, is a young person's game. The people who entered the tents were dressed like people with some education. Some wore Western clothing: for men, trousers and short-sleeved or long-sleeved shirts; for women, skirts and blouses or dresses. Other applicants wore African attire, mostly outfits made from colorful and striking Ankara prints. No unkempt or undergroomed persons walked into these tents. From the conversations I had with those coming out, all spoke English, albeit with different levels of fluency.

These were important visual and cultural clues conveying that the program was intended for a certain socioeconomic strata. The DV Program further entrenches class divisions in the countries where the visa lottery is played. Charity, a banker I interviewed in Ghana, was convinced that "the diversity visa is only for educated people." She was right. Those who play the lottery out of an abundance of excitement but without having the minimum educational qualifications are disqualified at the visa application review or interview stage. While I walked in the markets and busy motor parks, it struck me that so many individuals in these countries cannot win a diversity immigrant visa. The profile of visa entrepreneurs' customer base is dictated by the terms of the visa requirements: people over the age of eighteen who have at least a high school diploma or are skilled artisans.

Like neighborhood grocery stores and gas stations in the United States that offer easy-to-purchase jackpot tickets to shoppers, visa entrepreneurs' street tents offer convenience and easy availability to visa lottery applicants. The tents are a visual reminder for people who may have forgotten about the diversity visa lottery and a handy option for those going to or coming from work who have been too busy to apply for it; the tents make it easy to quickly pop in and get the application done on the spot. I spoke to a young man who said he had been wanting to register for the diversity visa ever since "a friend in America reminded me to register for it." He had forgotten to do so, "but on my way back from work, I saw the tent at Circle. So, before getting on my next bus to my house, I just walked here to register for the diversity visa." By placing themselves where people are bound to cross their paths, visa entrepreneurs encourage spur-of-the-moment decisions, similar to impulse buys. Another young man told me, "I just wanted to try my luck." The tent at Circle made it easy for him to go right in and register (see photos 4.1–4.5).

Street tents are not the only public venues where visa entrepreneurs operate. Internet cafés have also become spots for fee-based registration. Some visa agents hang banners and flyers advertising their services; others simply wait for potential applicants to walk in. In one café that was plastered with Vodafone marketing materials, a steady stream of people came in asking about the U.S. visa lottery. After clients paid their fee, the receptionist who had greeted them called out to an available staff member, who collected the client, walked them to an unoccupied computer terminal, and helped them fill out a lottery registration form. The process did not take a lot of time. In about fifteen minutes, the individual left with a slip confirming the submission of a valid entry via a unique confirmation number. In 2017, diversity visa entrepreneurs working out of internet cafés, or owners of internet cafés, charged individuals 15 cedis for this service—10 cedis to help them fill out and submit the online form and 5 cedis to take the digital image that has to be submitted with the form. Fifteen cedis in 2017 was equivalent to $4.

Photo 4.1   Street Tent near the University of Ghana–Legon Medical Campus, Accra, 2017

Source: Photo by Onoso Imoagene.

Photo 4.2   Street Tent near the Accra Mall, 2017

Source: Photo by Onoso Imoagene.

Diversity Visa Entrepreneurs in Ghana   83

Photo 4.3   Street Tent in Circle, a Major Public Transportation Hub, Accra, Ghana, 2017

Source: Photo by Onoso Imoagene.

Photo 4.4   The Circle Street Tent and the Intracity, Intercity, and International Motor Park, Accra, Ghana, 2017

Source: Photo by Onoso Imoagene.

Photo 4.5 Street Tent near Government House, Accra, Ghana, 2017

Source: Photo by Onoso Imoagene.

Targeting Secondary Schools and Universities

While street tents and cafés are ubiquitous in Ghana, many visa entrepreneurs operate in less visible ways. Some entrepreneurs carry out registration drives at secondary schools and tertiary institutions.[10] At secondary schools, the graduating (senior) class is targeted. Peter, a thirty-eight-year-old Ghanaian diversity immigrant turned health aide, explained:

> What they [diversity visa entrepreneurs] have been doing right now is just go around, especially in the high schools and universities, and take

[passport] pictures of people, and your particulars, because they know that if you win, there's a possibility that you'll qualify because you have the [education] qualification for the interview. They prefer [to register these groups of people] because they know that when you win, you have the [Senior Secondary Certificate of Education] and/or a university [degree] certificate, which will make it easier for you to get a visa than [it is for] ordinary people in the street.

It is explicitly stated on the website for the DV Program that any selected entrant without the required education or work qualification should not continue the process. As Peter noted, visa entrepreneurs know this: "They know that when you don't have the qualification and you win, it will become useless because you can't make it." That makes it less likely that a person will follow through and pay for further services from the visa agent.

Through recruitment drives at schools, visa entrepreneurs work the probabilities that the students will meet the minimum educational requirement (since secondary school seniors, by the following year, should have finished their O-level exams). Admission into a Ghanaian university requires that one pass at least five O-level subjects, including mathematics and English; this requirement is equivalent to the U.S. high school diploma and university entrance exams.

During my time in Accra, I talked to employees working for businesses that owned street tents, as well as owners of two businesses with street tents—Mr. Agyeman of Queens Consulting and Mr. Robertson of Link Tours.[11] Mr. Robertson was a young man in his early twenties who was just starting his diversity visa business. A university graduate, Mr. Robertson wanted to migrate to the United States and was making plans to earn a master's degree at a U.S. college. I interviewed him at a pizzeria near his busiest street tent. Mr. Agyeman, an immigrant himself, lived in the United States. He returned to Ghana frequently to oversee his business, especially during the diversity visa registration period. I spoke to Mr. Agyeman in his office in a large shopping mall in Accra. I had reached out to him through one of his employees by calling one of the phone numbers displayed on the company's advertising banners.

According to Mr. Agyeman, "We tell people, 'Don't waste your money if you only did junior high [the first three of six years of secondary school]. Don't even start [the application].'" He continued: "The diversity visa is not organized for people who would not go to America and fly. They don't want people who will crawl and use their resources."

Most Nigerian and Ghanaian diversity immigrants in this study who used diversity visa entrepreneurs to apply for the DV Program were recruited or enticed in secondary school or in college or university.[12] Sometimes respondents were persuaded less by the entrepreneur than by the encouragement and peer pressure of their classmates. While walking with a friend on their way to class, Peter stopped at a visa entrepreneur's table that was set up on the campus of the University of Ghana. "We were just walking on campus when we saw the banner." Peter's friend told him, "Let's go try our luck." Peter went with his friend to the table, though he was sure he would not win, as he had previously registered for the lottery "two times and never been successful." But since his friend "picked up the form," he too "showed interest in it and picked up the form" and "filled it out." The broker took a picture of him. Chuckling, Peter told me, "It didn't cost me anything. So why should I worry?"

While many study participants had given no prior thought to migrating, they were persuaded to register by a visa entrepreneur's urging. Gifty, a twenty-eight-year-old diversity immigrant who was a health aide in the United States, was in a class at the end of a lecture when some men entered the room asking people to register for the U.S. visa lottery. "In my school, there were these people who were going around taking pictures of people. I was actually running away." But because she knew the photographer who was working with the visa entrepreneurs (she had commissioned him to take pictures of her on several occasions), she listened when "he told me to come. So I waited and took the picture, and I didn't even know that was what they were using it for," she said (although she did recall filling out a form with her information). Gifty, who was already enrolled in a technical college in Cape Coast, Ghana, agreed to be photographed despite not knowing why because she knew the man who asked her to participate in his venture. She was not planning to leave school or to leave her country. She also did not mind because it did not cost anything. To her, "it wasn't that serious what they were doing. He took the pictures and that was it."

In Nigeria, Emem had a similar experience. She was about to write the post-UME exam—one of the three exams that secondary school students complete during their last year in order to be admitted to university—when she was approached by a visa entrepreneur. Until then, she had not heard about the U.S. visa lottery. She was trying to get into Obafemi Awolowo University in Ile-Ife, a top-five university in Nigeria.

> While we were sitting there, waiting for the exam to start, a young man came with an envelope, and he said, "These are visa lottery forms. I know you are students, or you are here for an exam, but fill this form—you never know what might happen." I didn't take it seriously. I was like, okay, whatever. So that was how I filled the form and that was in 2007.

Just like Gifty in Ghana, where "almost everybody in the class did it," Emem was not the only student who filled out a form: "Almost the full class filled the form," she reported. Because it was final exam season and they were there for an exam, "we had passport photographs. Almost everybody had passport pictures in their wallets or whatever they were carrying. So we just attached our passport photographs. I attached my passport photograph to my form and gave it back to the man." The visa entrepreneurs took passport photographs from individuals and scanned the photos to obtain digital images, which they used to complete the online registration.

Gifty, Peter, and Emem, like most diversity immigrants recruited during high school or college by visa entrepreneurs, did not pay any money for the lottery application—at that time. They did not give the experience much thought and almost forgot about it. Dreams of migrating to the United States or any other country "overseas" were, if considered at all, embryonic at best. The three students were busy with normal activities: taking exams, attending lectures, hanging out with friends, and otherwise participating in campus life. But by persuading all three to apply for the U.S. visa lottery, visa entrepreneurs changed the trajectories of these students' lives.

The respondents' accounts reveal much about entrepreneurs' school recruitment strategies and business models in both Ghana and Nigeria. Because of the DV Program's educational requirement, some visa entrepreneurs and their staff spread out across a given country, visiting the campuses of tertiary institutions—universities, technical schools, teaching colleges, polytechnics—and secondary schools in order to persuade students to "play" the lottery. Gifty was registered by an agent whose business was based in Accra, 146 kilometers (approximately 80 miles) away from her school in Cape Coast. To advertise the program some visa entrepreneurs set up tables and tents at campus hubs, where they call out to students to come apply. Some commission attendants in the computer rooms of these schools to give them access. Some contract with photographers already stationed at student residence halls to help them take the passport pictures and distribute their own "American lottery" forms to students. These forms ask for all the information needed to submit a valid online entry—the applicant's name, gender, birth date, city and country of birth, country of eligibility, mailing address, country of current residence, phone number (which is optional), and email address—with a passport photograph attached.

With student populations, visa entrepreneurs take a "no consequences" and "why not?" approach, relying on peer pressure or persuasion, lack of information, and the "fun" of "trying one's luck" to get students to apply for the lottery on a whim.[13] They bring the "impulse" decision they encourage in the street tents into the classrooms, where they count on students' adventurous or carefree natures to do much of the work for them. In this way, they repurpose the "language of luck" surrounding the DV Program and use it to transform and structure the luck and future of educated young West Africans.

Targeting secondary schools and tertiary institutions can be lucrative. The more students they convince to apply, the more chances agents have of getting their clients selected. Visa entrepreneurs increase the number of applicants by offering students free registration. Peter realized that "it is a big-time business. They go to universities and colleges and take pictures of people. They come with a banner . . . 'Diversity Visa Lottery.' Apply. It is for free. But that is the catch." The visa entrepreneurs who waive the lottery registration fee for students plan to recoup the money and make a profit by charging exorbitant fees to those selected in the lottery. They are able to charge these fees because they retain possession of the unique confirmation number that is given to each individual who successfully registers for the program. The visa entrepreneurs provide their own email address as the email address of the registrant and print out the confirmation page with the unique confirmation number for their own records. They are the ones who check the website when the results are released the following May. Then they get in touch with any individual they registered who was lucky enough to win and inform their "client" that their bill has come due.

This "big-time business" structure shapes the patterns of migration to the United States by targeting and facilitating the emigration of young men and women at a major inflection point in their transition to adulthood: they are either graduating from secondary school and about to enter college or already in college. But structuring the luck of these young people (by targeting students, bringing the lottery to their attention, getting them to register, and later tracking them down and pressuring them to proceed with the process) has negative long-term pre- and postmigration consequences—one of the most harmful migrapolicy interventions linked to the DV Program. The issue is timing: the stage (year) that a student has attained in their degree program determines whether they will have earned a bachelor's degree by the time they win the lottery, complete the diversity visa application process, and are required to enter the United States—a process that takes about a year and a half.[14] Only students who apply for the DV Program during their junior or senior year in college are likely to migrate to the United States with a bachelor's degree if they win. Students who register for the program before beginning college or in their freshman or sophomore year are unlikely to have completed their degree or graduated by the time they must emigrate. I discuss the consequences of this negative migrapolicy intervention and explore the experiences of this group of diversity immigrants in the next chapter.

Selling Expertise

I asked Mr. Agyeman why Ghanaians should use his company to register for the diversity visa lottery instead of doing it themselves, since registration for the program is free and the U.S. State Department cautions against using visa entrepreneurs, brokers, or middlemen. "Because we don't make mistakes," he answered. He then proffered that visa entrepreneurs create their own market or customer base by selling their "expertise" or "know-how" to people who do not have internet access, are not internet-savvy, or do not have competent computer and digital skills. Rather than promoting a "carefree" attitude (as they do when catering to students), visa entrepreneurs play upon this clientele's anxiety and their feelings of inadequacy. However, as I discuss later in the chapter, the requirements of the application process can and do cause similar anxiety among students in top universities, so there is a certain amount of overlap between these two markets.

With the application process now online, the U.S. DV Program assumes widespread internet access and computer skills among a nation's population. This assumption is unfounded for economically disadvantaged immigrant-sending countries, where internet access and computer ownership are not widespread. And even those who do have computer access sometimes find it difficult to navigate the registration website, take the required pictures, print and scan those pictures and other documents, and upload them as attachments. In 2018, 55.5 percent of Nigerians (111.6 million people) and 36 percent of Ghanaians (10.1 million people) were internet users. In comparison, 90 percent of Americans (293 million people) were internet users.[15] In 2020, only 7.9 percent of the Ghanaian population over the age of five owned a computer.[16]

"Many people don't know how to use a laptop," Mr. Agyeman said. "People don't have email addresses. How do we assume that high school–level diploma holders know anything about the computer?" His question reveals that, in its affluence, the United States myopically sets requirements that are harder to meet in developing countries in the Global South, with significant consequences for individuals hoping to emigrate. It might be natural for policymakers who live in the relative affluence of the United States to assume that everyone with a high school diploma has access to the internet and possesses digital fluency. Internet access is widespread in the United States, and typewriting and computer skills are taught in U.S. schools. Students in some K-12 U.S. schools use iPads and laptops for school learning and coursework. But what is common and taken for granted in the United States cannot be assumed to be common—or even happening—in economically disadvantaged countries.

The decision to move the diversity visa application process online, implemented in order to increase security and reduce fraud, has created conditions on the ground that allow visa entrepreneurs to profit from millions of people who lack computer access or internet fluency. Visa entrepreneurs also make money off of lottery winners by ushering them through the visa application process, which involves multiple stages in which additional documents must be scanned and uploaded. Mr. Agyeman succinctly summarized visa entrepreneurship as an unintended consequence (migrapolicy intervention) of the DV Program (and thus U.S. immigration policy) when he told me, "So we provide them with the internet, the computer, labor, everything, and we charge them only 10 cedis [about $3]."

Visa entrepreneurs have adapted over time and are always developing markets for their services. When the application process for the lottery was paper-based, all an applicant had to do was get a blank piece of paper, fill in the required biographical information, and append a signature and a passport photograph. Even then, because of widespread disinformation, many people did not know that using a blank sheet of paper was okay. They bought the lie that there were special forms to be used. Taking advantage of people's ignorance and the rampant misinformation, visa entrepreneurs sold forms that they themselves had designed and produced.

Theo, a forty-three-year-old Ghanaian diversity immigrant, laughed about it now, but his experience illustrates how visa entrepreneurs benefit from U.S. immigration policy by creating a market around the U.S. diversity visa. As Theo recounted, "They had a special form. Sometimes you could just grab a plain paper, write your name on it and your information, and then mail it. I did that, [but] that one didn't come [I did not win]." He came to believe that he needed an "official" registration form to improve his chances. "So this time I got the real one. On it was written 'THE DIVERSITY VISA' and whatever else was on it (*said with great emphasis and expressive hand movements*). That put some zeal inside me. I said, 'This is a fresh one.' To me, it was the original form." But it was not; it had been created by enterprising visa entrepreneurs who saw a way to make money off the program. Theo continued: "On it was written—'DIVERSITY VISA.' Beautiful. So that was why I said, 'Okay! Wow! This one, there is power in it.'" Theo felt vindicated in his decision to patronize the company when he won the U.S. lottery that year.

In a study of visa entrepreneurs operating out of internet cafés in Ghana, historian Carly Goodman found that before 2003, when the program was still receiving paper-based registration entries for the lottery, visa entrepreneurs created a market for their services by promising registrants that their entries would be delivered on time, even before the deadline, to the processing centers in the United States. To sound more convincing, visa entrepreneurs told people that they had private contacts who would ensure early delivery. This assurance was effective in creating a market because, in Ghana, the government-owned postal service was slow and unreliable. In fact, in several African countries, including Ghana, Nigeria, and Sierra Leone, there were rumors that the governments had ordered the postal services to destroy people's entries to deter emigration and impede a brain drain. Postal workers in Ghana denied any sabotage, claiming that the post office was making money from the millions of applications being mailed. Because shipping companies like UPS and DHL cannot deliver mail to post office boxes, and lottery applications were addressed to a U.S. P.O. box, applicants could not use those companies to mail their entries. Some applicants could send their entries to relatives and friends overseas, who would forward them to the processing center in the United States. People with no relatives or friends overseas, and those who were fearful that their entry would not be delivered—either because of inefficient service or deliberate sabotage—turned to visa entrepreneurs for help. Goodman's study provides additional evidence of how talented visa entrepreneurs are when it comes to using circumstances in their countries to create multiple markets for their services.[17]

Each day during my time in Accra, Ghana, I asked people I met while walking on the public streets and along the well-manicured pathways of the University of Ghana–Legon campus if they had heard of the U.S. visa lottery. I also asked people who were entering or exiting the U.S. visa lottery street tents why they had used a visa entrepreneur instead of registering themselves. They concurred with Mr. Agyeman, the owner of Queens Consulting: they needed to buy "expertise."

Many who had heard of the visa lottery and planned to register for it were puzzled by the digital image requirement, which is the first step in the application process and needed for a valid entry. That image had to be: "In JPEG (.jpg) file format/Equal to or less than 240 kB (kilobytes) in file size/In a square aspect ratio (height must equal width)/[and] 600 × 600 pixels in dimension." If they were using a preexisting photo, it had to be "2 × 2 inches (51 × 51 mm) [and] scanned at a resolution of 300 pixels per inch (12 pixels per millimeter)." All images had to be in color and "sized such that the head is between 1 inch and 1⅜ inches (22 mm and 35 mm) or 50% and 69% of the image's total height from the bottom of the chin to the top of the head."[18]

Many I spoke to asked me how were they supposed to know these things. "How does one keep a file size less than or equal to 240 kB?" A person who is somewhat knowledgeable about technology might be aware that cell-phone photographs are usually larger than 240 kilobytes, and they might know how to resize the file. But many would wonder,

"How do I resize a photograph? What is 600 × 600 pixels? Where is such information displayed?" And how could they to know if they had positioned the head in the correct ratio to the rest of the passport photograph?

Ghanaians I spoke to said that the experts in all this were the visa entrepreneurs, who reassured them that they knew how to format photographs and fill out applications correctly. Several undergraduates at the University of Ghana–Legon campus told me that they were going to use visa entrepreneurs to register for the program. These were students in the top-ranked university in Ghana. Presumably, they had access to the internet and were computer-savvy, but even they were defeated by the detailed requirements for the digital passport photograph. Some planned to use a street tent at Zongo Junction, which was near the campus. As Nick, a second-year economics major, said, "Since they are doing it for so many every year, they have a better understanding of the rules and all that, and the directions of the passport photographs to be taken and all that." Nick's words mirror how effectively visa entrepreneurs sell their services. He too alluded to visa entrepreneurs' know-how and expertise. He conferred even more accolades on them: they had a track record, as they had been doing it for a long time, and they would not make mistakes because they knew the rules.

The level of specificity required for the digital image contributes to conditions on the ground where, because many people need expert help, entrepreneurial individuals and businesses have taken advantage of this need to offer services, for a price, and a swarm of visa entrepreneurs and other MI actors has been launched, all servicing this one U.S. immigration policy. Mr. Agyeman described the market that has developed around the U.S. diversity visa: "The way we take their pictures, we do it professionally. It goes through [the online submission] successfully." His use of the word "professionally" is significant because it clarifies the service being provided and the service people are paying for, while obliquely giving voice to the fears motivating people to patronize visa entrepreneurs.

It is one thing for visa entrepreneurs to assert that they are offering people a needed service, but for a robust industry to manifest around the diversity visa, customers must accept that these offers of help and expertise are legitimate. Overall, customers I spoke to saw the street tents as "one-stop shops": for a small fee, the vexing questions of how to take the "right" digital image and how to fill out and submit the form were outsourced and "done right." However, as I discuss in the next section, this "short-term," "low-cost" relationship can sometimes unexpectedly expand into a long-term, higher-cost relationship if an applicant wins the lottery. The initial temptation to enter into a business relationship with a visa entrepreneur at the start of the application process makes it much more likely that a winner will feel compelled (by anxiety, superstition, or actual pressure) to return to that entrepreneur and continue to use their services after being selected in the lottery.

Serving as Record Keepers

Visa entrepreneurs also build a market for their services by acting, in the words of Mr. Agyeman, as "record keepers" for visa applicants. He claimed that his company and others like his "helped people keep track of their answers . . . of what they put down on their forms." Thus, if selected, they would not ruin their chances by providing inconsistent information in the subsequent forms they had to fill out. Visa entrepreneurs use different methods to ensure that they do not lose their clients' information. As self-proclaimed record keepers, Mr. Agyeman said, visa entrepreneurs promise to ensure that clients have all their ducks in a row.

> People win and forget what they used when registering. Our African culture, we don't keep receipts. Some register saying, "I was born so, so and so year," and forget. Others say they were born in Lagos. And then forgets, and fills [in the visa application form] he was born in Abuja, Nigeria. Then they get to the embassy and are disqualified. [So] we keep records for them.

Conveying a similar mistrust in his compatriots' attention to detail and record keeping, Mr. Robertson, the owner of Link Tours, told me, "Our people [Ghanaians] don't read. So they make silly mistakes. We help them keep track and make sure they don't, from these mistakes, lose their opportunity. We are helping them do it professionally." He added: "So many people make minor, minor errors." To pay the visa application fee, pay for medical exams, and cover the costs of gathering the required documents—at a minimum they need to supply a police report—"they spend all this money, get to the embassy, and get bounced. We do things the proper way. We provide all the documents required to prove [they are] who they say they are."

Mr. Agyeman concurred. When his clients say to him, "'I need a letter of invitation,' we say, 'Take this.' By the time you are going to the embassy, I have done my part. We say to them, this is the proper way to do it as it is drafted. These are the ingredients it must contain." Both Mr. Robertson and Mr. Agyeman told me that their goal was to ensure that their clients were seen as reliable by consular officers at the U.S. embassy in Accra. Mr. Agyeman said, "So many Toms, Dicks, and Harrys don't qualify, and we help them. We have helped thousands of people who are nurses, teachers, and military in the United States now."

"Record keepers" is a loaded phrase. It strongly suggests that the managing of information can be commoditized and given economic value, but in this context, it also intimates that visa entrepreneurs and their staff can help selected lottery winners obtain the documents they need during the visa application process. As record keepers, visa entrepreneurs are in the business of document acquisition and creation. This service helps them build a continuing relationship with clients. To review the process: Once an individual is selected in the lottery, the next stage is to submit the diversity visa application form. After they receive notification that the application has been reviewed, applicants must submit several required documents online, including a birth certificate (for all applicants), a police report, a sealed medical report (obtained by visiting a clinic or hospital on the U.S. embassy's approved list), a marriage certificate for married applicants, death or divorce certificates for those not in their first marriage, and the data page of a valid, unexpired international passport (a newly added requirement). After the visa registration form is deemed complete, applicants pay a fee to the U.S. government via a secure website and then receive notification of their scheduled screening interview, which they must attend with their spouse and qualified unmarried children. Individuals must acquire and bring to their interviews the originals and copies of all these required documents.

Visa entrepreneurs have contacts on the examination boards and councils that oversee secondary school O-level examinations and issue certificates of results. The agents have contacts in the government offices that issue and keep track of birth and death records, as well as in the judicial courts where marriage and divorce certificates are distributed, filed, and reproduced. Finally, visa entrepreneurs have contacts in the offices that grant international passports and at the police headquarters that produce official police reports. For a fee, well-connected visa entrepreneurs, especially the larger businesses, will help visa lottery winners acquire the documents they need for the application process by directing them to these agents or by liaising with the agents themselves to get the needed documents.

In the process, visa entrepreneurs are indeed record keepers in that they keep track of the information their clients provide on their registration forms and make sure that subsequent documents submitted (if the client wins the lottery) are consistent with the initial information given. More importantly, as record keepers, well-connected visa entrepreneurs work to ensure that their clients succeed and become diversity immigrants. To do so, visa entrepreneurs sometimes create false stories for applicants to put them in what they purport to be the best position to improve their chances of getting their visa approved. Mr. Agyeman alluded to this practice when he said, "So many Toms, Dicks, and Harrys don't qualify, and we help them." Visa entrepreneurs help make them diversity immigrants. And since, in the words of Mr. Robertson, they are not philanthropists, these agents charge significant fees because they are in the business of making money, even when paying these fees is a strain for winners, their families, and their communities. The fallout from these high fees is discussed in part 2 of this chapter, as are the gray areas and the sometimes illicit activities in which some of these visa entrepreneurs engage as they acquire documents for their clients.

Diversity visa entrepreneurs also sometimes act as a "nanny service." As Mr. Robertson details:

> Our people miss their interview dates. My staff have to call them to remind them. Many of them don't think; they think they can walk into any hospital to take their exams. We have to tell them no and send them to the right hospital. Sometimes we have to send our agent with them to accompany them to make sure they do it right. We [Ghanaians] don't read. Our people will win and they don't read. They don't know what they have to do and not do. We help them, and they are very pleased.

Through multiple services—from publicizing the U.S. diversity visa, to helping people register for it, to serving as record keepers—visa entrepreneurs facilitate the migration of thousands of people. At every stage of the process, entrepreneurial agents offer services to applicants for a fee. Some of these services are legitimate and helpful, while others have a more predatory and profiteering element to them.

Some of the respondents who used visa entrepreneurs did so because they had no choice: the visa entrepreneur they had hired subsequently refused to divulge their unique confirmation number without being paid an exorbitant fee. Such was thirty-one-year-old Adwoa's experience: the visa entrepreneur who registered her for the program located her after a lengthy search. Even though she was a "captive customer," in that she had to pay for the confirmation number to obtain it, the agent ultimately proved useful in helping her obtain necessary documents and ushering her through the visa process for an additional fee. "They did my birth certificate and my passport," she explained. The agency helped Adwoa organize her medical exams. "They have connections even where we went to do the medicals. The owner of the agency I used has connections everywhere. So like, when you go, it's like they know you, they know where you are coming from. So they don't go deep into the things you are supposed to go deep into because they have connections there."

No Needles Lost in the Haystack

To make a profit, visa entrepreneurs must be able to locate winners once the lottery results are released. Visa entrepreneurs collect a lot of phone numbers from applicants. In addition, they ask for the phone numbers of parents, siblings, friends, coworkers, pastors, relatives, and so on. Visa entrepreneurs do this because there is a lengthy time lag between the registration period and the selection of winners. If the visa application process begins in October of one year, it may be almost two years before the visa is obtained. For example, a student who applied at a college campus in October 2010 and was selected in the lottery in May 2011 would have had until September 30, 2012, to start and complete the visa application process. If they obtained their visa in the first six months of the 2012 fiscal year, they would be required to enter the United States before the end of the 2012 fiscal year. Their window to finish the visa application process and enter the United States is shortened, however, by the need to rush to process their visa so as not to run the risk of visas becoming unavailable, either because the annual visa cap of fifty thousand visas is reached or the cap for their country's visas is reached. Given that this is a multiyear process, visa entrepreneurs need to ensure that they can track down the winning applicant one way or another. After finding the lucky individual, visa entrepreneurs confirm the winner's information—name, date of birth, educational level, and so on—to ensure that they have the right person.

Emem, who had applied for the program while in her post-UME exam classroom, forgot that she had filled out a diversity visa form until she got a call from her mother.

> Yeah, it wasn't until two years after that. (*laughs*) I was in school. I just got back from class, and my mum had called me and she said, "Did you fill any lottery form?" I told her that yes, I did, but that was like two years ago. So I already forgot about it. But she told me somebody had called her and told her I was chosen.

Because Emem had relocated to a city 771 kilometers away from where she lived when she submitted the form, the staff of the visa entrepreneur had to contact Emem's mother using one of the numbers they had been given by Emem.

Not only are visa entrepreneurs dogged in their search for visa lottery winners, but they also pressure winners to seize the opportunity, even going as far as using family members to persuade reluctant winners. Visa entrepreneurs go to such lengths because their potential profits are tied to charging lottery selectees or their families exorbitant fees for releasing the unique confirmation number.

Intrepids and Doubters

Some study participants did not accept visa entrepreneurs' claims about their "expertise." These were usually those who had at least a bachelor's degree, rather than those who had only a secondary school education, or who were still in the process of attaining their degree, or who were artisans with at least two years of apprenticeship training. Those with a bachelor's degree felt that they were competent and could handle the entire process by themselves—from registering for the program to completing the subsequent stages of the application process if they won the visa lottery. (See table 1.1 for a chart detailing the stages in the diversity visa process.) I call this group the "intrepids." One would have the needed skills to complete the process, said one intrepid rather dismissively, "as long as you can read and write." But the factors involved clearly go beyond simply possessing the ability to read and write, since the other group—those who felt that they could not apply for the visa without getting help to avoid mistakes—included high school graduates and college students, who could ostensibly read and write too. I call that group "doubters."

Abena, a forty-four-year-old Ghanaian, was a doubter. She won the visa lottery in 1996, the second year that the program was fully operational. At that time she had just finished her A-levels (college-entry exams) and was working in her uncle's shop. Her friend in New York helped her register for the visa lottery; all Abena did was send her friend a passport photograph. Upon getting the notification letter from the U.S. State Department, Abena called her friend and asked if this was the outcome of what she had done for her. "My friend squealed and said yes. And then I called my father and told him. And we weren't sure of how to start it. Because we didn't know what to do, we had to pay somebody to help me fill it up." To "start it" Abena needed to fill out and submit the immigrant visa and alien registration form. Her family was introduced to an agent who was just "an individual that somebody told my mum knew how to do that stuff; he did it for somebody that she knew. It was the business that the guy was doing. Once anybody won the lottery, you could go to him and he will help you to fill it up." Abena paid the visa entrepreneur $800 just to help her fill out the forms. She paid such a huge sum for help in filling out the form "because we didn't know anything. We thought we could mess it up filing." That was the fear many doubters had—"that they would mess it up," as Abena said.

Intrepids tended to scoff at the notion of using visa entrepreneurs. Thirty-eight-year-old Bisayo and her husband, who was in the military and stationed in Alaska, were both intrepids. Both were Nigerian university graduates: she had a bachelor's of science degree in banking and finance, and her husband had a bachelor's degree in engineering. When asked about hiring a visa entrepreneur, Bisayo said:

> Oh, no, no. We did it by ourselves. Even though I remember when we got to the post office to pick up the parcel, they told us, "We have people that are expert in this, they can do it, you just have to pay them money." Then my husband was like, "What is there that I have to contract somebody for?" (*chuckles*) We have a computer in our house, we have a printer and a scanner. So everything was done in our house. We didn't have any difficulty doing that.

Having a computer and printer/scanner in the home is a marker of middle-class status, and knowing how to operate them was a sign that Bisayo and her husband had middle-class cultural capital as well.

Cultural capital is a defining feature of intrepids: it makes them confident that they will be able to understand and fill out forms and navigate the various government bureaucracies and institutions of both the United States and their country of origin. Drawing on insights from Pierre Bourdieu's definition of cultural capital as something that can be acquired through objective education qualifications, cultural capital can be understood as having skills and knowledge that become a valuable resource through their transferability to other domains of life and in dealings with institutions.[19] Put another way, intrepids possess a "repertoire of capacities" to draw from in navigating the application process by themselves.[20] Cultural sociologist Ann Swidler states that "within established modes of life, culture provides a repertoire of capacities from which varying strategies of action may be constructed." She also refers to the "repertoire of capacities" as "cultural toolkits" because "culture influences actions not by providing the ultimate values . . . but by shaping a repertoire or toolkit of habits, skills, and styles from which people construct strategies of action."[21] Looking at the dividing line between respondents in this study, degree attainment appears to be crucial to the acquisition of cultural capital, but it is not simply education that distinguishes between those who had cultural capital and those who did not; a combination of education, work experience in white-collar occupations, class, and wealth was also critical in their accumulation of cultural capital. Doubters did not have the "cultural toolkit" or "repertoire of capacities" developed and attained through a completed college education did not view themselves as "experts" and subsequently turned to visa entrepreneurs.

PART 2: EXPLOITATIVE CONSEQUENCES AND NEGATIVE MIGRAPOLICY INTERVENTIONS

The structure and requirements of the U.S. DV Program result in migrapolicy interventions that disrupt immigrants' lives (temporarily in the mildest cases and permanently in the most serious cases). The emergence of the visa entrepreneurship industry is, in itself, a migrapolicy intervention that can be directly linked to the DV Program's requirements and administration. In addition, the practices of visa entrepreneurs give rise to a number of negative and exploitative migrapolicy interventions, including the accumulation of debt, the creation of fictive kinship ties, the interruption of human capital accumulation, and more. Such exploitative interventions begin premigration, take place within immigrants' country of origin, and occur despite the legality of the DV visa itself. Effects are experienced far beyond the individual immigrant and can resonate well past their arrival in the United States. This section details a number of those interventions.

From 10 Cedis to Thousands of U.S. Dollars

In our interviews, both Mr. Agyeman and Mr. Robertson, as owners of diversity visa companies, described their role as "helping their people"; they felt that "we save people money" and prevented applicants from "being bounced [summarily rejected] at the embassy" because they lacked the right documents or were ill prepared for the interview. However, visa entrepreneurs are clearly in the business to make money and charge a range of fees. In 2017, street tent walk-ins were charged 10 to 15 cedis and internet cafés charged 15 cedis, or the equivalent of between $2.60 and $4.00. Given the thousands of people who patronize visa lottery street tents and internet cafés, these fees can add up and produce significant profits.

Visa entrepreneurs who operate in a gray area of legality by gaining and keeping possession of registrants' unique confirmation numbers can charge clients much higher fees. Martin, a thirty-nine-year-old Ghanaian diversity immigrant I interviewed in New Jersey, decoded the visa entrepreneur business model:

> If you win, in Ghana, if somebody tells you that you have won the visa lottery, so you are about to go to America, you feel so excited. Whatever it takes for you to get whatever money that they want from you so that they can process the document for the interview, you will do it because you know that you are going to get a green card. So whatever it will take, you work towards that. Whatever amount they want from you, you must come up with that money.

Less ethical visa entrepreneurs have lottery winners dead to rights because, if winners refuse to pay, they lose the opportunity to apply. Winners cannot move forward in the process without the unique confirmation number assigned to their case by the U.S. government; once someone else has that number in their possession, winners have only one other way to get it, but this option is blocked. Although there is a tool on the DV website that allows individuals who have lost their confirmation number to retrieve it by entering the email address they used to register and certain personal information, that avenue is blocked if the applicant does not know or have access to the email address used by the visa entrepreneur. Unscrupulous visa entrepreneurs not only retain applicants' confirmation numbers but also use their own email address in lieu of the applicant's, forcing those who use their services to register for the program to also use their services to process their immigrant visa. It is big business.

The diversity immigrants in this study who had used visa entrepreneurs to secure their visas were ultimately charged fees amounting to thousands of U.S. dollars. But the fees across visa entrepreneurs varied. In 2011, Kofi was charged $2,000, which his father paid since Kofi was a prospective undergraduate student. Gifty and Martin were each charged $3,000. According to my conversations with study participants in Ghana, Nigeria, and the United States, individuals who used visa entrepreneurs who retained their unique confirmation number were charged, on average, between $1,500 and $3,000. These fees were separate from the various visa processing fees, such as the diversity visa application fee of $330, the U.S. Citizenship and Immigration Services (USCIS) immigrant processing fee of $220, and medical examination costs.

Diversity visa entrepreneurs were cavalier about the pain they put clients through to raise the fees charged. According to Alfred, a Link Tour employee, "you have to find a way. You have won. Some people have not been able to pay, but very few. They forfeit it if [they] can't pay. We have had young boys like the ones you saw [come out of the tent] win it, and they have come up with the money." He was suggesting that if very young boys—the boys I saw come out of the tent had just finished high school and were hustling without regular employment—could find the money, older and more established lucky winners who had jobs had no excuse.

Agents who charged exorbitant fees used a variety of strategies to collect payment and prevent default. As Mr. Robertson, the owner of Link Tours, shared, "Before, we used to let people owe us.... We would process their passports, documents, and so on ... with the understanding that they would pay us once they got to America. But when they go to America, they forgot about us." As a result, he takes the payment up front, "no stories told." I asked him what he did if they told him they had no money. He responded, "They have family. I tell them to go borrow the money."

When Joy could not pay in full right away, she "had to go with this guy because he charged me sixty million cedis [equivalent to $1,500 in 2009]. I had to go to my screening interview with him." Her visa was approved. When she came out of the interview and told the visa entrepreneur that "the interviewer [a U.S. consular officer] gave me a yellow paper to use to come back to collect the visa," the agent confiscated it. "So, because I had to give the guy money, he kept that paper [that permitted her to collect her visa, stamped passport, and the package she was supposed to submit to the Border Patrol officer when she arrived in the United States] until I finished the payment." She was extremely motivated to make the payment, she said. "I went two days later to take my visa."

Mr. Agyeman said he advised clients on where to go to get financial help. He told me, "In Ghana, with the way the situation is now [tough economic times], if you sell your entire family (*said jokingly, to emphasize his point*), you cannot [raise] one thousand U.S. dollars." Expressing a sentiment similar to Mr. Robertson's, he told me that diversity visa entrepreneurs "are not charities. They cannot expect us to help them for free. So, if you have no money, you need people to help you. I tell them, take your winning letter to your chief [an ethnic group or village's traditional ruler], your assemblyman, to see if they can help. Some were successful."

A few interview subjects maintained greater control by not paying their visa entrepreneur until they had their visa in hand. It all depended on the visa entrepreneur used to register for the program. Some were more understanding and more willing to negotiate or delay payment until an applicant had obtained the visa or had migrated to the United States and earned enough to send dollars to pay what was owed.

The Accumulation of Debt

The specific requirements of the U.S. DV Program facilitate exploitative practices around legal migration. By establishing class-based requirements, such as education credentials, the diversity visa tends to attract those who might be considered the relatively privileged in their home country. Despite this privilege, many diversity immigrants and their family members are not spared from the yoke of debt, accrued either from the cost of the visa fees levied by the United States and the airfare to get there or because of added and sometimes exorbitant fees charged by visa entrepreneurs within their home country.

The families of the diversity immigrants I interviewed were definitely impacted by visa entrepreneurs. The exorbitant fees charged to clients to release their unique confirmation number or to help them process their application often made it imperative to involve family members. That visa entrepreneurs were clearly involved in a business transaction is exemplified in Mr. Robertson's statement to me: "So many people think the DV is free, [but] the only free thing is your [lottery] selection."

Diversity immigrants who had to pay the exorbitant fees ranging from $800 to $6,000 all needed the help of parents and extended family members. Some study participants, like Stanley and Gifty, had to borrow the money from family members. Whereas migration scholarship tends to focus on the sorts of debt accumulated by undocumented migrants who become beholden to coyotes and traffickers, we must acknowledge the burden of debt that accompanies this form of legal migration as well. As a consequence of obtaining financial help from family members, diversity immigrants become obligated to their relatives. The remittances they send back home can no longer be seen only as support for family members but now must also be seen as a form of debt for the money received from their families that helped facilitate their migration.

Creation of Fictive Kinship Ties

Sometimes visa entrepreneurs encourage single individuals who are selected in the visa lottery to add someone to their winning ticket. In fact, anthropologist Charles Piot's marvelous ethnography of a visa broker in Togo—cowritten with "fixer" Kodjo Nicolas Batema, a Togolese diversity visa broker—suggests that migration industry actors target young people *because* they are likely to be single and may thus represent another business opportunity. For a hefty fee, visa entrepreneurs in Togo added another person or persons as the diversity visa winner's spouse and/or dependent children. Often that person or their relatives, who tended to be wealthy people such as high-ranking individuals in the Togolese government or Togolese who lived abroad, picked up the tab.[22]

The scheme, a migrapolicy intervention that I refer to as the creation of fictive kinship ties, can look attractive to individuals who cannot afford all the fees associated with processing the visa. However, there is a risk involved. Suspecting fraud, U.S. embassy officials are wary of individuals who add someone to their application as a spouse after winning the visa lottery. But U.S. consular officers, on the whole, feel the United States cannot legislate against falling in love.[23] So individuals are not prevented from adding a spouse to their application, though doing so runs the risk of not having their visa approved and losing out on their opportunity to migrate. As Gifty shared:

> It is really true that [diversity visa entrepreneurs] would tell you, "Let's add somebody to your form." That person would pay for your ticket and things [the fees associated with processing the visa]. I heard about that, but because I had a boyfriend, I told my visa entrepreneur . . . I claimed I was going with my boyfriend. A lot of people were doing it. Brothers and sisters were getting married just because they both want to come to America. I had a friend who had to marry the brother, they had to do this fake marriage ceremony in Ghana, take pictures, and then they had to go for the interview, and they got the visa. A real married couple were denied the visa.

Gifty avoided this approach, however, because, she claimed, she was in a committed relationship and was considering adding her boyfriend (soon to be her fiancé) to her application so they could come to the United States together. But in the end, out of fear that her visa would not be approved if she did this, she decided not to. "I learnt a lot of people were being denied when they go as couples. So we decided that I will come. Then, if I am able to settle and get a good job and everything, then he will follow. So that is what we planned on doing, Unfortunately, we are now married to different people." I asked Gifty why her relationship ended, and she said, "It was the distance. The distance played a very big role in my relationship. There was no trust. So we had to go our separate ways."

According to Emmanuel, a Ghanaian diversity immigrant I interviewed in Philadelphia, some Ghanaians allow visa entrepreneurs to add people to their forms, creating pretend marriages out of desperation if they do not have the money to process the visa and need financial assistance. Because it makes them money, visa entrepreneurs also promote the practice.[24] As he details, in such situations, an exchange is made: someone is added to the winner's form—most commonly as a spouse—in exchange for paying the winner's full freight, including all visa processing fees and costs and the airplane ticket to the United States. Emmanuel gave an overview of the business of brokering diversity visa marriages:

> The thing is, you see, everybody wants his family or something like that to come here [to the United States]. You know, for that matter, getting the papers here is not easy. So there was a time that, with the introduction of the visa lottery, if people won, most of the time, we don't even have the money to pay for the visa fee or the processing fee. Before you process the other stuff, you have to go to hospital, they put you through a whole lot of tests. All those things you have to pay the money right away—cash. How can

you afford that? And those days, those, the monies was in millions of cedis in Ghana. I can't afford it. So somebody has to help you. So all that you want that time is to find a way, whichever way it happens to be, to get out from Ghana. And that was it. So there were some people that their relatives are already here or they are in United Kingdom or places like that—they can easily afford those monies because if they send their dollars and it is exchanged into cedis, it becomes very easy. So there are people who even create office for things like that back home. So if you win and then you don't have anybody overseas [especially in the Global North] or you don't have resources yourself, you contact those people. Then some of them will link you up with people who are ready—they have relatives here in Ghana and then they want their relatives to come to join them but they cannot give them the visa or their papers. So they know that through the visa lottery, they can easily bring that person. So things like that happen.

From Emmanuel we learn that some visa entrepreneurs have transnational connections. Their market is not only domestic but also international, as it spans across borders, in this case to the United States. These visa entrepreneurs serve as middlemen between individuals in the diaspora who are seeking ways to bring their family members over and desperate individuals in sending countries who have a legal migration pathway or solution to barter.

Because she was single, Emem was asked by the visa entrepreneur in Nigeria if someone could be added to her application in lieu of her paying the U.S. $2,000 she had been charged. "Oh, yeah! Oh, yeah! They were like, it's either you add a spouse or pay them the money. So my mum was like, 'My daughter! We don't even know you guys. I cannot just let you marry her off just because of a green card.' So we went ahead and paid them off."

According to Ghanaian and Nigerian diversity immigrants, the gray area between legal and illegal practices is a direct result of the contexts of desperation faced by many people in immigrant-sending countries and the increasing barriers to migration to countries in the Global North. When asked if he had difficulty during the application process, Emmanuel revealed that he had processed his visa through a visa entrepreneur who entangled him in a pretend marriage to cover payment.

EMMANUEL: Oh, my God? That was one interesting area of the visa lottery. A lot of problems men? A lot, a lot. At that time, I found it difficult to feed myself . . . things were very tough. I didn't have money to do anything for myself. It was a very difficult moment for me, and somebody had to

>   help me, and all those things had a very bad memory with me right now because you may end up not becoming a good person to somebody or things like that. So it's a hell.
>
> AUTHOR: You had to borrow the money? Or was it given to you as a gift?
>
> EMMANUEL: Oh, actually, the person [diversity visa entrepreneur] wanted to help me, and you know, those days, people will arrange that you have to bring them somebody and things like that. That was what happened. Actually, they wanted to sponsor us, to pay for the traveling. You have to bring the person as somebody that you have married.

In situations like Emmanuel's, visa entrepreneurs link winners of the visa lottery, who are single at the time of the win, to migrants in the United States who have relatives they want to bring over and who are willing to pay for the service. The clients in the United States pay both the principal winner of the visa lottery and the visa entrepreneur for providing the connection and overseeing the application process.

Emmanuel was aware that what he was doing was illegal and wrong. It shows in his words: the process was a "very bad memory," he felt he was "not becoming a good person," and the experience was "a hell." He was conflicted about entering into a pretend marriage in order to get the means to successfully process his diversity visa and come to the United States, but he did it anyway out of desperation, because "I found it difficult to feed myself . . . things were very tough."

Pretend marriages are not the only fictive kinship ties that may be created and added to applicants' forms before they are submitted. Derek had put his son's name on the form, but not the name of the mother of his child. Upon winning the lottery, he found that the visa entrepreneur had changed his form without his consent and knowledge.

> That was a problem. At that time I had one child. My second child was in the womb when I was coming. But the thing is, I don't know what happened. . . . I put my son on there. And I didn't put the woman on the paper because we weren't married and I didn't know what I was going to plan, so I didn't want to do anything stupid, so I think I left that blank.

Derek was not sure he wanted to marry the mother of his child and thus did not want to find himself in a situation where he would be forced to marry her or need to acquire a marriage certificate as proof of nuptials if he was selected. But "the guy [diversity visa entrepreneur] came, and for some reason, he changed, no, he went and canceled the kid's name [the name of Derek's child] because he put his sister on the form as my wife. He said he was thinking that his sister doesn't have a child, so he didn't want any trouble. . . . I came with her. I came with her as my wife."

The visa entrepreneur paid all of Derek's costs to process his immigration visa as payment for his agreement to add the agent's sister to his application as his wife and to go with her to the screening interview at the U.S. embassy in Accra. "He [the agent] paid the cost for the visa processing and everything." Along with covering the U.S. visa fees, the cost of Derek's medical exam, and the costs for obtaining his police report and international passport, the visa entrepreneur also paid for Derek's airplane ticket. It was a transaction satisfactory to all parties. "I was cool with it, and he got his sister here [in the United States]."

Derek did not quibble because he lived in a state of financial hardship and needed the financial assistance. His situation fit the conditions Emmanuel described. Derek came from a poor class background; his father only completed elementary school (to his parents' generation known as standard six). His mother was not educated. At the time of applying for the visa, Derek was working as a teacher in Ghana and making, when converted to dollars, "$40 a month or something." He could not afford to pay the visa processing fees, and his parents could not help him. The offer to have his payment covered, even with the risk of getting in trouble for fraud, was attractive and an opportunity saver.

Diversity Visa Entrepreneurs as Makers and Breakers of Luck

It is easy to read these stories and conclude that visa entrepreneurs have gambled with the luck of many individuals who won the lottery. By burdening them with fictive kinship ties that must be dissolved once they arrive in the United States, they tempt law-abiding but desperate and impoverished individuals to take risks that constitute falsehoods or fraud. Even I, as a sociologist, am tempted to react this way after hearing the accounts. This conclusion is valid, but it is not the whole story. The diversity immigrants I spoke to who entered fictive relationships to successfully leave their country of origin and enter the big prize country—the United States—did not regret their decision to agree to these temporary transactions. They felt that they had done what they needed to do to live in the United States. Challenging as it had proven to be, they believed that they still came out in a better position than they would have if they had remained in their country of origin. This might be true, but the finding still stands that visa entrepreneurs, in making luck for thousands of people, also put that luck at risk by making winners take one more chance: to trust that they will be lucky enough not to lose their opportunity to emigrate to the United States by getting caught.

I worried about writing about the illicit activities of some visa entrepreneurs and diversity immigrants because their stories could be used by critics as proof of rampant fraud and as a reason for terminating the program. I decided to go ahead, however, because these practices have been chronicled in other African contexts and, more widely, in studies of irregular migration in Latin America, Europe, and Asia. Piot's ethnography of the diversity visa lottery in Togo, *The Fixer: Visa Lottery Chronicles*, in detailing how visa brokers and Togolese people try to outsmart the U.S. embassy and their fraud detection officers, describes their formulation of the "game" as "the street vs. the embassy."[25] U.S. embassy fraud officers go to court registries to investigate whether the marriages presented by applicants are real, go to couples' houses to confirm evidence of cohabitation, and so on. It is similar to what U.S. immigration officials do in the United States when citizens and lawful permanent residents marry noncitizens; there couples must deal with the suspicion that their marriage is fraudulent and was only entered into for a green card. Piot defines visa brokers as people whose business is to "profit from someone else's good fortune by turning one visa into two."[26] Visa entrepreneurs are analogous to Togo's visa brokers, in that they make money by adding dependents to a "winning ticket," liaising with compatriots and Africans in the diaspora who want to bring over a loved one and are willing to pay thousands of U.S. dollars to make it happen.

In the process of writing a book about his coauthor's business, Piot draws back the curtain on almost all known illicit activities surrounding the U.S. visa lottery. He details how Batema created pop-up (pretend) marriages—pairing unmarried winners whom he registered for the program with fake spouses, describes how the fixer coaches couples for their screening interview, and reveals how Batema manufactures required documents. Such documents include marriage certificates and wedding pictures, which consular officers often ask for and view during the interview in addition to the apprenticeship training certificates that applicants must supply in order to meet the work experience requirement. Despite these revelations, one finishes Piot and Batema's book convinced that newer and even more cunning strategies will evolve in the battle to outsmart the U.S. embassy and beat the ever-expanding regulatory control and deterrence efforts of U.S. immigration officials.

Piot makes a crucial point: we should not read these stories of diversity visa entrepreneurs' and brokers' illicit activities and come away with a racist view of Africans as guilty of moral failure and Africa as a place of endemic lawlessness. Nor should we adopt a "deprivationist" view by assuming that the conditions of poverty, failed states, and low levels of patriotism have made Africans into pragmatists who believe that the ends justify the means in a world where opportunities for advancement and the good life are limited.[27] Rather, Piot, like his fellow anthropologists Jean and John Comaroff, argues that crime and the art of selling and "being fake," of misrepresenting oneself and taking advantage of loopholes, is global.[28]

One example of this is the self-help phrase "fake it till you make it," which echoes throughout all corners of the globe. This is exactly what some visa entrepreneurs and diversity immigrants are doing: faking it until they make it to the United States, where they settle and work hard. People create or buy fake followers on social media, or post fake comments written by themselves and their friends, to suggest that they have a greater impact, all in order to become a social media influencer and get sponsorship deals that will make money for them. This practice is becoming increasingly common in the West—and is just an example of fraud and false identity. Multinational companies that cache money in foreign lands and hire sharp tax lawyers to evade—or should we say "reduce"—their tax burdens, are violating the spirit of the law and operating on the very edge of legality, but they are often rewarded with rising share prices and unburdened by any real risk of prosecution. We should be clear-eyed about this global tendency to skirt the law rather than reflexively scapegoat Africans by adopting a racist or pitying posture.

Piot contends that it is the fees that lottery winners must pay that have engendered the migration industry around the U.S. Diversity Immigrant Visa Program. In his words, "if the fee weren't so high, there would be no fraud, no fixers, no trans-Atlantic finance, no debt bondage. It is the hefty interview fee that primes the pump in this economy."[29] The program was designed to be self-funding, so that fees collected from lottery winners who chose to apply for the immigrant visa would cover the cost of administering the program, which includes paying for the online system, the consular officers needed for screening interviews, and the fraud detection officers. In 2004, the immigrant visa application fee was $437. In 2006, it jumped to $755, in 2010 to $819, and then it dropped and has remained at $330 since 2012.[30] Diversity immigrants must also pay a $220 immigrant processing fee upon arrival in the United States.

Because of the U.S. government's decision to require diversity visa immigrants in poor(er) countries in the Global South to pay the same fees as diversity immigrants living in economically advantaged countries in the Global North (like the United Kingdom, Norway, and even within the United States), Piot argues, "the fraud in the visa lottery system—those backdated marriages of convenience that Togolese and other West African winners engage in to acquire money for the interview—is produced by choices made by Congress and the State Department in determining fee structure." Because most Togolese cannot raise the approximately $2,500 per individual needed to process their visas, they find "the market in marriage a strong temptation."[31]

I disagree with Piot, to an extent, because his claim pertains only to the business model of visa brokers who arrange marriages of convenience primarily solicited and bankrolled by compatriots in the U.S. diaspora who want to bring loved ones over. There are other types of diversity visa entrepreneurs who make their money from different business models and take advantage of other specific requirements of the program, such as the ones operating street tents and internet cafés. Even without high U.S. visa fees, migration industry actors like visa entrepreneurs will still proliferate to sell the dream of migration to thousands and make money from helping them pursue their migration dreams.

I argue that the issue is really one of poverty. Even if the United States reduces its visa fees to almost zero or uses a sliding scale so that diversity immigrants living in affluent countries pay more than those living in poorer countries, the cost of airplane tickets to the United States will still overburden many of those who win the diversity visa lottery. Consequently, winners will still turn to visa entrepreneurs or other MI actors to help them finance the trip.

America's reluctance to grant Africans entry visas also plays a role in efforts to "go around" the system. The significant limitations placed on African migration, combined with the sheer number of Africans living in countries where finding gainful employment is difficult, place Africans who want to move to the United States in an impossible position. Stuck between a rock and a hard place, they do what they need to do. Such difficulty explains, for example, why some individuals agree to pose as spouses or relatives of winners and to pay for the privilege of taking such a big risk—they can't see any other way to gain legal admittance to the country.

Although the stories of shady or ingenious practices (your point of view may depend on where you stand) are important, they are not this book's primary focus. That focus remains on exposing the overarching process of structured luck and the creation of migrapolicy interventions. Visa entrepreneurs, their business models, and their practices are only a part of this larger story.

Of course, not all visa entrepreneurs operate in the gray areas. But in evaluating those who do, we should ask: Whose luck are they jeopardizing? Who are they exploiting? There is no one, clear-cut answer to these questions, such as "the poor," or "the undereducated." The exploitation begins when agents retain applicants' unique confirmation numbers in exchange for free registration or just due to ignorance on the part of the registrants. In many cases, it is the young and naive who are exploited—those who register for the program on a whim, without giving it much thought. If they had taken their time to consider the situation, they could have applied on their own, or had a friend help them, or located a diversity visa entrepreneur who would charge only a reasonable fee and give them their unique confirmation number after they registered. In truth, it is the ignorant who are exploited, and both educated and undereducated people can be ignorant or act hastily.

But it is the poor who are most vulnerable to being exploited, as they do not have the money to pay the high costs involved in processing the visa, which, including the price of an airline ticket, can come close to $3,000 per individual. They either take on the yoke of debt or sell a spot on their winning ticket to fictive kin. The exploited are those who do not meet the education or work experience requirements—or again, depending on where you stand, they are those who are determined to travel abroad and to circumvent the regulations that seek to lock out the less-educated, as well as those who apply knowing that they do not meet the requirements but believe they will find a way to do so, even if it means paying steep fees to manufacture the qualifications that will make them "deserving" enough.

Finally, migrants without family or friends in diasporas in the Global North are the individuals shouldering the burdens associated with processing the diversity visa. The wealthy—both those still living in their home country and those living in diasporas within economically advantaged countries in the Global North—are complicit in this exploitation, as they partner with visa brokers to buy a spot on a winning diversity lottery ticket.[32] Thus, class, education, wealth, age, and both local and transnational social networks matter in several key ways.

Relations with the Government: "They Applaud Our Efforts"

I was interested in the relationship that visa entrepreneurs in Ghana had with the Ghanaian government, whether at the federal, regional, or local level. I found that visa entrepreneurs occupy a private space that attracts minimal oversight from government officials. That minimal engagement stems from entrepreneurs' companies being registered and having government authorization to operate in the country.

I asked Mr. Agyeman and Mr. Robertson about their relationships with the government. Both said that their company was registered in order to do business and that they had obtained the necessary permits to erect their tent in the public sphere—on the streets and in the markets of Ghana. Because their agencies were in the business of marketing and facilitating access to a legal migration pathway, their tents could be visible in society. Their marketing and registration drives were not carried out clandestinely, even if some of their practices would not have survived legal scrutiny. As entities registered with the government, their businesses paid taxes.

Visa entrepreneurs' relationship with the government is very different from that of some other MI actors—such as labor recruitment agencies in the Philippines, which often work as arms of the government, or MI actors who have received contracts from nation-states to control migration and border enforcement. In Ghana and Nigeria, facilitating the overseas migration of citizens is considered a private business. The business model of visa entrepreneurs is viewed more as citizens helping others migrate, one that has the "lucky" side effect of identifying opportunities to make money.

I asked Mr. Robertson and Mr. Agyeman if the Ghanaian government ever became hostile to visa entrepreneurs, out of a fear that they might be contributing to the brain drain out of Africa. Mr. Agyeman told me:

> I have no problems with the government at all. In fact, they see us as doing them a service. We are helping extract the unemployed youth of the country, and when they go abroad, they can send money back to help their families. In fact, I have many people in the government—commissioners—coming to me to help them get their children out of the country.

Like Mr. Agyeman, Mr. Robertson said, "I have no problems with them at all. They know what we are doing. In fact, they applaud our efforts. We are helping the people of Ghana."

Diversity visa entrepreneurs run the gamut from government-registered businesses with several staff to individual actors who, with just a computer and internet connectivity, register people for a small fee. They can be immigrants operating transnationally or nonmigrants. They earn their living by commodifying an immigration policy of the United States. Most are privately owned businesses, but a few are owned by highly positioned members of the civil service. While most visa agencies are independent of the government, those owned by high-ranking public servants blur the boundary between private business and the government, especially when such owners capitalize on their government contacts to assist their clients (particularly when it comes to document acquisition). Some visa entrepreneurs own travel agencies that do a very lucrative side business around registering people for the U.S. visa lottery and shepherding winners of the lottery through the application process. As one employee of such a business told me, "We are a travel and tours business. This diversity visa

Photo 4.6   Front View of Flyer Distributed by a Travel Agency, Accra, Ghana, 2017

Source: Photo by Onoso Imoagene.

business segues nicely into our main business. It gives us people to patronize our travel and tours business." The clients they get who win the U.S. visa lottery then buy airplane tickets from them. The double-sided flyer distributed by a travel agency and reproduced here (see photos 4.6 and 4.7) shows how visa entrepreneurs advertise the U.S. visa lottery and offer other services through their travel agencies.

Ironically, even as some visa entrepreneurs exploit their clients to make money, they are trying to obtain U.S. government contracts that will retain them to identify tricksters and fraudulent activities around the diversity visa immigrant program. Mr. Agyeman and Mr. Robertson lamented that the U.S. embassy and its consular officers did not contract with them to help ferret out visa applicants who were engaging in illegal practices. Both owners saw policing their own people while seeking to game the

Photo 4.7   Back View of Flyer Distributed by a Travel Agency, Accra, Ghana, 2017

Source: Photo by Onoso Imoagene.

system as a potential and very profitable new business. According to Mr. Agyeman,

> These embassies should be contacting us. We know our people. We know their tricks. The right thing the embassy can do is to bring the registered companies together. We can help them. We can help them fight terrorism. If they give us a permit from the embassy to do this, it will help. The embassies can come to us and ask us about certain basic information. "What do you think about this person?" We can verify. We can assist them on checking the paperwork, help them interpret foreign documents. The embassy has a desk that does this, and they can liaise with us.

Both Mr. Agyeman and Mr. Robertson told me that, with their local knowledge, they could easily help the United States and other nation-state governments weed out frauds and ineligibles, if they were contracted to do so. These owners were keeping an eye out for ways to evolve their companies to be in the business not only of facilitating migration but also of controlling migration. Mr. Agyeman was looking beyond the United States to how he could be of service to other countries in the Global North. His use of the buzzword "terrorism" suggested that he saw this as the pitch that might be successful in giving him access to and contracts from these countries' embassies, given the increased wariness about mass migration from the Global South and fears of terrorist infiltration from this region of the world. Both owners told me that they had sent out feelers through people they knew to the U.S. embassy to try to sell them on letting them take on this role but had yet to receive a response. Meanwhile, their actions showed how they were trying to position their businesses to adapt to a future characterized by stricter immigration laws and more stringent enforcement.

Removing Barriers

Diversity visa entrepreneurs play a huge role, both positive and negative, in the social organization of African migration to the United States. The promotional and recruitment activities of visa entrepreneurs bring the chance to migrate to the United States via the DV Program to millions of people who might never have heard of the program, or thought of leaving their country to go overseas, or had the wherewithal to do so. If they win the lottery, it is the diversity agent who can offer them options to succeed. Through all their activities, it must be acknowledged that visa entrepreneurs remove numerous disincentives to migration from many people's paths.

According to Martin Van der Velde and Ton van Naerssen, three crucial thresholds serve as geographical barriers to international migration and shape migration decisions and conditions for action: (1) the indifference threshold—before an individual crosses a border, migration must enter their psyche as a viable alternative to their current position (it makes a difference) and they take measures to leave; (2) the locational threshold—deciding where to go; and (3) a trajectory threshold—how the chosen destination is reached, whether via legal or illegal means.[33]

Diversity visa entrepreneurs push many people past these three thresholds via their publicity campaigns, recruitment strategies, and other services that help people meet the application requirements. In pursuit of profit, visa entrepreneurs help overcome the indifference threshold by making migration—to the United States in particular—seem possible. They spread news of the U.S. program far and wide. They literally deliver hope to the doorsteps of millions of their compatriots, in the form of an opportunity to migrate to the United States. The location threshold is already met, as visa entrepreneurs are creating a market around the U.S. Diversity Visa Program and migration to the United States. Then the trajectory threshold is met in a more complicated sense: if they win the lottery, people registering for the program are assured of using a legal pathway to enter the United States and possibly attain citizenship. Additionally, some diversity agents encourage obtaining that opportunity in illicit or even illegal ways.

Visa entrepreneurs also contribute to the *aesthetics* of migration through their banners, flyers, tents, recruitment drives, and other services—in short, through their visible presence in communities. The individuals they have helped to migrate establish social networks that encourage more migration to the United States, especially among family members who can reunite with relatives through the family preference system. As their activities contribute to the aesthetics of migration, visa entrepreneurs engender a desire among others to migrate, including those who, if they cannot enter the United States, may travel to countries in Europe, the Middle East, or Asia. As more people hear success stories about life in the United States or abroad, they find dreams of migration embedded in their psyche, further entrenching the culture of migration that exists in most sub-Saharan African countries.

Visa entrepreneurs structure the luck of thousands as they pattern migration. By targeting the young and educated population in their final year of secondary school or early years of college, visa agents enact migrapolicy interventions that reverberate for many years as they change the trajectories of students' lives, with transnational consequences.

But it is equally true that U.S. immigration policy, through its design, administration, and requirements, has created downstream effects that directly contribute to the creation, proliferation, and prosperity of visa entrepreneurs. Most agencies would not exist were it not for the ways in which U.S. immigration policy intervenes in economically disadvantaged countries in the Global South, thousands of miles away from U.S. shores.

The fact that the majority of diversity immigrants in this study applied for the program on their own does not minimize the ways in which the MI industry exploits potential applicants. Several respondents who registered for the visa lottery on their own still used visa entrepreneurs' services, whether to buy supposedly "official" DV forms when the program was paper-based or to get help filling out their visa application forms and acquiring needed documents. The fact that some of the lottery winners I interviewed who applied on their own but were still caught up in such business models—as were the crowds of applicants I observed making use of agents' services in street tents and internet cafés in Accra—suggests that a significant number of people are exploited in ways that often impede their integration in the United States.

Chapter 5 | Disrupted Undergraduates: A Created Category of Diversity Immigrants

IT WAS A SUNDAY morning. Kofi, a small man who still enjoyed the slenderness of youth and was personable and quick to smile, had a camera slung over his neck. As the pastor preached, Kofi walked quietly down the aisles of his church, taking pictures of congregants that would later be posted on the church's social media platforms. After the service, many congregants called Kofi over to snap their pictures. They posed outside, by the church door, in front of shrubs, on the green lawn, in the car park, giving Kofi a chance to capture their best looks. Kofi was patient. He waited for them to finish their numerous clothing adjustments, side conversations, hugs and kisses. Church was an important part of Kofi's life. Being in church, he said, "is the [most] precious gift my eldest sister ever gave me since childhood." It made him happy.

Yet Kofi was not where he thought he would be in terms of education and employment. When he won the U.S. visa lottery in 2010, he was just about to begin his first year as a chemistry student at the University of Ghana–Legon in Accra. Initially, Kofi did not want to take advantage of the diversity visa opportunity because he felt that he was "set," as he had been admitted to university. Migrating to the United States was not part of Kofi's vision for his future. But he was persuaded otherwise. After Kofi refused several times to take a call from the diversity visa entrepreneur who helped him register for the visa lottery, the agent came to his house and met with his parents. He convinced them to persuade Kofi to apply for the diversity visa since he had been lucky enough to be selected in the lottery.

Along with Kofi's parents, his eldest sister—who raised him because his parents were away from home for work—persuaded him to emigrate. The three convinced him that he could go back to school in the United

States. Kofi believed them because, like others in the educated class, his family valued education and had no doubt that he would earn his degree in the United States. According to Kofi, all his father cared about was that his children go to school. "He told us we shouldn't think about the things that he has achieved or anything, we just have to fight for our own. So we have to go to school and make ourselves." Because of the limited number of spots available in public universities in Ghana, Kofi's father had bribed some officials to push through his son's university admission. "My father paid something to other people, like giving them goats and rams, because of the course I wanted to do, and he had to pay something to other people." Kofi and his father dreamed that he would eventually become a medical doctor.

After a while, Kofi's motivation for migrating became about more than just familial pressure—he "also wanted to come" to the United States. "What really came to my mind was that I wanted to go to school." Kofi was afraid, like many other diversity immigrants mentioned in chapter 3, that if he stayed in Ghana he would not obtain a good job after graduation. He felt that he would "still have to pay money to other people to get a job." He engaged in "cognitive migration"—comparing his future in Ghana with a future life in the United States—and believed that, despite whatever difficulties he might experience as a diversity immigrant, he "could still come out with something."

Seven years after migrating to the United States, Kofi was still not a college graduate. Despite having a relative in the United States, his elder sister's husband, he got minimal support from him. He was told to "get a job and help pay the bills." Kofi was in community college. He had obtained enough course credits to receive an associate's degree in health sciences but was still in the process of completing all the course prerequisites he needed to gain admission into a premed bachelor's degree program in a four-year college. If he failed to gain admission to medical school, Kofi's fallback plan was to become a pharmacist.

Since he arrived in the United States in 2011, Kofi had worked in several hourly wage jobs. During his first year, he worked part-time as he tried "to get financial aid for school." For his first job, which was "miles away" from the house where he rented a single room, he had to wake up at 4:00 AM to catch the bus to work. His next job was at Target, where he worked for four years. He took on a second job to earn more money "for summer classes." Kofi now had a new job, which he described as a "really nice job": he worked in a nursing home where he "takes care of two clients who are mentally handicapped." His clients were largely independent: "They actually can do everything; they can talk; they can dance; they do everything." He described his responsibilities this way: "All you have to do is actually give them their medication and lock the kitchen so that they won't go there and eat all the food in the house. We have to control their diet."

Kofi acknowledged that he had not "realized" his dreams. He was twenty-eight years old at the time I interviewed him. During his visa interview at the U.S. embassy in Accra, the consular officer asked him why he was not in university, given his excellent high school grades. Kofi was asked, "What are you doing here?" He told the consular officer, "When I go, I am going to go to school. So, she said, 'Well, if you go and go to school, then I'll give it to you.'" His youngest brother was now attending university in Ghana, while Kofi is in the United States "still hustling" to get into college.

In Ghana, Kofi had been on course to graduate with a bachelor of science degree in four years; now he was an immigrant without a college degree, stuck in a poorly paid hourly wage job in the health care industry—the ethnic niche for many African immigrants in the United States. His peers back in Ghana—who were beginning their university program when he left—had since earned their bachelor's degree. Several had traveled to the United States or Britain to pursue a master's degree. In the United States, having a college degree has long been seen as the ticket to the middle class. The U.S. consular officer who interviewed Kofi was aware of this when she ended the interview by strongly advising him, again, to "go to school when you come up there [to the United States]." But Kofi was currently caught in a long and expensive journey to obtain a degree. In the Unites States, he had acquired significant student debt to pay the tuition fees for the courses he had taken at community college. He would be taking on more debt to obtain a college degree, and still more if he achieved his ultimate dream of attaining a medical or pharmaceutical degree. It is not uncommon for individuals to rack up more than $400,000 in student loans by the time they obtain a medical degree in the United States.

Kofi did not regret migrating because, "in Ghana, I was being taken care of, given money by my dad. That is not good. But here, I can call myself a man. I am working." Nevertheless, he conceded, "I have lost a couple of things, but at least I am standing on my own two feet." He also acknowledged that several of his peers in Ghana could be said to be doing better than he was. "The people I left behind, they have moved forward."

Kofi's story is not unusual: many Ghanaian and Nigerian diversity immigrants do not complete their college education so that they can emigrate to the United States. This chapter highlights the negative migrapolicy intervention of human capital interruption by revealing the experiences of "disrupted undergraduates": Ghanaian and Nigerian diversity immigrants who were on track to obtain a university degree but whose education was derailed when they won the U.S. visa lottery. I examine the immediate impact of a win on undergraduates before they migrate, along with the long-term consequences that hinder their educational experiences, employment, and social mobility after they migrate. The chapter elaborates on the concept of structured luck by showing how the design and administration of the DV Program, along with the activities of diversity visa entrepreneurs (discussed in chapter 4), result in high school and university students being targeted to play the visa lottery because they fit the educational profile required by the program.

Disrupted undergraduates are uprooted during their transition to adulthood. The language surrounding the DV Program—words like "luck," "play," "lottery," "good fortune," and "U.S. green card"—shrouds an important negative consequence of the program itself: by recruiting students when they are on their way to degree attainment into a global class of labor migrants, many of them are derailed at a critical juncture in their life course. The DV Program further structures the luck of such disrupted undergraduates by pushing them onto fragmented socioeconomic paths. In the United States, diversity immigrants become ensnared in an education boondoggle as they begin a lengthy and often unrealized journey to attain a college degree. That boondoggle results in burdensome student debt caused by the high costs of U.S. education and damaged self-esteem caused by a perceived failure to achieve their dreams.[1]

Economically advantaged countries in the Global North, such as the United States, tend to prize credentials, work experience, and skill training. Being a college graduate before emigrating helps immigrants skip a few rungs on the social mobility ladder. College graduates fare much better in the U.S. labor market than high school graduates and students who have discontinued their college education. A college degree carries a wage premium: college graduates earn on average $25,000 more per year than high school graduates and students who have left college.[2] Of course, there are some vocational occupations that do not require a college degree and are highly paid nonetheless. For example, long-haul truckers can earn between $60,000 and $90,000 a year; mechanics and plumbers also earn high wages. Business owners without a college degree, such as owners of restaurants and grocery corner shops, also earn income as high as, if not higher than, what some college graduates earn. But on the whole, college graduates are more likely to be employed and to have a wider range of job opportunities, while high school graduates and students without a college degree are more likely to be working in low-paying jobs.

For disrupted undergraduates from Nigeria and Ghana, the cost of not getting a college degree is not only economic but cultural and psychological. Nigerian and Ghanaian diversity immigrants, as members of the educated class in their country of origin, value education. A significant aspect of their dreams is to obtain more education in the United States, and their disappointment about their post-migration experiences is largely linked to not attaining a college degree. Few diversity immigrants realize before they migrate that it would be easier and less expensive to earn their college degree in their country of origin. To cope, many recast their American dreams to focus on ensuring that their children fulfill their potential. Immigrants' families expect them to get a college degree as much as they expect it of themselves, so they also face the disappointment of family members when they fail to do so.

This chapter brings into sharp relief the experiences and disappointments of a group of diversity immigrants who are largely invisible when we talk about educated immigrants in general, and about "lucky" diversity immigrants in particular.

STRUCTURED LUCK AND EDUCATION DISRUPTIONS

Social scientists usually model immigrants' pre-migration levels of capital, especially human capital (education and skills), as independent of the receiving country's migration policy, but immigrants' human capital levels are often affected by migration policies while they are still in their country of origin—as in the case of the DV Program.

Normally, dropping out of university is an unwise decision. In Nigeria and Ghana, securing a university spot is highly competitive, and students must work hard to meet the requirements by passing two or three national exams for multiple subjects. Sometimes parents must use their connections with prominent people to secure their child's spot or, as Kofi's father did, give gifts to officials. Giving up a hard-earned accomplishment is not an easy choice. But for someone who has the opportunity to move from a developing country in the Global South to the United States, leaving college no longer seems foolish. Chapters 2 and 3 discussed Ghanaian and Nigerian diversity immigrants' reasons for abandoning their college degree programs and migrating to the United States, including concerns about employment after graduation and a strong belief that life is better in the United States. In addition, disrupted undergraduates feel strongly compelled to make this decision by the U.S. Diversity Visa Program's policy of not allowing deferments.

When he was awarded the diversity visa, Bernie, a Ghanaian, was in his third year of a four-year degree in business administration. "I left because of the diversity visa. It wasn't an easy decision for me." Bernie remembered being torn over the decision. He knew he had just one year to finish his degree, but the diversity visa is valid for only six months from when it is granted. Bernie thought that after acquiring his U.S. green card he would be able to return to Ghana to finish his degree. But he had to discard that plan. "It was very difficult getting the finances to buy a ticket to come over here in the first place. So, thinking about going back again, it was going to be another issue because I was in school at the time. I had not raised enough money." Bernie borrowed $200 from his uncle to make up his ticket money. He felt that since he would have to work for a while in the United States to accumulate the money needed for a return ticket to Ghana and then back again, "that would mean that I would have to break my program for some time." He therefore decided "upon doing my own research and thinking, that furthering my education here [in the United States] will be the ideal situation." It took Bernie an additional six years from the time he migrated to the United States to earn his bachelor's degree in health administration. He works as a clinical research associate.

Benjy, a twenty-six-year-old hotel bellhop, had a similar experience. He felt he needed to emigrate and earn U.S. dollars to support his single mother and his siblings. He was in his second year of earning a commerce degree in Ghana when he won the lottery. But he felt compelled to seize the opportunity to help his family, and he knew he could not afford to travel back and forth to Ghana to finish his degree.

I interviewed twenty-three participants who won the diversity visa while in university. The DV Program structured the luck (and futures) of most of those winners, transforming them into disrupted undergraduates, because they could not defer the visa or they were unable to afford the airfare for going back and forth to maintain their schooling while also meeting the green card requirements. Only two managed to finish their degree program before migrating to the United States. Paul, a twenty-eight-year-old Nigerian, had just one semester left to get a computer science degree and so was able to complete the semester before the six-month window in which he had to use the diversity visa closed. The other respondent, Dozie, won the U.S. visa lottery in the third year of a five-year petroleum engineering degree. His family had enough resources to buy him the tickets he needed to travel to the United States to keep his green card active while remaining in Nigeria to finish his degree before finally settling down in the United States. Now Dozie earned a six-figure annual salary working for a petroleum company in Texas. He was a proud homeowner and took multiple vacations every year to Europe and Asia. The other twenty-one respondents were not so fortunate.

VISIONS OF AN EDUCATED SELF IN AMERICA

All of the disrupted undergraduates I interviewed believed that they would return to college and earn their degree once they reached the United States. Social psychologists Hazel Markus and Paula Nurius developed the concept of "possible selves" to describe "how individuals think about their potential and about their future. Possible selves are the ideal selves that we would like very much to become," as well as "the selves we are afraid of becoming."[3] Possible selves are visions of the self that often do not have to be verified or confirmed by social experience.[4] This concept helps us analyze immigrants who had to leave university after winning the diversity visa. There were positive possible selves they wanted to realize and negative possible selves they wanted to avoid. They hoped to become "the college graduate self," "the successful self," and "the family-supporter self." As university students in Nigeria and Ghana, they were on track to becoming graduates. And if things remained on track and they obtained a professional degree, like medicine and engineering, or if they earned a second-class upper degree or first-class honors degree, and/or if they had connections to get a good job, they could become "the professional self," earning a good wage. They could become "the successful self" who owned a car and a house, had money in the bank, supported their families, and enjoyed a rich social life. They wanted to avoid the negative possible selves, such as "the unemployed self," "the hustling self," the "poor self," or "the frustrated self."

Winning the diversity visa created a moment of disorientation that shuffled the possible selves hoped for and the possible selves dreaded. Lottery selectees experienced excitement and happiness over the win, which gave them an opportunity to imagine their positive possible selves in vibrant pulsating colors. They believed that they could achieve these possible selves more quickly in the United States, even as some winners, like Benjy, acknowledged that "it would not be easy." They still viewed the United States as "a land of opportunity." They had friends who had "made it" in America. They had heard stories that made them certain that life in the United States was better than life in Ghana and Nigeria. Their positive possible selves were now more tangible and the dreaded possible selves—like "the poor self" or "the unemployed self"—became more distant, more unlikely.

Possible selves present outcomes to be approached or avoided, while providing an evaluative and interpretative context for the current self. In these calculations, possible selves possess the power to incentivize and motivate individuals. Ghanaian and Nigerian disrupted undergraduates create an evaluative context and engage in "cognitive migration"—that is, they mentally travel to the hoped-for destination before leaving their country of origin and create a narrative about how their life is likely to proceed if they choose to migrate.[5] Then they decide to leave university. Their evaluative context is based on incomplete information, however, as they do not really have a good understanding of the challenges they will face to continue their education and become college graduates in the United States. None of the study participants, at the time they were leaving Nigeria and Ghana, imagined that they could become the possible self who failed to graduate from college. They all were driven to become the college graduate they were on track to become in their country of origin. They thought that it would be easy enough to get their degree in the United States and that their degree would be more prestigious than one earned in Nigeria or Ghana. In fact, employers in many sectors in Nigeria and Ghana prefer to hire individuals with a foreign degree obtained in the United States, Canada, or the United Kingdom. Thus, many respondents felt that having a U.S. degree would make them more employable in both the United States and their country of origin.

In reality, life in the United States had not been as they imagined before they migrated. Twenty-one of the twenty-three visa lottery winners left school to migrate to the United States. The impact on their educational attainment was not limited to their university degree trajectory in their country of origin; their pursuit of education in other countries was sometimes impacted as well. Nat, for instance, had gained admission to a university in England and obtained a student visa to earn a bachelor's degree in finance there.[6] His uncle had pledged to support his education in England, but over strong objections from his uncle, Nat chose to take the U.S. diversity visa opportunity because he could gain a pathway to citizenship and bring along his then-girlfriend. They married and migrated to the United States together.

Of the twenty-one respondents who left university, only seven had graduated with a bachelor's degree from a college in the United States. Of the fourteen who were unable to earn a bachelor's degree, two had earned an associate's degree in nursing (ADN), which is a two- to three-year nursing diploma.[7] Two had become licensed practical nurses (LPNs), which required one year of nursing education, and nine had some college credits and/or an associate's degree from a community college, as Kofi did. (See table 5.1 for a list of the study participants who experienced negative disruptions to their education; the table details the four-year degree courses they were enrolled in, the university year in which they abandoned their degree, the education they had attained in the United States, and their occupation.) In the U.S. context, dropping out of college decreases an individual's chances of eventually becoming a college graduate. One-third of those who enroll in college (33 percent) leave school entirely. In a National Student Clearing House study, only 13 percent of respondents who had dropped out enrolled in college again within the next five years, and only about half of them earned a degree or were still enrolled at the time of the study.[8] These statistics show that students struggle to finish college once they have discontinued their education for some amount of time.

Table 5.1 Disrupted Undergrads' Education and Work Experiences

Number	Pseudonym (N = Nigerian; G = Ghanaian)	Age at Time of Interview	Years Completed in University in Home Country at Time of Migration (Degree Course)	Education Level Achieved in the United States (Length of Time to Obtain Bachelor's Degree Post-migration)	Occupation/Job
1	Kofi (G)	28	Had been admitted but had not enrolled (biochemistry)	Associate's degree from a community college	Health aide in home for people with disabilities
2	Paul (N)	28	Earned a bachelor's degree (computer science)	No U.S. schooling	Computer programmer
3	Dozie (N)	39	Earned a bachelor's degree (petroleum engineering)	No U.S. schooling	Petrochemical firm engineer
4	Monica (G)	49	Had been admitted but had not enrolled (accounting)	Associate's degree from a community college	Home health aide
5	Nat (G)	41	Had been admitted to a university in England (finance) and obtained a student visa	High school graduate; attained several U.S. certificates	Warehouse manager
6	Mabel (G)	38	Had been admitted but had not enrolled (education)	Licensed practical nurse (LPN)	Nursing home LPN
7	Diana (G)	37	In second year (social work)	Associate's degree from a community college; dropped out of an ADN program	Health aide in home for people with disabilities

8	Shadrach (N)	36	In third year (banking and finance)	Master's degree in information technology (six years)	IT specialist
9	Benjy (G)	26	In second year (commerce)	Attended community college and earned some course credits	Hotel bellhop
10	Bernie (G)	37	In third year (business administration)	Bachelor's degree in health administration (six years)	Clinical research associate
11	Gifty (G)	28	In third year (marketing)	Attended community college and earned some course credits	Health aide
12	Brianna (N)	48	In third year (English)	Bachelor's degree in criminal justice (21 years)	Health care administrative assistant
13	Ada (N)	30	Second year (biology)	Licensed practical nurse (LPN)	Nursing home LPN
14	Eno (N)	26	Second year (social work)	Associate's nursing degree (ADN)	Hospital nurse
15	Maggie (N)	43	Third year (religious studies)	Bachelor's degree in health and society (12 years)	Research associate
16	Fred (G)	38	Third year (mathematics)	Enrolled in four-year college course	Telecommunications service tech
17	Gideon (G)	40	Second year (business administration)	Bachelor of science in nursing (BSN) (15 years)	Hospital nurse
18	Peter (G)	38	Third year (banking and finance)	In bachelor of science in nursing (BSN) program	Health aide

(Table continues on p. 126)

Table 5.1 Disrupted Undergrads' Education and Work Experiences (Continued)

Number	Pseudonym (N = Nigerian; G = Ghanaian)	Age at Time of Interview	Years Completed in University in Home Country at Time of Migration (Degree Course)	Education Level Achieved in the United States (Length of Time to Obtain Bachelor's Degree Post-migration)	Occupation/Job
19	Kobie (G)	37	Third year (business administration)	Bachelor's degree in engineering (nine years)	Employed in telecommunications
20	Joy (G)	29	Second year (political science and religion)	Associate's degree from a community college	Physical therapist
21	Emem (N)	29	Third year (history)	Associate's degree in nursing (ADN)	Nursing home ADN
22	Joseph (N)	46	Second year (engineering)	Several associate's degrees	Employed by a mobile phone company
23	Lara (N)	34	Third year (agriculture)	Bachelor's degree in health management (10 years)	Clinical research associate

Source: Author's compilation.

The disrupted undergraduates from Ghana and Nigeria had no idea of the lengthy journey they would have to embark on to earn a college degree in the United States. They did not know that getting their college transcript evaluated by members of the National Association of Credential Evaluation Services (NACES), a requirement put in place in the mid-2000s, would be such a prolonged process. They did not know that not all college credits from their universities back home would be accepted and counted as progress toward U.S. degree programs. Most did not know that they would need to obtain credits for course prerequisites in order to enter their desired college programs, such as medicine, pharmacy, law, and especially nursing. In fact, many respondents had been told while they were still in Nigeria and Ghana that nursing was the degree program that guaranteed a path to a stable job with good pay (a point explored later in this chapter).

Respondents did not know how difficult it would be to attend school while holding down a job in order to pay their bills. In the absence of significant financial support from family members and friends, it is nearly impossible to work full-time and go to school full-time. Most of the disrupted undergraduates I interviewed could not maintain that schedule. Instead, they worked full-time while taking a few courses every semester or intermittently, slowing the pace at which they could earn a their college degree. They also did not know how expensive it would be to get a college education in the United States and that their need for earnings or loans would be so great. Lastly, some disrupted undergraduates had difficulty getting student loans without cosigners.

The reality for most disrupted undergraduates is that they become almost indistinguishable from less-educated labor migrants, even as they still have a strong desire to earn a college degree. In fact, many continue in dogged pursuit of that dream. The hands-off approach taken by the U.S. government is encouraged and enabled by the language of "luck" and the designation of the DV Program as a "lottery" in which the U.S. green card is bestowed on worthy (educated) immigrants. After all, what help do immigrants need after they have won something so incredible?

The language of "play" further obscures the hard work facing winners once they enter the United States, renders their struggles invisible, and ignores the suboptimization of their talent and potential. The real "win" accrues to the U.S. economy, as U.S. employers obtain educated workers to fill low-level and low-wage jobs. Their education makes a difference in helping them perform well in these jobs, with minimal supervision.

BARRIERS TO BECOMING A COLLEGE GRADUATE
"I Was Just Working and Working and Working"

The reality faced by disrupted undergraduates upon migrating to the United States is that low-wage hourly jobs are the best they can hope for without a college degree or without going back to school to earn more credentials. In the U.S. labor market, the prospects (job opportunities and wages) of people who have not completed college are constrained and closer to those of high school graduates than those of college graduates. As a bellhop, Benjy earned about $1,300 a month. Diana, as a health aide, earned $13 an hour; with overtime, she earned just over $2,000 a month. Full-time health aides earn less than $2,500 a month. Yet low-income migrants face many financial demands: besides regular bills and rent, they are sending remittances back home to support family and trying to save money for school.

In response to these labor market realities, disrupted undergraduates work constantly. Some take on full-time jobs and add overtime. Some work two or three jobs to cobble together enough money to meet their needs. Ada, a thirty-year-old Nigerian, told me, "I was just working and working and working. But I was still living from paycheck to paycheck. It wasn't doing anything good to me. I was working two full-time jobs. There were times that I did three jobs." According to Monica, who worked in a nursing home, "I have to work two jobs just to have an okay life. It is not that I will be rich or anything. But at least I am able to take a vacation, travel somewhere if I work two jobs. I have to save every month towards it, though, and hope my car does not break down."

Many hourly jobs offer low wages, no fringe benefits, insufficient hours, and poor working conditions.[9] Gifty has held such jobs since she came to the United States in 2012. She told me, "My first job was through an agency. I worked as a packager in a Christmas ornament factory. You stand on your feet for the whole eight hours. It was hard." She was laid off from that job after three months because the Christmas season was over and "they said they were running low." She got another job at Walmart, but it was temporary. She held that job for six months and lost it too. She then got a job through her brother's friend as a health aide, looking after clients with "intellectual disabilities." Five years into that job, Gifty wanted to take a leave of absence because she had to travel to get married in Ghana. She said, "They didn't want me to go. So I resigned, and I went to Ghana." She was still employed as a health aide, but at another company that cared for disabled people.

For some of the respondents, like Kofi and Gifty, who had no work experience in Nigeria or Ghana because they had pursued their education (only to then leave university), there was excitement, as Gifty put it, in "working and earning my own money. I loved the money." The wages earned in U.S. dollars seemed large when compared to what they or their peers had earned, or could have been earning, back in their country of origin. Of course, when we consider that their expenses were also calculated in U.S. dollars, that impression proves rather hollow.

The opportunity to earn U.S. dollars made some disrupted undergraduates delay their schooling. Peter's first job upon arriving in the United States in 2005 was at a Wendy's. He recalled making $400 a month but did not mind because he had earned $100 a month as a secondary school teacher in Ghana after finishing a three-year course in teaching college. He said, "For $100 a month, I had to go to teacher's college. It wasn't that it was after high school and I was just teaching. No, I was trained and I was receiving $100 a month." After moving out of the home of his brother, who used to stress the need for him to go back to school, Peter rented an apartment with a friend. He recalled thinking, *"Oh, I'm on my own now, I need money. I need a house. I deviated a little bit to follow the money."* He kept on deferring starting school because "I was following the money too much instead of sacrificing"—by which he meant giving up his job and using the freed-up time to attend school.

College Is Expensive

The cost of U.S. higher education is a major obstacle that disrupted undergraduates must overcome to achieve their dreams of at least earning a bachelor's degree. Many are unable to do so. Gifty was unable to pursue her dream of becoming a nurse because she could not get anyone to cosign her student loans. "I asked everyone, my relatives here in America. I asked my pastors and members of my church. No one agreed to cosign a student loan for me, and I could not get one by myself." Gifty still hoped that she could return to school after she improved her credit score; for now she worked as a home health aide. Other respondents had obtained student loans and become burdened with debt, and some had nothing to show for it except some courses taken in community colleges over many semesters. Others had pinched their pennies to pay out of pocket for community college courses.

A few respondents, such as Bernie, had achieved success. Six years after arriving in the United States, Bernie graduated with a bachelor's in health administration. But it came at a cost of $60,000 in student loans. He said, "The cost involved in completing education here [in the United States] cannot be compared to completing a bachelor's degree in Ghana. When I compare the cost, it is something that would have taken me, like, let's say $8,000 to finish in Ghana. I ended up taking student loans of about $60,000."

Bernie would have paid much more had he been unable to transfer credits from his three undergraduate years in Ghana studying business administration. The transferred credits shaved off two years from his coursework. He was happy to have finished because "I was working and schooling at the same time."

Diana, a thirty-seven-year-old Ghanaian diversity immigrant, was still paying off over $10,000 in student loans even though she had not reached her goal of earning a degree. She had been admitted into a nursing program but was asked to withdraw because she twice failed a compulsory course.

Lack of Social Support

West African immigrants struggle to obtain educational credentials in the United States, as the currencies in their country of origin are extremely weak against the U.S. dollar and most do not have the familial resources to help pay for their U.S. schooling. Of course, many people in America who are not immigrants also struggle with the high and ever-rising costs of college. The average student borrower in the United States leaves college with a student loan debt of over $30,000. But research shows that the burden of rising debt has a racial pattern: a higher percentage of Black students take out loans, carry higher debt burdens, and receive lower economic returns compared to White students.[10] Educational plans are also delayed by a lack of social and emotional support while attending school.

Monica had started a program in community college when the uncle she was staying with in Texas gave her a week's notice to move out. With no other friends or relations in Texas, she had to move to Philadelphia to stay with another relative. "I had to drop out and then find several jobs to do in Philadelphia." She found employment at a furniture shop and stayed with her aunt for six months. Then she moved out and rented a room with other women immigrants from Ghana. Monica said, "It took me two years, after I moved from Texas, to save enough money and gather myself to start community college."

Nat, who, as introduced earlier, migrated with his wife in 1998, said that the family friend with whom he and his wife were staying got tired of them in the second month. "He wasn't happy with us to the point that he saw us as a burden on him." The couple had to move out by the end of the second month and Nat had to find a job quickly. This scrambled his plans because "all I kept on thinking is the bill, the bill, the bill, because you don't have that much, you have to earn more." Because of the pressure to pay bills, Nat kept postponing a return to school. He had earned several vocational certificates but never enrolled in college to pursue a degree.

Another factor that delays a return to schooling in the United States is the pressure to send money back home. This pressure can be self-imposed or applied by relatives explicitly demanding remittances. Peter strove to make money to "build his house in Ghana and invest," but he was under pressure to remit money to support his family. Mabel, a thirty-eight-year-old LPN who migrated to the United States during her first year of an education degree, stated:

> The family demands back home are so many, and at the same time you want to go to school here. So it's like a type of war. Nobody told us that you can't just be here working, you have to go to school. So we started working. And then, from back home, there is pressure because, in their mind, especially my family, "you are in America; so now you have to start giving us money." That pressure also became a burden that you had to work. I would say that I was being verbally abused and things were being said to me that made me feel like I was just useless. So you work and you work.

Disrupted undergraduates like Peter and Mabel blamed themselves for never getting their act together enough to go back to school. Mabel regretted that "someone did not grab [me] and tell [me] to go back to school." She told me that,

> if you tell me to go back to 1997 and when I arrived in '98, I will tell you immediately, I get here, the next week I'm in school. You see, we played around with our time. We struggled because we didn't have somebody who was older tell us, "I'm taking you guys under my wings. You two are going to school. Stop this working and craziness." We had no guidance. I mean, I was twenty, my husband was twenty-three. I mean, how wise could we be?

Peter strongly believed that if he had stayed in his brother's house and not moved out, "I would have been out of school long time." At the time of our interview, Peter had been in the United States for twelve years and was still in nursing school. Later he would drop out.

A few disrupted undergraduates, like Shadrach, told their families that they would have to wait on remittances. As a result, they were able to save more money for school and finish faster because they could afford an uninterrupted program. Shadrach earned both a bachelor's and a master's degree in computer science. He was now married, with a son, and owned a newly constructed townhouse in a nice neighborhood in New Jersey. He told me, "I didn't have to send money back home. I told them that this is the condition—whatever I am earning, I am paying rent, and I need to eat. Basically, they understood. So the expectations of me even sending money home wasn't there during that time, till the time I finished school." Temi, a clinical research associate who emigrated three years into earning her agriculture degree, enjoyed a similar leeway. She said, "My parents were pretty understanding. They didn't really need the money and so gave me breathing space."

CONSTRAINED OPPORTUNITIES

Even as disrupted undergraduates negotiate a labor market with prospects contrary to what they had believed, they are also discouraged by community members from pursuing goals that are judged as unattainable for an immigrant. Some respondents were told by coethnics that foreign accents made it difficult to excel in many jobs, and they were discouraged from pursuing degrees in certain fields. Brianna had wanted to go into broadcasting, maybe get a radio host gig. She said:

> When I started school here [in the United States], that was the first thing I was going to do. I tried, but people started discouraging me, saying, you know, because of our accent and things like that, you won't do well, and apart from that, it won't yield good money. To get a job depends on people you know. It would be really hard to get a job. It completely discouraged me.

Paul, who was a computer programmer, wanted to become a filmmaker in Hollywood and was overjoyed that Nevada, the state in which he arrived, was close to Los Angeles. But after doing his own research and talking to friends, he decided that

> my background as an immigrant—someone with an accent and all of that—would have been a liability or a disability for me. So I ended up ditching my initial passion for filmmaking. I wanted to be a director. I was like, okay, for now, let me just focus on whatever I can lay my hands on to make money, maybe in the future, I can become a filmmaker, a producer, because it's still my first love.

Rather than opening up a range of career opportunities to immigrants, migration seems to funnel them toward a few career choices—particularly nursing, which, in Nigerian and Ghanaian communities in the United States, seems to go hand in hand with the idea of "making it." Indeed, the health care industry in general has become an ethnic niche for African immigrants.[11] Nursing is promoted as one of the best jobs an immigrant can retrain for in the United States. One reason is that it pays well. An individual with an associate's degree in nursing earns between $27 and

$33 an hour, which comes to $77,000 annually, and the individual will earn more if he or she obtains a one-year RN to BSN degree.[12] Such wages situate an individual solidly within the middle class. As Gideon, a forty-year-old Ghanaian, explained, nursing is almost fully "recession-proof": an individual is unlikely to lose a nursing job during economic recessions, even when many other workers are laid off or cannot find jobs. Eno said that her Nigerian friends "started talking to me about nursing, that if you become a nurse, you make good money." She took their advice and was now a registered nurse with an ADN.

Before they leave their country of origin, many immigrants are advised to go into nursing once they arrive in the United States. Emem, a twenty-nine-year-old registered nurse, said, "I had learnt from some people before I came to the United States that nursing was one of the best careers to start with here. So I had that in mind." During her first nine months in the United States, Emem stayed with her aunt, who was a nurse. Her aunt helped Emem get her first job, in the cafeteria of the rehab center where she worked. Emem worked in the kitchen, served meals to the elderly, and "did the dishes too, whenever they were done eating, and [I] cleared [the tables] and waxed the [floor]."

Becoming a certified nursing assistant (CNA) is the first stepping-stone to becoming a nurse, especially for those who lack a college degree. College graduates have more and faster options available to them, such as completing a limited number of course prerequisites and then applying to enter an accelerated nursing program, which takes between one and two years, depending on the program. Since Emem had not finished college, she balanced working in the cafeteria with taking a CNA course, which takes about two months to complete. She then started working as a health aide, looking after elderly clients through a staffing agency. From there, she entered "the LPN program that was like a one-year program. So I did that, and then, from there, I proceeded to the RN, the associate degree program for nursing. So that's how I got my RN license." Though still committed to earning a bachelor of science in nursing (BSN), at the time of our interview Emem was on a brief hiatus because she had a young baby. She planned to return to school in the next year to get her BSN.

Emem's path—working hourly wage jobs, completing a CNA course, becoming a health aide, then either earning an LPN or entering straight into an ADN program and finishing with a BSN program—is the prescribed pathway followed by many disrupted undergraduates. Some, like Gideon, successfully completed the journey. Others, like Mabel, Peter, Eno, Ada, Emem, and Monica, obtained an LPN or ADN but had yet to earn a BSN. Others, like Diana and Gifty, were stuck at the beginning, still working as home health aides. Starting the CNA course represents an explicit or implicit commitment to proceed on this path. As Emem said, "Immediately I started the CNA; I already knew I would end so." Having arrived in the United States in 2011, she was finally nearing her end goal when we spoke in 2018. It had taken her seven years to get an associate's degree in nursing.

Mabel started along the same path Emem did, but stopped after earning an LPN:

> From the day I arrived here [in the United States], I worked as a cashier in a big retail shop [Sears]. I did that for about two years. Then I did home care. I did home health aide, and then I moved and did the CNA. I was doing both home care and the CNA together. I did that for a long time. I was a CNA from 2000 to 2012. And then I did the LPN. I worked as an LPN for three years, and then I moved into the residency service supervisor. So I'm like in administration now.

Getting quickly up to speed in science subjects is difficult for disrupted undergraduates who were not on the science track in their home country. As such, many of the study participants who were advised to go into nursing or pharmacy struggled with the science requirements. Although she really wanted to obtain a bachelor's degree in nursing, Mabel could not make it past the LPN program because she could not pass the science course requirements. She explained, "I was taking crazy courses. I was doing precalculus, biology, chemistry in the same semester, and I was working full-time. It was too difficult."

Another interview subject, Monica, could only afford to enroll for one semester per school year. She used a combination of student loans and personal funds to pay for her courses. She was shattered when she learned that she could not be admitted into a nursing (ADN or BSN) program because she got a C-minus grade in a required science course. All her effort and the money had gone down the drain. She entered a physical therapy program, taking out more student loans and paying more money out of pocket. But several years after graduating as a physical therapist, Monica could not find a physical therapy job. She remained a home health aide. In 2018, she was back in school again, this time doing an LPN program. She said, "I was told this is a better path to getting a better job than being a home health aide." The irony is that Monica had been dissuaded from pursuing an LPN degree when she arrived in the United States. She said people told her that "the LPN program is being done away with. If you do it, you won't find a job. Nursing homes and hospitals will not hire you. They are looking for RNs." Fourteen years later, after spending so much money and expending so much effort, she was back in school, paying fees for a one-year LPN course.

Some disrupted undergraduates change their minds before earning certification. Brianna dreamed of being a radio host but took the advice of her Nigerian mentors and tried to train as a nurse. She said:

> I actually applied for nursing on three different occasions, and I got accepted. I did all the course prerequisites I needed to start the associate nursing degree program. But I withdrew when I started the program because I got scared that since I did not really want to do nursing I would get midway, get bored, and say I can't do this anymore.

Brianna decided not to "waste all that money." Because she loved investigating, Brianna "decided to do a bachelor's in criminal justice. But the thing is, I finished and the jobs are not out there." It took Brianna twenty-one years to get a bachelor's degree after she entered the United States in 1997. Despite her dedication, she remained an administrative assistant in a health care service.

For some, the advice to pursue nursing puts them on a positive path. Although Mabel was now an administrator, the health field was a good fit for her because she wanted a nurturing job. She had wanted to become a teacher but felt she would not enjoy teaching in the United States. "So I said, 'Okay, so, plan B.' So that's how I started searching to find something that I will enjoy doing." She wanted a job that had a nurturing aspect "because I had grown up taking care of my siblings, my cousins, taking care of the home."

Gideon also didn't mind being steered into nursing. He saw it as a blessing that he had the opportunity to do nursing in a new country.

> I was a business major, and being a business major back home, there's no way you can divert to any other field. When I came here, when I saw the opportunity, I also consulted people who have been here a while, and they all told me, "Oh, you can do whatever you want." So even beginning, I wanted to go for pharmacy, and I checked all the prerequisites needed for pharmacy, but during the admission process, it was so difficult and I had to use my credit. So that's why I diverted to nursing.

Gideon came to the United States in 1999 and attained his bachelor's degree in nursing in 2015. It took him fifteen years. He told me passionately, "There is opportunity in America. You can become anything you want." His statement is somewhat surprising since he was diverted into nursing and away from a degree in pharmacy, his first choice.

Some respondents did not follow the advice to enter nursing, despite the general sentiment in the community that it was the best way to make it in America—easier, faster, and with a guaranteed pathway into the middle class—and the best way to become the positive possible selves migrants dream of: the "successful self," the "asset-owning self," and the "family-provider self." The pressure to go into nursing is community-wide, as it is the general sentiment that nursing is the golden ticket to the middle class for African immigrants.

Calling himself a contrarian, Paul said that he had refused to be steered into nursing. The friend he stayed with when he first arrived in the United States was a registered nurse and also going to school to earn a BSN. "So that was what he was recommending I do. It is like, that is the biggest thing you can do if you want to be able to make decent money in this country." Paul described the general sentiment well: "The churches that I went to, they were like, 'Hey, you should do nursing, take this path,' and all of that. For me, it seems I am a contrarian. When I got this advice, the first question I asked was, 'Is that the only thing somebody can do and make it in this country?'" He ignored the advice. "I already have a background in computer science. I already have a background in programming, so I guess I could build on this."

ECONOMIC AND ETHNIC NICHES

Before many disrupted undergraduates even leave their country of origin, their luck is structured by the advice and information they are given by coethnics in their immigrant communities. This advice leads many on the path to nursing. As more coethnics follow this path successfully, they pass on their advice to newly arriving immigrants, as well as to immigrants whom they feel are wasting time pursuing other options that will not lead to a steady job or pay good money. In addition, some new immigrants get jobs via referrals by friends, family members, or coethnics that often establish them in occupations similar to the occupations of the people referring them. According to social scientists, immigrants seeking employment benefit greatly from ties to others in similar semiskilled occupations, especially those in the medical field.[13] But one consequence of this pattern—for immigrants generally and specifically for African immigrants in the health industry ethnic niche—is that their career choices and decisions are constrained. They rarely have the opportunity to explore other options and careers, partly because those other career pathways are unknown or unexplored in their community, and partly because they are under pressure to do something, to become something, to "make it" in America, so that they can send money back home to help their family members, many of whom have very high expectations regarding the blessings that such "lucky winners" will bestow upon the family.

For instance, from my discussions with Ghanaian and Nigerian diversity immigrants, I found that pursuing credentials in information technology (IT) in areas such as coding, database security, or management was another successful pathway to obtaining well-paying jobs and entering the middle class. Ghanaian and Nigerian diversity immigrants who had an IT background before migrating had fared very well in the U.S. labor market. Others who had retrained in IT since arriving in the United States were also doing well. Perhaps as more coethnics succeed in IT, more people in Nigerian and Ghanaian communities will be advised to follow that course.

The nursing pathway, which relies on a pattern of encouragement and compliance among new immigrants and more-experienced coethnics, illustrates how ethnic niches are created and maintained. An ethnic niche is defined as a concentration of members of an immigrant or minority group in a particular area of the labor market.[14] Sociologists Richard Alba and Victor Nee go a step further, defining an "ethnic niche" as "any economic position—a type of job, say—where a group is sufficiently concentrated to draw advantage from it, typically by being able to steer its own members into openings."[15] This form of ethnic inclusivity can sometimes result in members of other immigrant groups, who are regarded as outsiders, being blocked from occupations in a particular ethnic niche. A related concept is the "ethnic enclave economy," defined as one in which members of an immigrant or minority group concentrated in a particular occupational field are not just employees but also owner-employers and customers.[16] Some ethnic enclave economies that come to mind are the Chinatown districts that exist in most U.S. cities and Little Havana in Miami.

Ethnic niches can be created in response to discrimination when members of an immigrant group find it difficult to break into the mainstream economy and so end up being concentrated in particular jobs. They can be created as immigrant groups take advantage of opportunities to enter a particular career field that arise when demographic and structural changes in the economy cause another (often already established) immigrant group to move out of that field, creating opportunities (more jobs) for other immigrant groups to enter the niche.[17] Some niches are created by government policy that grants certain types of visas to immigrants to work in particular industries and occupations; at one time in the United Arab Emirates, for instance, Filipinos were admitted as domestic workers and nannies. Examples of ethnic niches in the United States include Hispanics as laborers in construction, field-workers in agriculture, and workers in the meatpacking industry; Filipinos as nurses in health care organizations; Asians as workers in the garment industry in New York; and Black immigrants as health workers.

In the past, ethnic niches among minorities were associated with poverty, ethnic neighborhoods, and exploitation by coethnic owners (some of whom would pay very low wages with a promise that they would reward the worker with start-up funds to launch their own business in the same field). That said, working in an ethnic niche does not always entail bad jobs; it can be an advantage and lead to upward social mobility and entry into the middle class. For example, African Americans are over-represented in U.S. government jobs, through which they enjoy good benefits and careers.[18]

For West African immigrants, the structural opportunity of a nursing shortage, coupled with their higher levels of education and English fluency (for those hailing from ex-British colonies), has allowed them to become health care workers in both low- and high-end jobs in the industry and to become owner-entrepreneurs in the industry.[19] I believe that the long tradition of U.S. health care employers hiring immigrant health care workers did not hurt West African immigrants but rather facilitated their entry. U.S. employers have long hired Filipino nurses trained outside the United States. They also have a long tradition of hiring West Indian health care workers. West African health care workers are just a more-recent group of foreign-born health care workers in an industry long used to and comfortable with hiring non-White immigrants. A study of West African immigrants in New York and Boston found that one-third of African women held a health care position, ranging from nurses, nursing assistants, and orderlies to respiratory and lab assistants.[20]

However, while West African immigrants are creating an ethnic niche in health care, their entry into this industry is unlike that of Filipino nurses, who mostly complete their training before migrating to the United States. West Africans tend to train in the United States, in stages, to become nurses. In the Philippines, government policy encourages migration through transnational labor recruitment firms that operate almost as government parastatals: they recruit, train, and place Filipino nurses in global health care organizations (including organizations in the United States). That government policy shapes their path into the U.S. health care industry. West African nurses' paths into U.S. health care are largely private and community endeavors. In response to the local context of nursing shortages in the United States (due to increasing populations of the aged, chronically ill, and disabled) and the conclusion reached within West African communities that nursing is a well-paying, recession-proof job that leads to a middle-class lifestyle, African immigrants themselves have "become labor brokers who tap into their local ethnic and immigrant communities to channel coethnics into" nursing and other health care occupations.[21]

Since African immigrants hold jobs at different levels of the health care industry, it is likely that they remain congregated in this occupational field as it continues to offer the possibility for upward social mobility. That makes the field attractive to newly arriving coethnics and to the second generation. Research that focuses on the children of immigrants finds that members of the second generation tend not to pursue jobs in a given ethnic niche or ethnic enclave economy, but largely because they are not drawn to the sorts of physically demanding, poorly paid jobs that their parents and other coethnics had to accept upon their arrival in the United States. For example, many second-generation Chinese, unlike their parents, would rather not work in Chinese restaurants, and second-generation Asians avoid working in nail salons and health spas, as their parents and other coethnics have done. In fact, while the ethnic niche is maintained by newly arriving coethnics, many immigrant parents encourage their children to focus on education so that they can enter the mainstream economy and take up white-collar professional work instead. With the niching of Africans in the health care industry, however, this pattern might be avoidable because there is room for the African second generation to enter the higher-status occupations in health care, becoming nurses, nurse practitioners, dentists, doctors, and owners/entrepreneurs of health institutions.

DISRUPTED UNDERGRADUATES: A CREATED GROUP

The subgroup of diversity immigrants I refer to as "disrupted undergraduates" is a *created* group, that is, one structured by the terms of the diversity visa. Disrupted undergraduates are young people disadvantaged at the transition to adulthood, just prior to the point of degree attainment. This disruption affects their experiences at work and in school in the United States.

These diversity immigrants have been rendered invisible because the disruption they experience is obscured by the rhetoric of "luck" and "good fortune" for winning a U.S. green card, which so many people seek. They have also been rendered invisible because once they arrive in the United States, they are used as fresh bodies to meet the labor needs of U.S. employers, just as immigrants have been treated throughout U.S. history. Their experiences warrant a critical examination of the downstream effects of immigration policies that are promoted by economically advantaged countries as benign gestures of goodwill toward economically disadvantaged countries. The migration experience of disrupted undergraduates also offers a clear example of the two sides of the coin of winning: negative migrapolicy interventions (interruption of educational attainment) combined with positive migrapolicy interventions (gaining legal status) can produce suboptimal outcomes and unforeseen challenges for immigrants. The impacts on educational attainment of these interventions influence not only the careers and schooling prospects for immigrants abroad but also how much assistance they can send back home. Additionally, completing a degree, finding a job, and earning money are key to immigrants' incorporation in the United States.

For disrupted undergraduates, the discord between the possible selves they dreamed of and the reality of how their lives in the United States unfolded exacts a psychological toll. Having placed great value on becoming college graduates, they felt the loss or failure to attain their core educational goal most keenly. In the 2018 Pew Global Attitudes Survey, 92 percent of Nigerian respondents cited better educational opportunities as the reason why they wanted to emigrate, illustrating that, for most of these immigrants, the goal of becoming better educated was paramount. Disrupted undergraduates felt that way even as the declining economies fortunes of Ghana and Nigeria allowed them to earn more money in the United States than in their country of origin, and even though they were able to send monetary remittances to their families.

The Ghanaian and Nigerian diversity immigrants who won the U.S. lottery as high school graduates or skilled artisans also wanted to return to school, but because they were never enrolled in university in Ghana or Nigeria, they did not feel as disappointed by their educational experiences in the United States as those immigrants who were on their way to earning a degree at the time of emigration. Diversity immigrants who had a college degree before emigration, even those who wanted to pursue further degrees, were also largely satisfied with their migration experiences, because they were still better off financially in the United States. The lack of degree attainment was thus most damaging to disrupted undergraduates.

As social stratification scholars show, the value of a college degree extends throughout an entire family, as children whose parents have college degrees are more likely to attain college degrees themselves than children whose parents do not have college degrees. Thus, having a college degree not only helps individuals economically but gives them a sense of achievement and worth. It also raises the likelihood of future generations' higher educational attainment.

The experiences of disrupted undergraduates raises a crucial question: Can changes be made to the DV Program to prevent the suboptimization of immigrants it allows into the United States? Broadening the focus of that question, how can we change the stance of economically advantaged countries in the Global North so that they become more cognizant of migrapolicy interventions and more responsive to the consequences for immigrants of logistical requirements, such as time frames to migrate? This issue is addressed in the concluding chapter of the book.

Chapter 6 | "We Are Talking About American Citizenship"

"IF I TELL YOU, don't laugh," was Alaba's response when I asked how many times he had played the U.S. visa lottery before winning. "Seventeen times," he said. Religiously, for seventeen consecutive years, from 1993 to 2009, Alaba played the visa lottery. "The funniest part of it is that 2009 was the last time I planned to apply for the diversity visa." Alaba was on the brink of giving up: he was getting married and felt that migrating was no longer for him. "But as God will have it, it was the last one I won."

In the parlance of U.S. immigration, Alaba, a forty-four-year-old Nigerian, was an independent immigrant, so he would have had difficulty migrating to the United States without a diversity visa. He did not have family members in the United States, such as a parent or sibling, who could sponsor him for an immigrant visa. Even though he had a college degree, he was not a highly skilled professional, such as a doctor or nurse, whose skills are coveted in the United States. And he had limited prospects of obtaining an employment-based visa.

The DV Program gave Alaba his chance to migrate to the United States "with papers." In doing so, the program lived up to its objective: to give independent immigrants from countries historically underrepresented in immigration flows an opportunity to legally migrate to the United States. "I heard that if you win the lottery," Alaba said, "you get everything right away. So something within me just told me that that is my opportunity. I don't know, I just believed that this was my only way."

Alaba had been "desperate" to leave Nigeria. He had a bachelor's degree in engineering and a job, but his salary was inadequate. "I could not even feed myself, settle down and afford a wife, three, four years after graduating." He believed that when one moved to America, "you get the whole thing: flashy cars, money, a good job, and money to build a house back in Nigeria." Alaba ended our interview by telling me, "America has been good to me." At the time I interviewed him, Alaba was doing well in America. He had a stable, well-paying job. His wife had just finished a nursing program and gotten a job in a hospital. They owned their home in Houston, Texas, and what they earned in their jobs put them in the middle class. Alaba had become one of what I call "affective Americans": the many immigrants who, even as they identify with their ethnic group or national origins, feel emotionally attached to the United States and thankful for the better life they have found there, especially when compared to the lives of those they left behind in their country of origin.

This chapter explores some of the outcomes of migration for diversity immigrants—revealing dreams both fulfilled and deferred. It discusses two positive migrapolicy interventions: the higher status gained by "having papers" and the benefits of immigration for an immigrant's children. Also discussed, however, is one negative migrapolicy intervention: marital and familial instability.

A PROMISE KEPT: LEGAL ENTRY

According to the study participants, the DV Program met their expectations in some ways and not in others (though only one participant felt disappointed enough to wish they had not migrated). Perhaps the DV Program's greatest success lies in fulfilling immigrants' dreams of legally settling in the United States and allowing them to escape the frightening and demoralizing situations that face the undocumented.

Concerns about illegality and an awareness of the vulnerability of undocumented status in the United States informed West African emigrants' decisions to migrate. Many of those with some idea of how difficult life is in the United States without papers were unwilling to emigrate without legal documentation.[1] In 1993, a family friend offered to help Alaba migrate to the United States but candidly told him that it would "destabilize his life and that it might take some long years to stabilize because he would not have papers." It was Alaba's first time hearing about the importance of papers or of needing a Social Security number to work and live well in America. After a few days of research and soliciting advice from friends and family, Alaba decided not to take up the offer. He tried to go to school in Canada in 1997, but his father could not afford to pay the fees. In 2003, Alaba "had the opportunity to travel to Russia and China, but I turned it down too because I made up my mind that anything that will not make me a legal person in any country, I'm not going to do it." Instead, as we saw earlier in the chapter, Alaba entered the United States on the diversity visa that he won in 2009.

Debo, a forty-five-year-old Nigerian, felt similarly. "I wasn't going to relocate out of Nigeria without a legal stay. That was not on the table. Nothing was going to make me leave Nigeria and come and be in the shadows here [in the United States]." Shormeh, a thirty-nine-year-old Ghanaian diversity immigrant, recalled telling her mother, "I will not live abroad without papers. I always promised myself that I will not do it because I couldn't imagine myself going through life using people's papers and not being able to visit my mum [back in Ghana], not being able to do the work I want to do." Solape, a Nigerian in her late forties, concurred. "No, no, no. I won't come because it's not easy staying here without papers, you won't be able to move freely, you won't be able to work. It's not easy, because I've seen a lot of people suffering without good papers." Not having papers "just makes it very hard!"

Others were not as picky. They were willing to get a visa and overstay the visa and thus become undocumented in order to remain in the United States. Peter told me, "Back home right now, people just want, like, an invitation to visit, just to visit for like six months. They spend huge sums of money to get an invitation visa. They can pay up to $5,000. Because they know that when they come, they are gonna overstay. And when they come over here, they know that they came through visa. Some even come here illegally knowing they can find somebody to do their papers through marriage."

Some were willing to engage in stepwise migration by trying to enter another country first, such as England, one of the European countries, China, or a country in the Middle East, such as the United Arab Emirates. By winning the U.S. diversity visa lottery, they did not have to take such an elaborate path. Ambrose, a thirty-nine-year-old Ghanaian diversity immigrant who came to the United States in 2005, described migration on a diversity visa as "looking forward to a greener pasture, enjoying this greener pasture."

As Alaba's story shows, the DV Program offers pathways to migration that would be otherwise unavailable to certain individuals. Patrick, a forty-two-year-old Ghanaian diversity immigrant said, "For me, I didn't even have a family member here. So I did not have any intention to come here [the United States] because I thought the only way you could get here was through a family." Patrick was not wrong. Every year, immigrants in the family-based category comprise, on average, about two-thirds of the approximately one million immigrants legally allowed into the United States. (The rest arrive with refugee/asylum status, employer-based sponsorship, or a DV Program visa.) In 2018, 41 percent of all legal immigrants were immediate relatives of U.S. citizens—spouses, children, and parents. Another 20 percent of legal immigrants in 2018 came under family-sponsored preferences, which include siblings, their spouses, and their underage children.

Far more than one million people enter the United States every year. In recent years, the number has reached more than forty million annually. They enter without visas as citizens of countries that are part of the U.S. Visa Waiver Program; with temporary visas, such as visitor and student visas; with work visas, such as the H-1B and H-2B for agricultural workers; with immigrant visas; and as undocumented migrants, most of whom cross the U.S.-Mexico border. Many of these individuals who enter the United States without immigrant visas choose to stay and are classified as unauthorized, illegal, or undocumented persons in the United States.

The diversity visa helps place the recipient on the legal side of the legal-illegal divide and protects them from experiencing the worry and fear that comes with being vulnerable to deportation and immigration enforcement in the United States. The diversity visa also has other advantages. Diversity immigrants come to the United States wanting to "better themselves," by which many mean completing their education. Unlike those on student visas, diversity immigrants who enroll in educational programs are not under time and financial pressure to complete school as soon as possible and without any detours. To obtain a student visa, an individual must provide proof of significant financial resources, usually in the form of bank account statements or a notice from the U.S. school that tuition has been paid. A diversity visa has no such requirements for recipients who might decide to attend school once they are in the United States.

However, diversity immigrants often experience frayed social ties and insufficient assistance. Twenty-nine study participants had seen their social support networks fail after they arrived in the United States (see table A.3). Their situations ranged from having a strong social network (a parent or sibling in the United States) to having a social network made up of extended family members (uncles, aunts, cousins), to having no relatives in the United States and relying on friends of friends, who sometimes turned out to be less than reliable. Nat had no family members in the United States. His wife's family had friends in New York who said that they would sponsor the couple. But after arriving in the United States, Nat and his wife did not get a warm welcome or much help from their sponsors. "The moment we arrived, what I was expecting wasn't what I met—in terms of where to stay and who we were living with." Their sponsor told them after the first month that they had "to move and find [their] own place." Within six weeks, they "got an apartment and then [had] to start paying." To afford the new apartment, Nat had to take a minimum-wage job in a shoe factory. He could no longer afford to be picky.

Bisayo, a thirty-eight-year-old Nigerian, migrated to the United States with her husband and their two toddlers. Their sponsor, with whom they were supposed to stay in New York upon arrival, failed to meet them at the airport. "When we got to the airport, we tried to call her several times and the number wouldn't go through." They were stranded but had some money to stay in a hotel. "We tried calling her many times, but the number did not go through. So we started calling families and friends." They finally were put in touch with "a friend to my friend's husband." That family, whom they did not know, drove down to New York to pick them up. "They really impressed me. They came in two cars because we had a lot of baggage, and they carried us, took us to their house in Maryland." They stayed with this family for six months before getting their own place.

Weak social support networks are a feature and not a bug of the DV Program, not only because the program, by design, is more likely to give independent migrants a pathway to migrate to the United States, but also because no consideration is given to whether lottery winners have strong or weak social networks to help ease their transition into the United States. As shown by the experiences of some of the study respondents with the DV Program, nation-states can impact immigrants' social capital via immigration policy. The concept of social capital, developed by French sociologist Pierre Bourdieu and American sociologist James Coleman, originally centered on individuals or small groups as the units of analysis.[2] With some significant variations, both scholars focused on the benefits accruing to individuals or families by virtue of their ties with others. Bourdieu's treatment of the concept was instrumental, going as far as noting that people intentionally build their relations for the array of material and informational benefits that they bring later.[3] The sources of social capital are clearly associated with a person's networks, including those that they explicitly construct for the purpose of gaining social capital.

Governments can and do play a positive role in boosting social capital. A clear example is the support, both pecuniary and nonpecuniary, that governments provide to refugees. Such support helps create communities and bridging ties to wider non-ethnic social networks that assist refugees in finding jobs, housing, and schools for their children and in settling into U.S. society. Admittedly, diversity immigrants are not internally displaced persons resettled by the U.S. government, but they too face new, often bewildering environments and could use some assistance as they settle. Research on immigrant incorporation makes clear that strong social networks are a significant factor in successful immigrant integration.[4] The U.S. government should consider how to bolster the social capital of diversity immigrants, especially for those who have few if any family or friends in the United States.

HETEROGENOUS AND STRATIFIED: TODAY'S DIVERSITY IMMIGRANTS

Among Africans in the United States, diversity immigrants are part of the wave that began in the 1980s as a result of political and economic crises in Ghana and Nigeria and other sub-Saharan African nations. In the culture of migration that emerged during this time, most people in these countries have come to see moving overseas as their only way to achieve upward social mobility, since their governments have failed to provide jobs to the citizenry and to maintain already inadequate social infrastructure built during colonial times. Significant portions of this wave of African immigrants have been members of the educated class trained to meet the labor needs of the United States and other rich countries in the Global North.[5]

Less-educated immigrants have also been a part of this wave. These immigrants have found myriad ways to enter the United States and other rich countries, most often by overstaying a visitor or student visa that had given them temporary legal status. Others have engaged in stepwise migration that eventually enabled them to cross into the United States, though without authorization. Members of this group were not as fortunate back home as those in the middle class and found it harder to find gainful employment. Many were locked into an underclass in the urban centers in their home countries.[6] These immigrants have had to use various channels to become lawful permanent residents in the United States. Some have married for papers, either by entering into a business agreement by which they pay money to someone to marry them so as to regularize their stay via the family reunification system, or by pretending to enter a loving marriage and then surprising their spouse by filing for divorce once they get their papers. Other undocumented migrants have regularized their stay by applying for asylum.

Diversity immigrants do not have to worry about the time-consuming process of regularization that faces immigrants who are legally in the United States but on a temporary visa. Even irregular immigrants who are as educated as diversity immigrants (or even more so) confront the challenge of regularizing their stay and gaining lawful permanent resident status. Some DV Program winners started out in the United States on a temporary visa, such as a student visa or an employment-based visa, and were fortunate to avoid the issue by winning the lottery. These lucky winners did not have to find a job with an employer who would sponsor them for an H-1B visa and help them apply for a green card. They did not have to consider marrying for papers or taking other drastic steps to stay in the country. They did not have to apply for asylum. There is no doubt that having papers is an important and life-altering component of the DV Program that can only be envied by other classes of immigrants. However, despite all the advantages they enjoy as legal, educated immigrants, diversity immigrants still face significant hardships and setbacks owing to how they came into the United States.

Ghanaian and Nigerian diversity immigrants were preceded by Africans who came to the United States from the 1960s to 1980s. Some of those who arrived during this period belonged to their country's educated elite, a class that emerged during colonialism and the independence movements. Some members of the educated elite were sent overseas for postgraduate studies, sponsored either by their family, their village, or their government. They were expected to return to their home country after they earned their degrees and to work in high-ranking civil service positions. Many who went to the United States for further education, however, chose to stay there. A significant number had children in the United States, and even children who were taken back to their parents' country of origin when they were young have since returned to the United States. This group of Africans, who are some of the most-educated immigrants in the United States, have bought homes, settled in suburbia, and sent their children to college.[7]

Ghanaian and Nigerian diversity immigrants, as well as other African diversity immigrants, join Africans who transitioned from undocumented to lawful permanent resident status and citizenship thanks to the 1986 Immigration Reform and Control Act (IRCA), which offered amnesty to undocumented immigrants who had entered the United States by 1982. Among those granted amnesty under IRCA were 300,000 Africans. Their transition to lawful permanent resident status transformed the African population in the United States. African migrants were able to come out of the shadows, and many went to school to improve their credentials so as to get better jobs and achieve upward mobility.[8] These newly legalized immigrants could and did file requests to bring over their relatives, both near and far.

Ghanaian and Nigerian diversity immigrants also join a growing African population whose members are undocumented, hold temporary protective status (TPS) (such as the Liberians and Sierra Leoneans allowed into the United States during the Ebola pandemic of 2013 and 2014), or hold student or work visas (a population that can easily become undocumented if they overstay their visa).

As part of a stratified and heterogenous African immigrant population in the United States, Ghanaian and Nigerian diversity immigrants know they are fortunate: until they want to become U.S. citizens or file for spouses, children, parents, and siblings to join them, their dealings with USCIS end when they receive their green cards soon after arriving in the United States. They belong to churches and other places of worship where prayers for people to get green cards are common. They sit in conversations with friends and undocumented family members strategizing how they can regularize their stays (get papers). Some work with undocumented immigrants in their place of work. Most sympathize with their coethnics because they know that, "but for the grace of God," they might have been in the same situation. The declining economic and political fortunes of African countries constantly push Africans to find any possible way to enter economically advantaged countries like the United States. The diversity immigrants I interviewed for this book are sympathetic and hope that their coethnics are able to get green cards. On the whole, they are not supportive of immigration restrictions, as they know how tough life is for people back home. A common refrain on the lips of both Nigerian and Ghanaian diversity immigrants is "people are really suffering back home."

AN UGLY SIDE OF HAVING PAPERS

Sometimes the process of getting papers turns ugly: it can reveal hidden truths about family members or lead to deception on the part of others who want to secure papers for themselves (proving that illegal immigration has negative impacts on legal immigrants). That was Moses's experience. He married his girlfriend after he was notified that he had won the visa lottery. He added her to his immigrant visa application, and she arrived in the United States with him. "I didn't know she was pretending because she was coming to the United States. So when we got here, first day, she told me there was going to be nothing between us. I said okay, I can respect that, we are already in the United States and there's nothing I can do." They were divorced within a year of their arrival and went their separate ways. Being a divorced man made it challenging for Moses to enter new relationships. He recounted having to spend months trying to convince his current wife that his divorce had not been the consequence of anything he had done, like mistreating his wife, but rather that he was a victim of a love imposter. Though stressful, this courtship was successful. They got married and had three children.

Zeke, a thirty-seven-year-old long-haul trucker from Ghana, was applying to sponsor his two children when he learned that one of them was not his biological child. "The second was my biological child, but the first one wasn't." He learned this through the DNA test required by the U.S. government to identify fraudulent family reunification cases. "I did everything, and the DNA came, and that was the result. I spent all that money for nothing." He could not bring the first child over because, "if it's not your biological child, they won't even allow the kid. But the one who was my son actually came." Zeke subsequently divorced his wife. He was unemotional when he recounted the story, but the experience seemed to have left some scars on him, as a decade later he remained unmarried.

Though the situations described here might seem unique to the individuals involved, widespread ignorance among winners and their communities about what is allowed under the DV Program's rules, combined with how the program is administered, can also disrupt and separate families. Fear of being disqualified for committing fraud against the U.S. government sometimes prevents lottery winners from adding a new spouse to their visa applications, forcing them to leave their partner behind. Some couples are able to withstand the separation and its stresses; others are not.

Stanley, a thirty-four-year-old computer programmer from Ghana, got married to his girlfriend in the time between registering for the visa lottery and winning it. He decided not to add his spouse to his application because he did not want to risk being accused of entering into a fraudulent marriage and have his application denied. Upon entering the United States, he discovered that if he applied for a spousal visa as a green card holder, it would take a very long time for his wife to get the visa and join him. He was advised by several immigration lawyers and other Ghanaian immigrants that it would be best to wait until he became a U.S. citizen and then apply for her under the U.S. citizen spousal visa category. However, it takes years for a diversity immigrant to qualify for citizenship.

If someone registers for the lottery while single, they are justified in worrying that they will be disqualified for subsequently adding a spouse. If U.S. consular officers are able to uncover fraud in a relationship, the couple will lose their chance for a visa. Stanley was unwilling to take that risk. Looking back, he believed that, instead of marrying his girlfriend, he should have applied for her to join him immediately after he arrived in the United States, using the fiancée visa option.

> We could have done the fiancée one. With that one, we wouldn't do the marriage. I will come here, after that then, I will file for a fiancée visa from within the U.S. So, in three months, she will come here, and we do the wedding. Once you have a green card or citizenship and you are dating somebody, you can file for your fiancée. And the fiancée visa, they give her a ninety-day visa and you must marry within that ninety days.

It is not guaranteed, however, that this process is faster than filing for a spouse as a lawful permanent resident.

Stanley's lack of definitive facts points to a central problem with the DV Program: few winners clearly understand how the United States deals with changes in marital status after registration. Stanley did not know of the fiancée option at the time, but more importantly, he was unaware of the delay in the processing times for a spouse who wishes to join a diversity immigrant who holds only a green card. At the time I interviewed Stanley, he had already been apart from his wife for three years and would have to wait at least another two years before she could join him. For each month he spent in Ghana to be with her, he delayed the date by which he would satisfy the physical presence in the United States requirement in order to apply to become a U.S. citizen.[9] So their wait could be even longer. The year before our interview, Stanley spent four months in Ghana to be with his wife. He managed to keep his computer software job because "they know my stress, so they keep themselves tight [are accommodating of his absences]."

Davis, a thirty-six-year-old clinical research associate from Ghana, left his girlfriend (now his wife) behind when he came to the United States. "When I got the visa, we weren't married." He and his girlfriend did not want to rush the wedding.

> Going to the embassy with your documents, you have to show your marriage certificate and stuff like that, and with the church [we attended] before you get a marriage certificate, you just can't walk in there. They schedule a time, you have to go through counseling, like maybe two to three months, before you set a wedding date, and you know, you can't just get it right away.

Also, the diversity visa entrepreneur who helped Davis put together his immigrant application was unwilling to add a new spouse because it would imperil his application. Davis thought there would be no problem getting his girlfriend to join him in the United States. Like Stanley, he did not know how lengthy the process was. Had he known, Davis said, he and his girlfriend would have considered a quick wedding—a registry wedding in a judicial court. As it happened, he had to wait six years before he could bring her over.

COST AND THE CREATION OF TRANSNATIONAL FAMILIES

Financial constraints imposed by the DV Program are another factor that commonly forces winners to leave spouses and children behind, creating transnational families. Because a visa lottery win cannot be transferred from one fiscal year to another, either for the primary winner or their derivatives, diversity immigrants who cannot pay the visa processing fees and airfare costs to bring their families over by the entry deadline have to leave their families behind. Research on transnational families finds that distance and absence impact the stability of marriages, parental relationships, family formation, and the well-being of family members left behind in the home country.

Samson, a fifty-six-year-old cook who worked in the oil shale fields of North Dakota until he lost his job during a slump in the price of oil, left his wife and three daughters in Ghana. "I came alone because you know . . . the financial constraints about money. So I came in. Then later the family followed up when I became a citizen." Samson was married at the time he registered for the program, and he added his wife to his immigrant application, but "it was expensive coming with three girls and a wife. You don't know how the place was going to be like. So we came to the agreement that, okay, let me take a lead. That was the system we adopted." He migrated in 2001 and visited Ghana in 2003. His wife joined him in the United States in 2008, and his daughters came in 2011. He was aware that he could file for a fiancée visa for his wife and that she would be given a Social Security number and work authorization.[10] But, Samson said, "you have to work to do that. Pay lawyers, more money, fight! I didn't use that method. Once you become a U.S. citizen, it's just easier."

Mamle and her husband left their two children back in Ghana when they migrated in 1995.

> We decided to leave them because of financial problem, because we could not get the money to do all those papers in Ghana, to bring them with us for us to come together. Our brother and uncle helped us with the money to get over here. Then, when we came, we had to work hard and go and get them. It was as a result of financial problem that we couldn't come as a family.

The two children finally joined their parents in 2001. It took Mamle and her husband six years to bring their daughters over because "when we got here, we found out that it is not easy. It's not like what we expected in Ghana, where things are easier. In America, we came to find out that you have to work hard, unlike in Ghana. It took us a long time to secure a job and save money to do the kids' papers."

In sum, having "papers" through the DV Program does not always spare diversity immigrants from difficulties associated with legal status. In most cases, the problems are temporary: families reunite, and those in broken relationships move on and enter new ones. But some situations leave permanent scars, such as divorcing, or learning that a child is not one's biological offspring, or that a spouse has been unfaithful, or even entering into additional relationships and establishing several families. Diversity immigrants with minimal or no social ties over time are eventually able to bring over their family members, thus expanding their social networks and making new friends in the United States.

REVISED EXPECTATIONS: "I HAVE ACHIEVED SOME OF MY DREAMS"

Diversity immigrants migrate to the United States with big dreams, some of which are realized, others of which are revised. One of those dreams is to help their families back home, though the extent to which this familial responsibility weighs on them varies. For some diversity immigrants, the help they give their family is ancillary to their primary purpose of advancing themselves and achieving their goals. Such goals include going to school, attaining degrees, finding good jobs, earning a lot of money, buying new cars, owning houses both in the United States and in their country of origin, starting businesses back home, and belonging to the upper-middle or elite social classes.

Moji, a thirty-three-year-old Nigerian, occupied a spot on that spectrum: her goals and dreams came first, and she made no apologies for it. Before emigrating, she was selling clothes in Lagos because she could not get a job after graduating with a three-year diploma in accounting from a polytechnic. Now, in the United States, she worked as a nursing assistant. "I have passion to travel, I just wanted to travel out. That is my own. I wanted to change the environment." She was secretive about her win. "I didn't even tell them [my family] that I won it until I finished everything. If you tell them, you have people asking you for things. I didn't tell them until I passed the interview, and I collected the visa. When I got my ticket is when I told some people, not everybody." In America, she was pacing herself to achieve her goal of becoming a nurse. "Everything is step by step. In this country, you do not need to be rushed." When I interviewed her, she was focused on taking care of her two young sons.

Moji helped her family in Nigeria when she could afford to do so. "I call them, if they ask me something, I will give if I have it. If I don't have it, I won't kill myself. They have been calling me now, they called me yesterday . . . 'Ehm, my daughter wants to go to computer school.' I don't have the money. I said I cannot afford it. He still texted me. When I woke up this morning, I saw the text . . . 'Eeh, please o. . . .'" Moji ignored the text.

> You know, I can't do more than myself. If I have the money, I send to them. But Nigerians, their problem is too much. They will be calling you, demanding all the time, demanding, demanding money. If I have, I give them. But if

> I don't have, you know any money you have here, you have to pay your bills. After your bills, what is remaining? You don't have savings. When you finish paying your bills, there is nothing remaining.

She tried her best to help but knew that gratitude is fleeting.

> If you have been giving them money every month, and the day you did not give them, they'll be complaining that, 'Hmm, she doesn't help o. If you ask her, she will not give.' The day you refuse to give them, you are nothing to them; they will be saying all kinds of nonsense, all kinds of rubbish. So within myself, I know I care for them. I try my best.

Some migrants whose family members are better off are able to avoid the pressure to send money back home. And some of them, like Efe, receive help from their parents, which eases their integration into the American middle class. I spoke with Efe's father. He was aware of the pressure that parents put on their children to remit money and goods but said that it depends on how well the parents or other family members are doing back home.

> If you come from a family where things are rather hard for them in Nigeria, and they manage to put resources together to send you to America, it's like they sent you for the Golden Fleece, so you have to support them back. Fortunately, I think we are not in that position because by the grace of God, we are rather comfortable. Also, when she came in, we were able to . . . as soon as she settled down and got a job, we were able to pull some resources to enable her pay for a mortgage for a house because we thought about it and we sensed that we have to be coming more often.

Efe's parents knew that, as they grew older, they would want better health care than they would get in Nigeria. So the help that they were able to provide for their daughter would help them as well, as they planned to visit her in America, stay with her, and avail themselves of U.S. health care. "So we said, 'Okay, how much do you need to tender as down payment to get a mortgage for a house?' So she told us, and we could do it. So, we did, and we also helped her to settle down so that there will be no stress and pain."

Martin was happy being in the United States and pleased with what he had been able to provide for himself and his family.

> I should say that half of them [my dreams] have been realized. The only thing I've not achieved is education. But I'm working towards it. But in terms of

building a house, it's been achieved; having a family, it's been achieved. Now my wife is investing, which is money, it's been achieved. So I think that for ten years that I have been here, I have achieved a lot, and I've been able to build a house too for my dad.

Katherine, a thirty-one-year-old Ghanaian, fell near the other end of the spectrum: her focus was firmly on helping her family back home. She worked as a midwife in Ghana, but because of an error by the credentialing organization in the United States, her degree was not recognized as transferring in value. She wanted to build a house for her mother and felt that,

> since the dollar is always ahead of the cedi, when it is converted you get something bigger than you already get back at home. And whatever was in your mind to do to help your family you could do faster. At that time I had already planned on building a house for my mother. So being here would be faster for me to build a house than being back in Ghana and practicing as a midwife.

For Katherine, pursuing her own dreams was secondary to helping her family.

> My dream was that I would get a better life. I had a friend I went to high school with who will call me and tell me about her good life, that she had a car and a house. So that was on my mind, but I never even dreamt for anything. I was just like, okay, the opportunity is here, I'm gonna take that opportunity and then, whatever comes up from that stage, I'll take it up from there. But I didn't have any big dream, like hoping I was gonna buy a big car or a big house, no. My only aim was just to be able to support my family, that's it.

Katherine broke down how her family was able to use the money she sent home every year:

> If I send only the feeding fee for my mother, that is U.S. $2,400 in a year. But then if any of my siblings are in school, their school fees are different from that. If their rent is due, I need to pay for that as well. And recently I was trying to get them a house; so for the past three years, I would say every year, I send for the house alone around $6,000. So, in all, about $8,000 to $9,000 average.

Zeke also viewed winning the diversity visa as primarily a family win, with him in the role of his family's channel for blessings and upward social mobility.

On the dreams aspect, all my life, all that I have been able to think of is just to be able to support my family. Being here and getting a job and being able to send money to my mother every two months was just something that I was satisfied with. Once I can have something for myself, have a place to lay my head, I am fine. My family not being taken care of is something that will hurt me. So being able to send money, that is just it for me.

Zeke emphasized that "anything that comes out of it is a secondary issue. The most important thing ever is to know that my mother is being taken care of. That's the whole height of the vision that I had and that was what was met. So every other thing that I have been able to achieve outside of that, I would say that it was a bonus for me."

Ultimately, the responses of the diversity immigrants I interviewed when asked whether they had achieved their dreams differed according to their view as to who ought to be the primary beneficiary of their visa.

"MY KIDS ARE SUCCESSFUL"

Diversity immigrants are generally happy to have migrated because they believe that their children have better opportunities in the United States than in their country of origin. The disappointment of not achieving their personal goals is lessened when they look at their children. Because diversity immigrants are drawn from the educated class, any disappointment with their lives in the United States largely stems from not getting more education. Ghanaians and Nigerians prize education highly and see it as a surefire path to upward social mobility and entry into the middle class.[11] In my first book on the adult children of Nigerians in the United States and Britain (the second generation), I found that a prevalent belief among respondents was that it is un-Nigerian to not go to college.[12]

Mamle was happy to move to the United States but was worried because she was poorly educated. "I was the person who, because of financial problems, didn't go further in school." She had only finished elementary school. She was working as a teaching assistant and doing a tailoring apprenticeship when she won the visa lottery. She got the visa in 1996, when the requirements were less stringent. She said she could not achieve her dream to become a nurse because "I have a problem with math and science. I have a little problem with English. I can't do those physiology and anatomy and all that stuff." She had worked for twenty years as a health aide and was now a phlebotomist.

Yet Mamle's children were successful, which made her immensely proud. She told me, "Oh, God is so great! My children are successful . . . all of them. My oldest finished a master's degree. The second one finished her master's degree. Then, the other one [a third child she and her spouse had in America] is the one I'm working with. She is in college right now." Mamle passionately believed that her children would not have been college graduates if she had stayed back in Ghana. She asserted, "I never regretted being here in America."

Even though Nat felt that he had not achieved his dreams in the United States, he consoled himself by looking at his daughter and the opportunities she had.

> I have fallen behind on all my goals because I wasn't expecting that I'll be kind of struggling by now. I had my goals that by the age of this, this is what I'll be and then, from here to here. I kind of programmed everything. So as I moved to America, everything has kind of like fallen back in terms of our education, of having money, the types of jobs we wanted to have. We cannot just get up and do things.

Nat had some regrets. "In terms of America per se, if somebody would have asked me if I would come again, I would think twice." His sole focus now was making sure his daughter had all she needed to excel in school. "I think about [our daughter] first. Our goal is to make sure she has all the possible education that she wants. That's [what] we are kind of like working on. So if somebody calls me for money from back home, I tell them my daughter is about to go to college, hold on."

Children of diversity immigrants who remain in their parents' country of origin also enjoy better opportunities than they would have if their parents had stayed behind. Their parents can send money and goods back home to make their lives easier. The children can attend good private schools because their parents can afford the tuition fees. Peter sent his children to the most expensive school in Ghana, "because I want them to get that kind of a little bit of American education. So that when they come over here, it wouldn't be like, too hard on them." Many parents dream that their children will eventually migrate to be with them. They send clothes, food items, pocket money, and other goods to their children and their caregivers. Some of the parents bring their children over for vacations. These are transnational families, but the children enjoy the goods and benefits of immigrant remittances.

However, while they are proud that they can send money and other resources back home to improve the lives of their children, these parents find it emotionally challenging to be separated from them. Seye, a forty-three-year-old nurse from Nigeria, said, "When I came and left my kids there, it was tough because I was always thinking about them over there." In this way, the "family win" becomes somewhat complicated.

THE IMPORTANCE OF LEGALITY

The status systems and struggles "back home" structure how Ghanaian and Nigerian diversity immigrants view their win and their experiences in the United States. They see their luck in securing a U.S. green card as giving them (and their children) opportunities that would have been unavailable to them had they remained in Africa. On top of those benefits, they can freely move around and visit their country of origin because they are lawful permanent residents, and most eventually become U.S. citizens.

In the United States, diversity immigrants enjoy a higher status in their ethnic communities because those communities are stratified by class and legal status. But diversity immigrants also enjoy a higher status in their country of origin, where they are seen as family champions, not only because they have successfully managed to migrate overseas, but because they have the ability to sponsor their relatives to join them in the United States.

The experiences of diversity immigrants recounted in this chapter reveal the importance of legal status in delivering overall positive socioeconomic outcomes not only for these immigrants but also for their children.

Chapter 7 | Conclusion: Making Sense of the Lucky Win

IF BEING LUCKY is defined as being selected when selection is outside of one's control and the chance of selection is infinitesimal, then one is indeed lucky to win the U.S. visa lottery.[1] Because this worldwide lottery attracts, on average, more than fifteen million entrants per year, one's chance of being picked is 0.0067 percent. In the second phase of the process, one's chance of successfully making it through the visa application process is halved.[2] For diversity immigrants hailing from countries with declining economic and political fortunes, winning the U.S. visa lottery is a momentous occasion filled with immense promise of bettering oneself and one's family. Winners are overjoyed when a "prize" that so many people seek—the possibility of obtaining a green card—is awarded to them by chance. Suddenly, the fears that have kept them awake at night—fears of failure, unemployment, poverty—seem to dissolve in the light of the limitless benefits to come (riches, success, fulfillment).

The United States promotes this discourse of luck regarding the DV Program. And it is true that diversity immigrants are fortunate to avoid the overwhelming struggles facing migrants who enter the United States without papers or those who risk becoming "undocumented" by overstaying their visas. With a diversity visa, independent immigrants—individuals who otherwise have limited opportunities to migrate to the United States—can pursue a legal, permanent path to citizenship that is not afforded to many migrants. However, as this book has revealed, there are two sides to the winning coin: one side is upward social mobility and benefits for family members, but on the other side are numerous unforeseen difficulties that complicate any simple understanding of the terms "winners" and "losers," "lucky" and "unlucky."

Chapter 1 touched on former president Donald Trump's accusation that the DV lottery delivers into the United States a random pool of low-quality immigrants from "shithole countries." The chapters that followed established that the U.S. DV Program actually does an excellent job of selecting the best and the brightest from countries that often can least afford a national brain drain. Although I believe that we should acknowledge the DV Program for what it really is, a visa for highly skilled immigrants, the language of "play," "luck," and "winning" used to describe the lottery and the immigrants it allows into the country has become part of America's immigration zeitgeist.

At first glance, it seems notable that the United States is able to obtain such well-educated immigrants from a program that is founded on a lottery, a methodology that is supposed to ensure random selection. But as I have asserted, that outcome is not coincidental or simply fortunate—it is the result of the "structured luck" that underlies the entire program. This book has argued that scholars, supporters, and critics of the program must begin to question the structures, language, and policies that shape the DV Program and the lives of those who "play" the lottery.

SUCCESS VS. SUBOPTIMIZATION

The mythology of America depicts it as a place where everyone can thrive, make something of themselves, and provide an even better future for their children. The fact that most Africans have a positive image of the United States and that so many Ghanaian and Nigerian diversity immigrants describe it as a "land of opportunities" speaks to the greatness of America's image in the world. The United States holds special value to many immigrants because of the freedom and upward mobility (social, economic, occupational) it offers. And the DV Program can definitely serve as a tool to enable such success stories, as can be seen in the sample of diversity immigrants I interviewed for this study.

One perfect example is Shormeh, who left Ghana after winning the U.S. visa lottery in 2003. Shormeh grew up poor. Her mother had only an elementary school education, and her father, who left high school before earning his degree, did not live with them. In Ghana, Shormeh was a nurse. After starting out in the United States working as a ticket agent at the Houston airport, she was able to get her nursing credentials certified and begin the process of returning to the health care field—where she felt she "belonged"—by becoming a CNA, and then a registered nurse. Shormeh did not stop there: she decided to pursue her dream of becoming a medical doctor. At the time I interviewed her, she was a consultant in pediatrics. Even as she worried about the huge student loans she had to pay back, Shormeh was glad because, "since I came to America, I have been able to do my bachelor's in nursing, I did premed, I was able to go to medical school. Now I have my doctorate degree. So it has really pushed me up."

Along with experiencing upward mobility, Shormeh had been able to sponsor her mother and two younger sisters to join her in the United States. She also supported her other siblings in Ghana, helping them attend school and establish lucrative careers. Shormeh was convinced that winning the diversity visa was why she moved up in life and was able to pursue a "possible self" unimaginable in her home country.[3] "The associate degree in nursing probably was going to be the end point for me [in Ghana]," she observed.

Like Shormeh, all of the Ghanaian and Nigerian diversity immigrants I interviewed saw winning the U.S. visa lottery as a "turning point" in their lives. The diversity visa can offer immigrants a new start, better educational choices for their children (and sometimes themselves), and the ability to help family members back home. Even respondents who were unable to achieve their educational dreams often earned far more money than they would have if they had stayed in their home country. They also succeeded in other ways: they built houses, started businesses, and acquired the trappings of success. For these reasons, only a few of the Ghanaian and Nigerian diversity immigrants I interviewed regretted their choice to migrate to the United States. They compared their situation to the lives their "possible selves" would have been living back home. In light of the desperation and the worsening economic climate in Nigeria and Ghana, they concluded that they had exceeded what they might have achieved if they had not emigrated.

However, success stories are only one part of the DV Program narrative, and they offer a somewhat incomplete picture. A full assessment of the program reveals a persistent and troubling pattern of suboptimization. I use the term "suboptimization" to refer to the system's failure to ensure that diversity immigrants reach and fulfill their true potential. As I will explore in greater detail in this conclusion, the United States benefits significantly from the DV Program in that it receives skilled and educated immigrants who are prepared to work hard upon arrival. They are grateful to the United States for the opportunity to come here and quickly become "affective Americans" who are emotionally dedicated to their new country. So it is disheartening when their hopes and dreams are dashed, delayed, or recast and transferred to their children.

While America celebrates stories of immigrants making something of themselves, the struggle of many diversity immigrants to do just that raises pressing questions about the DV Program. Why did it take Gideon fifteen years to become a nurse in the United States after leaving Ghana during his third year as a business major? Why had Monica, who left

Ghana just as she was admitted to university, been unable to complete a bachelor's degree in the United States despite being in the country for seventeen years? Instead, she worked as a health aide in an elderly residential facility, and her attempt to earn a nursing degree had left her with hefty student loans for a still-incomplete course of study at a community college.

When I asked Monica why someone might choose to play the U.S. visa lottery, she responded, "Maybe, better their lives or something." Her response communicated her doubts and disillusionment as to whether an immigrant would necessarily have a better life in the United States than in their country of origin. The possible self that Monica dreamed of had not materialized, as she had not been able to build a house for herself back home. Currently renting a one-bedroom apartment, she no longer foresaw a future for herself as a transnational homeowner, since she was not making enough money and had no savings.

The figures and analysis presented in chapter 1 of this book revealed that diversity immigrants experience a wage penalty in the U.S. labor market in the early stages of their arrival and that, surprisingly, they do less well than all other categories of legal immigrants, including refugees, who generally have been displaced from their homes and enter the United States with low levels of financial, human, and social capital. But diversity immigrants recover to attain parity with most other legal immigrants. Subsequent chapters detailed diversity immigrants' experiences of disrupted educational paths, frustrated career aspirations, accumulated debt, and family separations, all of which compromise and delay their full and gainful incorporation into U.S. society. The findings suggest that something about the design and administration of the Diversity Immigrant Visa Program is shaping these immigrants' outcomes in the United States.

MIGRAPOLICY INTERVENTIONS AND THEIR TRANSNATIONAL EFFECTS

The DV Program has created what I call "migrapolicy interventions"—a set of intended and unintended consequences that take positive, negative, and neutral forms. Table I.1 identifies the migrapolicy interventions discussed in this book.

Migrapolicy interventions have transnational consequences for immigrants, nonmigrants, and countries of origin. Not only do their impacts begin long before lottery winners emigrate, but their ripple effects continue to be felt long after by the people and places they leave behind. Yet such impacts rarely receive attention, primarily because migration scholars and policymakers usually focus on immigrants within their receiving countries rather than on potential immigrants and communities in the Global South. This book has attempted to remedy that omission.

As discussed in chapter 6, one example of a positive migrapolicy intervention is that diversity immigrants receive lawful permanent resident status, which grants them higher status in their communities in their country of origin and allows them to function as benefactors and role models for those left behind. But getting papers also can function as a negative migrapolicy intervention for families when it leads to divorce, separation, and the creation of transnational family units. Other negative migrapolicy interventions, as discussed in chapter 5, include the disruptive impact on immigrants' human capital obtainment, which is felt not just when they arrive in the United States but even before they leave their country of origin. The effects of lowered attainment filter back home as well, in the form of decreased remittances.

One major transnational consequence of the DV Program is that it creates conditions on the ground for the emergence, proliferation, and prosperity of diversity visa entrepreneurs, who greatly affect the social organization and patterns of migration. In chapter 4, I discussed how visa entrepreneurs make money from the DV Program. These agents have a significant effect on structuring the luck of thousands of potential immigrants as they publicize, register, and help people apply for the DV Program. Their omnipresence is clear evidence of the intrusive effects of U.S. immigration policy on less-developed countries in the Global South thousands of miles away from America's shores. As I explained in chapter 5, visa entrepreneurs play a key role in one of the most detrimental negative migrapolicy interventions—interference in the human capital accumulation of what I call "disrupted undergraduates." By targeting educated youth in their final years of secondary school and early years at tertiary institutions, visa entrepreneurs change the trajectories of countless potential graduates, with consequences that reverberate for many years as disrupted undergraduates try to get back on track in the United States.

The study of exploitative practices targeting immigrants has often focused on undocumented migration or migrant labor contracting. Yet close study of the U.S. DV Program reveals that exploitative practices emanate even from *legal* migration.[4] Visa entrepreneurs play a significant role in the accumulation of debt, the falsification of marital and familial bonds, and the acquisition of required qualifications. They also put intense pressure on visa lottery winners who are not inclined to pursue the migration process, sometimes enlisting family members to persuade them. Some agents charge exorbitant fees, and others trick applicants into paying for unnecessary forms and services. Lottery winners often must borrow from friends and family in their home country and in the diaspora to pay agents' fees, accumulating obligations that they continue to feel long after their arrival in the United States. Often diversity immigrants' long, difficult, and at times unfulfilled path toward upward mobility is shaped by these debts.

Thus, I reframe notions of "debt," which migration scholarship has typically associated with irregular migration via human traffickers, such as coyotes in Latin America. Even though most diversity immigrants belong to the educated class and all enter the country legally, many diversity immigrants and their family members are not spared from the yoke of debt. Scholars must expand their conceptualization of "cost" to look beyond the debt associated with illegal migration and trafficking and include the obligations incurred with legal migration that cannot be easily resolved once an immigrant arrives in the United States, such as debts owed to diversity visa entrepreneurs and family members.

Although it must also be acknowledged that visa entrepreneurs sometimes offer crucial lifelines for aspiring emigrants who lack the confidence or wherewithal to pursue the process on their own, it is nevertheless the case that their practices, both pernicious and useful, stem from the requirements and structure of the DV Program itself. The technological and documentation requirements, the lack of deferment options for students or for families struggling to afford airfare and fees, and the education requirement all place lottery winners in potentially desperate or untenable situations before they have even left home.

SELECTIVE ADMISSION, STRUCTURED MIGRATION

The DV Program structures not only the luck of its participants but also the very flow of global migration. It shapes migration patterns from the African continent in particular because it offers a key route for Africans to enter the United States. The citizens of most countries in the Global North can enter the United States visa-free for a visit of less than ninety days, but the citizens of sub-Saharan African nations are not afforded this same opportunity. For these African citizens, outside of being a refugee from a war-torn land or being fortunate enough to have a legal and established close relative in the United States (the percentage of sub-Saharan Africans with relatives in the United States is small, however, owing to the historical exclusion of African migrants), the diversity visa is the major, and often the only, migration path to the United States.

The rules for applying for the diversity visa include class-based requirements, such as education credentials, that result in an applicant pool drawn from those who might be considered relatively privileged in their home country. Thus, the DV Program reproduces and codifies the deliberate division of citizens in the Global South into two classes: the worthy (members of the educated class who can be given permission to enter the United States) and the unworthy (members of the uneducated class and urban and rural underclasses who are legally locked out).

Compare this to how policies toward other countries legally allow for more class diversity. For example, under the Visa Waiver Program, the United States admits citizens of countries in Europe and Asia without obtaining an entry visa and thus without having to meet various education or skills requirements. Since the United States does not extend this privilege to Africa, the demands placed on African migrants who are seeking authorization to enter the United States are far greater than those placed on other groups. The result is greater class diversity among certain nationalities. Simply put, African migration is managed through stricter criteria for legal entry.

One stereotype that sometimes arises in scholarship and popular commentary is that African immigrants are somehow intrinsically oriented toward success and upward mobility, especially compared to other immigrants or U.S.-born Black Americans. However, Black African immigrants' relative socioeconomic success (be it imagined or actualized) is in fact indicative of the extreme selectivity and much more stringent rules applied to African migrants via U.S. immigration policy.[5] This book helps us understand the selection process for Africans and how it continues to shape the African population in the United States. It provides additional answers as to why African populations are often highly successful. But it also pulls back the curtain on the limits and barriers to that success, the ethnic niching and funneling of diversely talented individuals into constricted career fields, and the resulting frustration and suboptimization of highly educated and highly skilled individuals who come to this country with what should be achievable dreams.

Immigration policy has profound implications for immigrant integration. In this epoch, scholars pay the greatest attention to the impact of U.S. laws and enforcement strategies on undocumented persons. Theories such as the concept of "legal violence" highlight the negative impact of the combination of U.S. immigration and criminal laws on immigrants with tenuous legal status.[6] For example, some laws grant or restrict immigrants' access to driver's licenses and state IDs, welfare benefits, public employment, and so on, all of which have significant impact on immigrants' integration into society. But migration scholars' study of immigration has been too singularly focused. We have lost sight of the impact of U.S. immigration policy on migrants with lawful permanent resident status—in other words, the people the U.S. government technically defines as immigrants. *Structured Luck* reveals the ways in which even a program that offers legal entry (and does not seek to bar, deter, detain, or deport immigrants) can nonetheless have detrimental and exploitative effects on both the personal and transnational levels.

THE GEOPOLITICS OF MIGRATION: WHO ARE THE *REAL* LUCKY WINNERS?

We must not lose sight of the fact that, for many, crossing international borders is a difficult necessity. Migrating takes you away from all that is comfortable—your home, your family, and your friends. It is not an easy path, but people are often driven to leave their country owing to the intractable problems of poverty and blocked upward mobility. Endemic corruption along with the failure of many African leaders to harness their country's resources to deliver economic development, sufficient infrastructure, jobs, health care, and a social safety net for their citizens have created the conditions that many seek to escape via emigration. Those leaders' failures should not be erased or excused, but we must simultaneously attend to the ways in which their countries' economic decimation was triggered and exacerbated by neoliberal systems imposed by global organizations, such as the International Monetary Fund and the World Bank, and the imperialist activities of wealthy and powerful Western countries (I discussed these points extensively in chapter 2). That immigrants sometimes engage in fraudulent practices to migrate, such as pop-up marriages or the manufacture of qualifications to render them "worthy" of receiving a visa, is only further evidence of desperation and systemic inequality. Focusing too much attention on fraudulent practices can distract from a key truth: immigrants are coming to economically advantaged countries *because there is demand for their labor and these countries benefit from their presence.*

The United States needs immigrants. Immigrants power its economy. The rhetoric of immigration restriction and the attempts to enforce immigration laws with concomitant deportation wither in the face of employers' demand for immigrant labor. In 2013, when the Obama administration ramped up workplace immigrant enforcement raids, agricultural producers and their associations told the administration to stop because crops were rotting in the field. They could not find enough labor migrants, most of whom are undocumented, to work as harvesters. California U.S. senator Dianne Feinstein wrote a letter in response to lobbying by a farmers' group from California's Central Valley, asking officials in the Department of Homeland Security to "redirect" their enforcement activities from labor migrants to immigrants associated with "serious violent crimes." Senator Feinstein noted, "The reality is that the majority of farmworkers in the U.S.

are foreign-born and unauthorized, which is well-known." She added that she was "afraid that this aggressive worksite enforcement strategy will deprive the agricultural sector of most of its workforce."[7] Indeed, the use of undocumented workers in the agricultural industry is a poorly kept secret.

U.S. politicians often speak out of both sides of their mouths—appeasing opponents of immigration with tough talk about building walls and strengthening enforcement, while reassuring agricultural employers and other U.S. companies that a continued stream of immigrants will be permitted so as to not disrupt their capitalist endeavors and profits. Ex-president Donald Trump, known for his tough talk on immigration, his pledge to build a wall on the U.S.-Mexico border, and his immigration bans targeting Muslims and citizens of some African (Black) countries, was found to employ undocumented immigrants in several of his businesses.[8] The seeming inability of the United States to control migration is partly a product of these opposing forces that U.S. politicians and policymakers have to navigate.[9]

Another factor that necessitates an influx of immigrants is the reality that the American population is aging. The U.S. Census Bureau projects that by 2034 the United States will have more people over the age of sixty-five than children, and that by 2040 one out of every five U.S. residents will be sixty-five or older.[10] In the face of such demographic changes, the United States needs immigrants, most of whom are young and in their prime working years, to bear the fiscal burden of supporting retired seniors by funding Social Security, Medicare, and Medicaid. Immigrants in the United States generate revenue for local, state, and federal governments through paying taxes. Importantly, they also serve as health care workers and caregivers who assist American seniors. Without immigrants, U.S. residents would see their taxes increase out of necessity to cover all these costs.

The 2020 U.S. census reports that the United States experienced its slowest population growth in a century, growing by just 0.35 percent in the previous decade (2010 to 2020).[11] The White population shrank in that decade for the first time in U.S. history; thus, the observed growth rate was powered by recent immigrants and their subsequent generations. In short, without immigrants, the United States would be a country with a declining and aging population, labor shortages, dying towns and neighborhoods, an uncared-for elderly population (unless children quit their jobs to care for their parents), and budget shortfalls due to high expenditures on retirees. Few avenues would be available to the country to balance its budget outside of tax increases, which some argue could discourage people from working and thus exacerbate labor shortages.[12]

The United States benefits from immigration. A comprehensive report on the economic and fiscal impacts of immigrants in the United States found that immigrants do not affect the overall employment levels of native-born workers. In fact, new immigrants largely replace older immigrants in the workforce, suggesting that fresh migrant bodies are used to replenish the migrant labor supply.[13] Skilled immigrants boost the wages of both college- and non-college-educated natives, and the presence of immigrant labor helps to keep the prices of food, housekeeping, childcare, and construction low.[14] Immigrants and their children start businesses and create new technologies. It is noteworthy that Steve Jobs, the founder of Apple, was the child of a Syrian immigrant.

Does the cost of supporting immigrants outstrip the gains they provide? It does not. In terms of fiscal impact, the federal government gains from the presence of immigrants, largely via tax contributions, but the burden of supporting immigrants and their children (mainly by providing education and health care) is borne by local and state governments. From 2011 to 2013, "the net cost to state and local budgets for first-generation adults (including costs generated by their dependent children) was, on average, $1,600" per immigrant per year.[15] But local and state budgets benefited from second- and third-plus-generation adults. Second-generation adults (children of immigrants) generated a net positive of $1,700 per immigrant per year, and the third-plus generation generated a net positive of $1,300 per immigrant per year. According to these estimates, the total annual fiscal impact of first-generation immigrants and their dependents, when averaged across 2011, 2012, and 2013, was "a cost of $57.4 billion, while second- and third-plus-generation adults create[d] a benefit of $30.5 billion and $223.8 billion, respectively."[16] In short, after absorbing significant costs to support first-generation immigrants, the United States benefits fiscally at all three levels of government—federal, state, and local—from subsequent generations of immigrants.[17]

Ultimately, the facts show that the United States and its residents benefit from *all* immigrants of every race, ethnicity, and religion—uneducated, poorly educated, somewhat educated, highly educated, labor migrants, highly skilled workers, and professionals—and from their children and subsequent generations.

WIDENING THE LENS

I have focused here on the U.S. DV Program, but the process of "structured luck" and the consequences of multilevel migrapolicy interventions are not limited to the United States. Other economically advantaged countries in the Global North pass and enforce policies that define and select "worthy" (often well-educated) immigrants and block "unworthy" immigrants.

Canada's migration policy, including the Express Entry program, uses a points system to grant migrants permanent resident status, with points awarded based on educational qualifications, age, language skills, and work experience. The more educated one is, the more points one accrues, so individuals who hold doctorates or medical degrees are awarded the maximum number of education points. Being married to an educated spouse earns an applicant more points, as does being between the ages of twenty-one and thirty-five. Like the U.S. DV Program, Canada's Express Entry program selects the elites from less-developed countries in the Global South. The Canadian government is clear in its intention to recruit millions of skilled-labor migrants and encourage them to settle in sparsely populated regions.[18] In 2017, a sampling of the top ten occupations among Nigerian Express Entry applicants to Canada included information system analysts and consultants, software engineers, computer programmers and interactive developers, cooks, food service supervisors, and university professors and lecturers.[19] Nigeria is one of the top ten countries whose middle-class citizens are migrating to Canada via the skilled-workers immigration policy.[20]

The United Kingdom terminated its highly skilled migrant program in 2008, only to find itself suffering from a scarcity of workers post-Brexit. Subsequently, the United Kingdom reinstated a points-based immigration system that seeks highly skilled workers. In early 2020, Germany instituted an immigration policy that admits highly skilled workers from around the world, whereas previously it admitted only migrants from the European Union. Middle Eastern countries are engaged in similar efforts. The Kingdom of Saudi Arabia is recruiting medical doctors and other health professionals from Nigeria.[21]

Human beings are the greatest resource on Earth, and economically advantaged countries are benefiting tremendously from people's domestic and global labor. Though this book focuses on skilled immigrants, the division of workers into such categories ignores the clear evidence that receiving countries benefit from all immigrants who enter their workforces. There is a long and troubling tradition by which receiving countries demonize immigrants while denying that those same immigrants make significant contributions to their adopted homeland. But why should wealthy countries in the Global North grow richer off skills and talents that were developed and subsidized by the economically disadvantaged nations left behind by emigrants? To promote the virtues of global capitalism and the free flow of capital, trade, and ideas while working against the free flow of the labor of human beings is hypocritical.

INVESTMENT AS A SOLUTION

One sure way in which the Global North could reduce the flow of migrants to its shores (if that were truly what it wanted to do) would be to assist in the development of immigrant-sending countries.[22] As they develop, countries that are net-emigration states become net-immigration states, since their citizens no longer need to migrate out of economic necessity. In fact, those nations become attractive to citizens from other countries who are seeking greener pastures. This has happened to Ireland, and it is in the process of happening to Mexico. In the past decade, fewer Mexicans have been crossing the border to the United States to look for jobs, and more Americans have been moving to Mexico seeking lower retirement and health care costs.

Beyond investing in countries of origin, economically advantaged countries must invest in immigrants themselves by committing to minimizing the suboptimization of immigrants' talents. With suboptimization, the exploitation is tripled: first, the development of immigrant-sending countries is sabotaged by preventing them from competing on a level playing field in global free trade; second, the best and brightest in these countries are lured away via immigration policies that target the educated classes; and third, highly educated and highly skilled immigrants are underutilized when U.S. policies compel them to take jobs for which they are overqualified without helping them achieve and realize their full potential. Responsibility cannot end with the excuse advanced by most receiving countries, and even many immigrants: that migrants are better off than they would be at home because "at least they are earning money." The fact that money earned abroad makes a big difference in the lives of those left at home points to a further injustice: the huge disparities in national currency values are exacerbated and reinforced by the system itself.

When Caribbean immigrants in Britain were told by White Britons to go back to their countries, they replied, "We are here because you were there."[23] They meant that, as citizens of Britain's ex-colonies, they had a right to come "home" to the "motherland" of Britain. As a colonial power, Britain established historical and exploitative links with many countries around the world—in well-known words of that long era, "the sun never sets on the British Empire"—and its imperial relationship with these countries made it a destination country for many immigrants.

In the twenty-first century, migrants entering more economically advantaged countries—including growing powerhouses like China—can make a similar claim: "We are here because you are there," "there" being a reference to the ongoing interventions of wealthier countries inside the borders of net-emigration countries. Such interventions include military operations, capitalist penetration, trade, and immigration policies that impact countries of origin and their citizens. Rather than endorse such predatory investments, economically advantaged nations should consider investments that would simultaneously benefit themselves *and* countries that are still developing.

FROM MACRO TO MICRO

What we learn from the stories of the Ghanaian and Nigerian diversity immigrants interviewed in this book is that we must pay greater attention to the downstream effects of *all* immigration policy coming out of economically advantaged countries in the Global North. We must understand how these policies are reshaping the patterns of migration, how they are affecting the lives of immigrants both before and after they arrive in the receiving country, and how they are impacting the people and countries that emigrants leave behind. We must challenge the widely accepted notion (which hides a more complex reality) that immigrants are better off in their receiving countries than in their countries of origin. We must trouble the notion that immigrants with lawful permanent residence status do not merit scholarly study and do not need assistance transitioning and incorporating into their new country just because they are better off than undocumented immigrants, who are forced to live in the shadows under the ever-present threat of deportation.

Refocusing our critical lens will reveal the complex ways in which economically advantaged countries exploit immigration, thus allowing for more focused and effective solutions and mitigation strategies. It will also enable scholars to learn more about different migrant groups and add to our understanding of the specific challenges and motivations of immigrants from a wider variety of races, nationalities, social classes, and economic backgrounds.

There are, of course, certain commonalities among immigrant groups: most migrants leave home because they can earn more and access a higher standard of living in receiving countries. Many emigrate because they believe that their children will have better educational opportunities. But the specifics also matter. For example, Nigerian emigrants are drawn to countries in the Global North by the promise of uninterrupted electricity, which would allow them to escape the noise and air pollution of generators (if they belong to the middle class), end their reliance on wax candles and kerosene lanterns (if they are less affluent), and avoid spending hours in darkness (if their lack of money makes even these alternatives a luxury). They can safely run errands or simply be social at dusk and at night without worrying about being robbed or killed. These seem like simple things, but they are important facts of daily life that influence people's decisions about whether to migrate, remain, or return. Improving and developing infrastructure, with the contributions of receiving countries, could eliminate one cause of migration.

Fewer people would choose to leave their homeland if they knew that the circumstances at home would soon improve. Clearly, countries like Nigeria and Ghana can do better too; they can endeavor to provide more gainful employment opportunities, improve infrastructure, and reinforce security. There are the fixes that leaders of those countries have the power to make, and then there are the problems implicated in the larger global system of capitalism.

For the immediate future, I would argue that a greater responsibility for change lies with receiving countries that rely on immigrant labor (even when they do not admit that fact), because they are recruiting the best and brightest away from the countries that have subsidized those individuals' education and acquisition of skills. Receiving countries not only deprive sending countries of valuable citizens but also stand poised to benefit from immigrants' talents and the talents of their descendants. As such, receiving countries need to take more responsibility for owning the disruptions in people's lives caused by their immigration policies. They must seek innovative and fair ways to tackle these issues. In particular, they must address the suboptimization of immigrants' potential and discard the transactional mentality that views immigrants as easily replaceable (after all, more are rushing to come) and as necessary grist in the mill to fill unattractive, but essential, jobs.

POLICY ISSUES

The close analysis of the DV Program in the preceding chapters sheds some light on current demands for change and policy ideas regarding U.S. immigration. The United States is often criticized for making a family preference system the foundation of its immigration policy. Critics want to increase the percentage of immigrants who enter via professional and skills visas and drastically reduce the percentage of immigrants who arrive via the family preference system. Such a readjustment would put U.S. immigration policy in closer alignment with the immigration policies of Canada and Australia, countries to which it is often compared. Both countries admit lower percentages of immigrants because of their family connections.

But this book's examination of diversity immigrants does not support that course of action. By analyzing longitudinal New Immigrant Survey data to understand how diversity immigrants from around the world compare to other legal immigrants and by collecting empirical firsthand accounts of West African diversity immigrants' experiences, *Structured Luck* reveals that immigrants and refugees who receive social support in the United States fare better than educated diversity immigrants, who struggle to adjust and achieve, particularly in their early years in the United States. This finding suggests that the United States should be cautious in overhauling its current system and replacing it with one where the majority of immigrants come in via skills visas and where little to no attention is paid as to whether they have social ties in the United States.

It is not incidental that diversity immigrants face no requirement to have family connections or social networks in the United States. One of the program's goals is to give independent immigrants an opportunity to migrate to the United States, which is otherwise unavailable to them. However, since the diversity visa is also reserved for nationalities that are underrepresented among U.S. immigrants, it is likely that the coethnics in the United States of diversity immigrants from certain countries are very few in number. This book emphasizes the importance of coethnic communities, which many new immigrants rely upon to access resources that facilitate integration. Diversity immigrants are not required to have employer sponsorship or a job in order to emigrate, so they do not necessarily find workplace support early on, and non-profit aid organizations are focused on refugees and asylum seekers rather than skilled legal immigrants.

In the U.S. context, the importance of having social networks to assist immigrant integration is crucial because the United States spends far less than comparable countries, such as Canada, on immigrant integration. The United States takes a laissez-faire approach to its immigrants, essentially leaving it to immigrants to figure out for themselves how they will integrate and incorporate. Canada, which takes a multicultural approach, supports immigrants' integration with both financial and nonfinancial assistance. Whether the United States would be willing to invest similarly in its immigrant population is highly questionable—and might not be needed, given that U.S. immigrants are faring well enough compared to immigrants in Canada—but the solution to the problem clearly cannot be to restrict family-based immigration while seeking more skilled immigrants who lack support and family connections.

The experiences of the Ghanaian and Nigerian diversity immigrants interviewed for this book reveal the importance of legal status. Despite the challenges many had faced, from lack of preparation to migrate to being Black in the United States, these immigrants had largely experienced success in the United States and succeeded in helping their families. Even though, like other diversity immigrants, they earned the least of all legal immigrants in the early years after arrival, they did not remain disadvantaged. They were able to recover because their legal status kept them out of poor jobs in the secondary labor market, in which they could have been exploited, and facilitated their job mobility, which gained them higher wages and avenues to additional educational credentials. Most of their children were keeping the immigrant bargain, rewarding their parents' sacrifice by finishing high school, going to college, and getting well-paying jobs in mainstream U.S. society.

A consequence of undocumented status is poverty, as undocumented workers are often limited to low-paying jobs with unsafe working conditions.[24] They are vulnerable to exploitation because of limited rights and the threat of deportation if they report workplace abuses. Their constrained financial situation also affects their children's life chances. Immigrants with legal status do not have to suffer these injustices.

It is good news that the Biden administration is looking to expand legal pathways for migration to the United States, but apart from plans to increase the number of refugees from the Caribbean and Latin America, the administration plans to grant only temporary one- to two-year work authorizations.[25] These actions are an attempt to reduce the flow of undocumented immigrants across the U.S.-Mexico border and blunt Republican political attacks on Democrats as weak on border security. But they also represent a recognition of the country's need for labor migrants. What is needed are more pathways that grant immigrants lawful permanent residence status; such policies would stop the proliferation of undocumented immigrants caused by the move into undocumented status when immigrants' work authorizations expire, imperiling their own and their children's socioeconomic assimilation. It would be heartening to see the Biden and subsequent administrations make a positive case for legality, as this book does.

A COLLEGE EXEMPTION FOR DIVERSITY IMMIGRANTS

The DV Program is a functional and beneficial program in that it provides the United States with highly skilled immigrants and helps many people who need to migrate but are not eligible for migration through other categories. But the program's problematic structures and the problematic structures it creates must be acknowledged so that improvements can be made.

Many elements of the program could benefit from attention and reform. The high incidence of brain waste among college-educated immigrants across the United States reveals a failure to maximize their potential and leverage their skills and reflects poorly on all levels of the U.S. government and on private-sector employers. If immigrants were assisted via bridge programs in improving their English fluency and other practical skills, or in getting U.S. state licenses that would allow them to use their foreign health or education credentials, some who would otherwise wind up in poorly paid jobs could find work in well-paying white-collar professions. Such jobs would ease their integration into U.S. society; help meet U.S. needs for highly skilled workers; improve standards of living for immigrants and their families, both in the United States and in their country of origin; and increase the amount of the remittances they send home, which could allow a younger family member to go to school or enable another family member to get needed medical care.

I raise several issues that should be reviewed and changes that should be made, though I will leave the details for experts in the policy field to work out. The technological requirements of the visa—especially the DV photo requirements—should be reviewed, as should the effects of the "no rollover" policy on kinship ties and on family separation. Also open to review are possible improvements to information dissemination about the program and to the program's requirements and accommodations (rights) for winners of the visa lottery. Visa processing fees should be reduced. Other issues that are not specific to the program but impact diversity immigrants and all other immigrants include reducing the difficulty of getting degree and course accreditation for overseas education.

I propose one key modification to the diversity visa that would optimize the potential of its immigrants and facilitate their successful incorporation into American society. The United States should create a college students' exemption that permits those who win the U.S. visa lottery while attending a four-year, degree-granting college to complete their bachelor's degree before using their diversity visa. The exemption should apply to recent and current high school graduates who have managed to get accepted into a tertiary institution in their home country but have not yet started their program (matriculated). The U.S. government could issue directives to the relevant administrative bodies, in particular the State Department, that winners currently enrolled in a bachelor's degree course be given an exemption that grants them the diversity visa if they meet all stated requirements, but allows them to defer usage of the visa and entry into the United States until they graduate. Immigrants with a college degree, even one from a foreign school, fare better in the U.S. labor market than migrants without a college degree.[26] This slight change to the program would eliminate the negative migrapolicy intervention of disrupting immigrants' acquisition of human capital. The change aligns with the stated U.S. interest in recruiting high-quality immigrants to meet its economic and labor needs. If more than 50 percent of all diversity immigrants and 62 percent of African diversity immigrants already had at least a college degree, this change would raise that percentage.[27]

Critics might argue that this adjustment would only accelerate the brain drain already underway in immigrant-sending countries. Although it is clear that countries like Nigeria and Ghana would benefit from retaining their most-educated citizens, especially after investing in and funding much of their schooling, not all aspects of the loss are negative. There is evidence of a "brain gain" from highly skilled migration in immigrant-sending countries in the form of increased remittances; improved standards of living (such as new or upgraded housing), bankrolled by emigrants overseas; increased human capital accumulation by family members via emigrants' contributions to their school fees and education; transfers of information on study and work opportunities; and return migration.[28] A college exemption could benefit immigrants' countries of origin in similar ways.

However, a college exemption policy would exacerbate the inequities caused by wealthy countries recruiting individuals whose education has been subsidized by their country of origin. In fact, it would virtually ensure that countries of origin absorb the costs of educating individuals who are definitely planning to leave. This is a dilemma that government officials and policymakers in both the sending and receiving countries would need to address.[29]

The current gridlock in the U.S. Congress does make changes to immigration policy seem nearly impossible. Comprehensive immigration bills have languished in Congress for decades because of the lack of appetite for providing concrete solutions to the problem of having more than ten million undocumented persons in the United States. The last immigration bill that granted undocumented immigrants a pathway to citizenship was the 1986 IRCA bill, signed into law by President Ronald Reagan. During the Trump administration, there was an increased appetite in Congress to end the DV Program. By contrast, the immigration bill written by the Biden administration in 2021 would increase the number of diversity visas awarded annually to eighty thousand.

With such a huge disconnect between policies, I am rather pessimistic that lawmakers from opposing parties will be able to reach an agreement, but the call and the case for policy change should be made anyway. And this book makes it. Because a college exemption would require further changes in how many visas are awarded annually, possibly necessitating the creation of a reserve of visas for those remaining in college until they earn their degree, and because of the existing "no rollover" requirement that diversity visas be used in the fiscal year they are won, legislation that clearly lays out the new processes would have to be passed by Congress.

OPTIMIZING THE DV PROGRAM

Structured Luck has offered a critical examination of the U.S. DV Program, revealing its positive aspects, its intended and unintended consequences, and its inequalities. This book in no way argues that the policy should be terminated, only that it be modified to reach its full potential. There is no need to accept suboptimization for either the policy or the people it admits.

One of this book's major objectives has been to fill some of the ongoing gaps in migration scholarship that have resulted in researchers overlooking the plight and experiences of legal immigrants, including those who enter via the DV Program. Since the visa lottery offers the main route into the United States for immigrants of African origin, this seems especially important given the lack of insight into the experiences of African immigrants. *Structured Luck* has sought to remedy that deficit in some small way.

The book's other major objective has been to awaken the "better angels" in those of us who live more fortunate lives in economically advantaged countries in the Global North. Let us challenge ourselves and our governments to shift from a stance of unconcern and renew our commitment to helping each other live our best lives. Policies like the DV Program hold great promise, but governments and citizens in the Global North must awaken to and take responsibility for their immigration policies. With due deliberation, the United States must game out all the potential consequences of a program that has been largely characterized as a game itself.

Methodological Appendix

Table A.1 How Diversity Immigrants Fare in the U.S. Labor Market: Mixed-Effects Linear Models Predicting Ln Income in the United States

	Pooled Sample	Europe, Canada, Australia, and New Zealand	Latin America and the Caribbean	Sub-Saharan Africa	Asia, the Middle East, and North Africa
Class of admission * Time (Reference: Time 1 class of admission)					
Diversity Migrant * Time	2.381***	2.946***	1.784†	2.618***	1.170
	(0.406)	(0.647)	(0.567)	(0.612)	(0.546)
Class of admission (Reference: Family-sponsored)					
Employer-sponsored	1.721***	1.395*	1.359*	2.818**	1.969***
	(0.136)	(0.200)	(0.203)	(1.071)	(0.269)
Refugee	1.029	0.869	0.868	0.937	1.123
	(0.102)	(0.137)	(0.189)	(0.214)	(0.258)
Diversity migrant	0.362***	0.366***	0.887	0.340**	0.619†
	(0.053)	(0.097)	(0.425)	(0.123)	(0.173)
Age	1.095***	1.206**	1.048	1.141*	1.043
	(0.029)	(0.072)	(0.063)	(0.067)	(0.037)
Age squared	0.999***	0.998**	0.999	0.999†	0.999*
	(0.000)	(0.001)	(0.001)	(0.001)	(0.000)
Years of education abroad	1.056***	1.054**	1.037**	0.989	1.067**
	(0.011)	(0.020)	(0.015)	(0.027)	(0.022)
Years of U.S. education	1.046**	1.066*	1.017	1.178***	0.998
	(0.015)	(0.034)	(0.023)	(0.040)	(0.030)
Speaks English well or very well	1.240*	1.538	1.159	1.019	1.175
	(0.116)	(0.465)	(0.200)	(0.227)	(0.172)
Switched jobs after time 1	1.062	1.107	1.045	1.043	1.050
	(0.151)	(0.296)	(0.276)	(0.477)	(0.220)
Female	0.687***	0.544***	0.685***	0.994	0.706***
	(0.043)	(0.065)	(0.074)	(0.199)	(0.068)

	(1)	(2)	(3)	(4)	(5)
Made at least one prior trip without a visa	1.016 (0.112)	0.967 (0.187)	1.006 (0.188)	1.076 (0.287)	1.092 (0.256)
Self-employed	1.247 (0.319)	0.756 (0.257)	1.071 (0.213)	1.125 (0.397)	2.661 (2.243)
Continued education after time 1	0.998 (0.106)	0.878 (0.158)	1.067 (0.240)	0.865 (0.167)	1.128 (0.192)
Region (Reference: Europe, Canada, Australia, and New Zealand)					
Latin America and the Caribbean	0.603*** (0.060)	—	—	—	—
Africa	0.737** (0.077)	—	—	—	—
Asia and the Middle East	0.679*** (0.051)	—	—	—	—
Years in the United States	1.043*** (0.008)	1.028† (0.017)	1.027* (0.013)	1.013 (0.017)	1.083*** (0.018)
Time	1.401*** (0.083)	1.331** (0.135)	1.311* (0.145)	1.526** (0.227)	1.510*** (0.162)
Constant	1,771.652*** (950.217)	241.557*** (280.898)	4,997.316*** (5,710.724)	1,007.226*** (1,219.813)	2,158.761*** (1,631.269)
Random effects parameters					
$\sigma(\alpha)$	0.475*** (0.024)	0.482*** (0.060)	0.455*** (0.042)	0.405*** (0.066)	0.423*** (0.040)
$\sigma(\varepsilon)$	0.526*** (0.029)	0.417*** (0.047)	0.482*** (0.055)	0.467*** (0.065)	0.597*** (0.044)
Observations	946	240	240	122	344
Intraclass Correlation Coefficient	0.573	0.412	0.537	0.584	0.735

Source: Author's analysis of New Immigrant Survey data, 2003–2009.

Note: Standard errors are in parentheses. The response variable was *income*, measured in U.S. dollars. Before estimating the results reported here, I opted to transform *income* by taking its natural logarithm. Transforming the response variable in this way allows us to interpret exponentiated regression coefficients in terms of percentage changes in income.

***p < 0.001; **p < 0.01; *p < 0.05; †*p* < 0.10 (two-tailed tests)

Table A.2 Post-Hoc Differential Analysis by Class of Admission

	Pooled Sample	Europe, Canada, Australia, and New Zealand	Latin America and the Caribbean	Sub-Saharan Africa	Asia, the Middle East, and North Africa
Class of admission (Reference: Employer-sponsored)					
Family-sponsored	0.776†	0.711†	0.806	0.489	0.650
Diversity migrant	0.307***	0.263***	0.661	0.165***	0.357**
Refugee	0.792	0.673*	0.784	0.498	0.671
Class of admission (Reference: Refugee)					
Family-sponsored	0.980	1.056	1.027	0.981	0.969
Diversity migrant	0.388***	0.390***	0.843	0.331***	0.532
Employer-sponsored	1.263	1.486*	1.275	2.006	1.491
Class of admission (Reference: Diversity migrant)					
Family-sponsored	2.528***	2.708***	1.218	2.960**	1.821
Employer-sponsored	3.258***	3.809***	1.512	6.053***	2.802**
Refugee	2.579***	2.563***	1.186	3.017***	1.879

Source: Author's analysis of New Immigrant Survey data, 2003–2009.
Note: Standard errors are omitted.
***p < 0.001; **p < 0.01; *p < 0.05; †*p* < 0.10 (two-tailed tests)

Table A.3 Selected Impactful Experiences of Study Respondents

Events	Number of Respondents (Percentage)
In possession of insufficient information during diversity visa application process	57 (77.0)
Failure of social support network post-migration (kicked out earlier than expected or had been told; moved in with another relative or friend; turned to church and church members for help; abandoned or postponed acquisition of more education or occupation credentials because of need to cover housing costs earlier than planned)	29 (39.2)
Interrupted tertiary education	
Won a diversity visa while in college in country of origin	23 (31.1)
Remained in college after winning a diversity visa and graduated with a bachelor's degree	2 (2.7)
Abandoned tertiary education to migrate to United States	21 (28.4)
Gained admission in a university but did not enroll	3 (4.1)
Enrolled in a university but did not finish	18 (24.3)
Of the twenty-one respondents who abandoned their tertiary education to migrate to the United States:	
Those who obtained a bachelor's degree in the United States post-migration	7 (33.3)
Those who failed to obtain a bachelor's degree	14 (66.7)
Of the fourteen respondents who did not obtain a bachelor's degree post-migration:	
Those who had some schooling—course credits or an associate's degree from a community college—in the United States	13 (93.0)
Marital and family instability (directly linked to moment of winning the diversity visa)	24 (32.4)
Unexpected divorce (used for papers and asked for a divorce upon arrival in the United States; evidence of adultery when DNA test proved the child in the marriage was not the biological offspring of both parents)	4 (5.4)
Planned divorce (dissolution of temporary marital alliances)	7 (9.5)
Creation of transnational families (family separation)	13 (17.6)
Feelings of dislocation or emotional trauma	12 (16.2)

Source: Author's compilation.
Note: N = 74

Notes

INTRODUCTION: LUCKY WINNERS

1. Nationals of countries that received more than fifty thousand immigrant visas in any preceding five-year period become ineligible because their citizens are no longer considered underrepresented in the United States.
2. There is a small body of literature on African diversity immigrants in the United States. Kremer (2011) is one of three studies I discovered that examine how diversity immigrants fare in the U.S. labor market. Comparing the employment outcomes of diversity immigrants to outcomes for all other legal immigrants—those who came via family unification, refugee, or employment— Kremer finds that diversity immigrants are slightly less likely than other legal immigrants to be employed. Kremer (2011, 2014) shows that educational attainment has an insignificant effect on employment status, while experience in the United States is the most important positive predictor of employment. The third study, by Ilana Restone Akresh (2006), concludes that, while all U.S. immigrants experience an initial period of downward occupational mobility, diversity immigrants are more unlikely to have seen an improvement in occupational status between their first U.S. job and their current job. Because all three studies use data from the first wave of the New Immigrant Survey (NIS), which conducted interviews with lawful permanent residents (LPRs) six to eighteen months after they were granted their green cards, it was impossible to draw definitive conclusions about diversity immigrants' long-term labor market prospects. However, Akresh's study was a red flag that diversity immigrants' socioeconomic attainment is not as predicted by usual models of immigrant economic assimilation. This study and another by Akresh treat diversity immigrants as a homogenous category, thus failing to incorporate their actual diversity into the analysis (Akresh 2006, 2008). These studies also do not speak to any effects of winning the lottery on diversity visa immigrants. I build on Akresh's studies using restricted longitudinal data from the NIS (see chapter 2). My results show that diversity immigrants were

significantly disadvantaged in the U.S. labor market in terms of earnings in the early years. The few micro-level studies on African diversity immigrants focus only on their experiences in the United States (Ette 2012; Hailu et al. 2012; Kremer 2014).
3. Kessler 2018. See chapter 1 for ex-president Trump's full comments on the DV to Jeanine Pirro.
4. Hereafter, I refer to "diversity visa immigrants" as "diversity immigrants."
5. American Community Survey 2022.
6. Ibid.
7. Lorenzi and Batalova 2019. Between 1980 and 2018, the African population grew to 265,000 in 1990, to 671,000 in 2000, and to 1.33 million in 2010.
8. Lobo 2006; Logan and Thomas 2012.
9. Roger Waldinger makes this critique in the introduction to *A Century of Transnationalism* (Green and Waldinger 2016).
10. See Chavez 2013; Hagan 2008; Hernández-León 2008; Menjívar 2006; Menjívar and Abrego 2012.
11. Menjívar and Abrego 2012, 1383.
12. Ibid., 1381. See the work on undocumented Chinese immigrants by Hsin and Aptekar 2022.
13. Jasso 2011; Massey 2007.
14. Massey and Bartley 2005; Menjívar 2006; Menjívar and Abrego 2012.
15. Gonzales 2016; Painter, Gabriel, and Myers 2001; Walter, Bourgois, and Loinaz 2004.
16. There are a few studies of refugees in the United States (see Gowayed 2022; Holtzman 2000; Ludwig 2013). However, U.S. refugee policy is shaped by U.S. foreign policy.
17. That same year, 6,218 Nigerians and 5,105 Ghanaians, representing the top two African countries, received notice of being selected in the lottery out of the 105,000 entries selected. In fiscal year 2014, the last year in which Nigerian citizens were eligible to register for the diversity program, 2.4 million Nigerians, including their derivatives (spouses and unmarried children under the age of twenty-one), submitted applications. For fiscal year 2020, 1.9 million Ghanaians applied for the program, along with 183,000 derivatives, bringing the total to 2.1 million Ghanaians, which is 6.7 percent of Ghana's population. This made Ghana the second-ranked applicant-sending country, just behind Uzbekistan at 2.5 million.
18. Ketefe 2013; Logan and Thomas 2012; Rotimi 2005. However, there is evidence of a "brain gain" in countries of origin as well, in that the improved living standards of emigrants overseas filter back home. This improvement typically takes several forms, including: increased human capital accumulation among immigrants and relatives in the home country; remittances; the transfer of information about study and work opportunities to individuals back home;

and return migration (see Clemens 2007; Gibson and McKenzie 2012; McKenzie, Gibson, and Stillman 2007).
19. Newton 2005.
20. Kremer 2011.
21. The cost (payment) comes later, as will be discussed in detail in chapter 4.
22. "Human capital" refers to the amount of education (training) and the skills that an individual possesses.
23. Nina Glick Schiller, Linda Basch, and Cristina Blanc-Szanton (1995, 6) define "transnationalism" as the "processes by which immigrants forge and sustain multi-stranded social relations that link together their societies of origin and settlement."
24. I follow Carly Goodman (2016, 2019) and Charles Piot (2010; Piot and Batema 2019), who, in their studies of diversity visa agents in Ghana and Togo, use the word "entrepreneur" to capture the business-for-profit activities of these MI actors who help people register for the U.S. visa lottery.
25. From cognitive and psychological research, we know that human memory is not always perfect, which can compromise the quality of retrospective data. However, cognitive, memory, and psychological research find that individuals have clear and detailed memories of "landmark events" (events with high emotional involvement; Berntsen and Rubin 2002; Talarico, Labar, and Rubin 2004), events associated with positive emotions, events experienced for the first time, events with high relevance to the individual, and events that the individual retells frequently. All such memories hold up particularly well, whether they occurred recently or a long time ago. Such events are encoded for storage in ways that facilitate easy access and retrieval. Also, because memory is organized in networks (Spada 2006), "more important events serve as anchor points that enable coherent structures and recall to memory of less significant events" (Muggenburg 2021, 309; Brückner 1990; van der Vaart and Glasner 2010), even events that happened a long time ago. Consequently, to capture accurate data from individuals, it helps to ask about events that are rare and long-lasting, that have had severe consequences, and that are of high emotional and cognitive significance to them (Muggenburg 2021; Oberauer, Mayr, and Kluwe 2006; Thompson et al. 1996). Winning a one-in-four-hundred chance in the U.S. visa lottery to become a diversity immigrant is a landmark event that leads to profound changes in a winner's life. Thus, diversity immigrants remember the events associated with the win very well.

Scholars can improve the quality of retrospective data and reduce problems of retrieval and bias by using various aided recall techniques (Muggenburg 2021). I used the aided recall technique of asking respondents for events in chronological order within a theme, which research finds "facilitates memory retrieval because related events in different partial biographies only need to be remembered once" (Muggenburg 2021, 308). For example, I asked my study participants to walk me through their entire U.S. employment history, starting with their first job upon arrival. My interview questions were focused on understanding the whole context of how winning the visa lottery and becoming a diversity immigrant had changed the course of their lives. Cognitive research shows that asking respondents about the whole context often leads to more detailed memories (Muggenburg 2021; Sudman, Finn, and Lannom 1984). From what we know about the various processes of memory, I believe I elicited high-quality data from study participants, reducing the problems of retrieval and the biases that are usual concerns for retrospective data.

I decided to interview Ghanaian diversity immigrants who had been in the United States for at least three years because I wanted them to have spent some time in the United States. This decision was informed by research finding that immigrants need approximately three years to become acclimated to U.S. life. In my analysis of the pilot NIS, I found it took legal immigrants three years to adjust and begin to recover from downward occupational mobility. Akresh's (2006, 2008) results showed a similar recovery time (see Imoagene 2006). None of the Nigerian diversity immigrants were recent arrivals because Nigeria became ineligible for the diversity visa in 2013.

26. Kremer 2011.
27. Goodman 2016, 2019.

CHAPTER 1: THE DIVERSITY IMMIGRANT VISA PROGRAM AND STRUCTURED LUCK

1. In addition to being grouped according to legal status, immigrants can be categorized as belonging to three distinct migrant streams: namely, traditional labor immigrants, human capital immigrants, and undocumented immigrants. Traditional labor immigrants have low levels of education and are limited to poorly paying manual jobs at or near the bottom of the U.S. labor market. They tend to work in agricultural fields and on poultry farms, construction sites, and simple manufacturing assembly floors. Immigrants from Mexico and Latin America, the largest group of contemporary immigrants, tend to be traditional labor immigrants. Their challenges in becoming integrated into America worsen if they are undocumented because that status makes them vulnerable to exploitation, limits their job options, and constrains their ability to negotiate higher wages and better job conditions.

2. To qualify with work experience an individual "must have two years of experience in the last five years, in an occupation which, by U.S. Department of Labor definitions, requires at least two years of training or experience that is designated as Job Zone 4 or 5, classified in a Specific Vocational Preparation (SVP) rating of 7.0 or higher." U.S. State Department, Bureau of Consular Affairs 2017. The U.S. Department of Labor provides information on job

duties, knowledge and skills, education and training, and other occupational characteristics on their website http://www.onetonline.org/. The O*Net online database groups work experience into five "job zones."
3. Alba and Nee 2003, 231.
4. Ibid., 229–36.
5. The label "immigrant" is used by the U.S. government to distinguish individuals who have been permitted to reside permanently in the United States and to apply for citizenship if they choose to do so (Kretsedemas 2012). The definition creates two distinct camps, the second of which includes millions of individuals within the United States who are categorized as non-immigrants (those with temporary legal status, such as those with visitor or student visas) and undocumented immigrants. It is very easy to move from the legal non-immigrant category to the undocumented category by overstaying a visa. And individuals from all groups on the other side of the immigrant divide constantly seek myriad ways to become immigrants because having legal status makes it easier to succeed in America and live outside of the shadows.
6. Alba and Nee 2003, 231–32.
7. The Hart-Celler Act created the following preference system, which is still the law of the land today. Preference 1: immediate family members of adult U.S. citizens—spouses and minor children—with no numerical limitation. Other preference categories are subject to numerical limitation, and each nation is eligible for the same number of visas. Preference 2: Unmarried adult children of U.S. citizens. Preference 3: Spouses and unmarried adult children of lawful permanent residents. Preference 4: Married adult children of U.S. citizens. Preference 5: Brothers and sisters of U.S. citizens. Preference 6: individuals with professional skills and exceptional abilities that could benefit the United States (20 percent of all visas). Preference 7: Eastern Hemisphere refugees fleeing persecution or in fear of persecution (6 percent of visas). No more than twenty thousand immigrants per year could come via the preference system (excluding spouses and minor children) from a given nation.
8. Fitzgerald and Cook-Martin 2014.
9. Ibid.; Goodman 2016; Law 2002.
10. Goodman 2016.
11. Law 2002; Goodman 2016.
12. Goodman 2016.
13. Ibid., 41. Congressman Donnelly represented the eleventh district of Massachusetts, which consisted of lower Boston, Quincy, and the South Shore. It was the most Irish district in the country in the 1980s. In 1987 and 1988, the Donnelly visa program, known as the NP-5, made 5,000 nonpreference visas available each year. These visas were for citizens from countries that were "adversely affected by the 1965 Immigration Act." They were distributed on a first-come, first-served basis, and the application period opened and closed

in one week. Just over a million applications were sent in. The program was widely publicized in Irish communities throughout the United States. Over 250,000 Irish nationals applied for the Donnelly visas, and of the 10,000 visas granted, the Irish won 3,112 (Ibid., 47–53). Multiple applications per individual were submitted, as the application was not limited to one application per individual. IIRM leader Sean Benson, for instance, submitted more than 400 applications. He won one of the Donnelly visas. Congress extended the Donnelly visa program for 1989 and 1990 and increased the number of immigrant visas to 15,000 per year. A new application period was not allowed; thus, visa recipients were chosen from the initial pool of applications sent in 1987. Carly Goodman describes the visa program as "a gift for the IIRM" (ibid., 49–70, 77).

14. Ibid., 81–87.
15. The program was included in an immigration bill sponsored by Senators Kennedy and Simpson.
16. Fitzgerald and Cook-Martin 2014; Goodman 2016, 49–107, 108.
17. Oceania includes Australia, New Zealand, and surrounding islands such as the Christmas Islands, Fiji, Kiribati, Micronesia, the Marshall Islands, Papua New Guinea, Samoa, Tonga, Tuvalu, and Vanuatu.
18. Goodman 2016.
19. Fitzgerald and Cook-Martin 2014; Goodman 2016; Law 2002.
20. For fiscal year 2022, citizens of the following countries were not eligible to enter the DV Program because their country was no longer underrepresented in the United States: Bangladesh, Brazil, Canada, China (mainland-born), Colombia, Dominican Republic, El Salvador, Guatemala, Haiti, India, Jamaica, Mexico, Nigeria, Pakistan, Philippines, South Korea, United Kingdom (except Northern Ireland) and its dependent territories, and Vietnam. Several exemptions are available to citizens of these countries who can claim citizenship with another country whose citizens are eligible for the program. Ineligible countries total 18 out of 195, which means that citizens of 177 countries can apply for the program.
21. Wilson 2019; Goodman 2016.
22. Dawsey 2018.
23. Watkins and Phillip 2018. In November 2017, the Trump administration announced that it would end the TPS designation for Haitians by July 2019. This designation had allowed approximately sixty thousand Haitians to live in the United States after the 2010 earthquake in Haiti that killed 200,000 people (Tatum 2017).
24. Watkins and Phillip 2018.
25. Bierman 2018.
26. Ebba Kalondo, spokeswoman for African Union chairman Moussa Faki, quoted in Dwyer 2018.

27. A statement released on the Botswanan government Twitter account, reproduced in Dwyer 2018.
28. Kessler 2018.
29. Wilson 2019; U.S. State Department 2020.
30. With the fiscal year 2021 rule change requiring applicants to submit a number for a valid, unexpired international passport, the number of Ghanaian applicants plummeted to 298,000 applicants and 82,000 derivatives, bringing their total to 380,000 applications. I expect that more people will be prepared and not caught by surprise in future rounds of the program.
31. U.S. State Department 2020.
32. Kretsedemas 2012; Teke and Navarro 2016. Teke and Navarro used filled-in I-94 forms to estimate that 42.7 million individuals entered the United States in 2016, but this number is an undercount because certain visitors are not required to fill out an I-94 form. Canadians visiting the United States on a B1/B2 business or tourist visa and Mexicans entering with a border crossing card (BCC) or a B1/B2 visa who plan to remain in the border region are not required to provide I-94 data. In light of these exceptions, we know that the number of non-immigrants admitted to the United States is much higher than 42.7 million because Canadian and Mexican tourists and business travelers make up the majority of non-immigrant admissions to the United States.
33. Fiscal year 2017 is the most recent year for which the United States has a full set of statistics about who applied for the lottery, who was selected, and who was issued a diversity visa by country. According to that data, 2,715 Norwegians applied for the program, along with 1,622 derivatives (spouses, unmarried children, and children under age twenty-one), bringing the total of Norwegian applicants to 4,337. By contrast, 1,953,577 Ghanaians registered for the program, plus 245,444 derivatives, bringing the total to 2,199,021 Ghanaian applicants. Immigrants from less-wealthy European countries, such as Moldova, Belarus, Azerbaijan, and Uzbekistan, register for the U.S. lottery in higher numbers than do immigrants from European countries with which the United States has a long history. For example, in 2017, 876,875 Uzbekistanis registered for the program, along with 699,304 derivatives, bringing the total to 1,576,179. In comparison, even though Germany has a long history of migration to the United States, only 52,373 Germans registered for the program, along with 39,525 derivatives, for a total of 91,898.
34. From 2008 to 2017, the total number of diversity visas issued to Africans was 22,960 (49 percent) in fiscal year 2008, 24,648 (51.3 percent) in fiscal year 2009, 24,745 (48.2 percent) in fiscal year 2010, 24,015 (47 percent) in fiscal year 2011, 13,582 (39.4 percent) in fiscal year 2012, 23,607 (45 percent) in fiscal year 2013, 22,703 (43.4 percent) in fiscal year 2014, 19,686 (39.9 percent) in fiscal year 2015, 20,706 (44.3 percent) in fiscal year 2016 and 19,211 (38.4 percent) in fiscal year 2017. The total number of diversity visas issued

to Europeans in the same period was; 14,788 (31.7 percent) in fiscal year 2008, 14,241(29.6 percent) in fiscal year 2009, 16,083 (33.5 percent) in fiscal year 2010, 16,378 (31.9 percent) in fiscal year 2011, 13,093 (38 percent) in fiscal year 2012, 17,296 (32.9 percent) in fiscal year 2013, 18,904 (36.1 percent) in fiscal year 2014, 19,811 (40.1 percent) in fiscal year 2015, 15,207 (32.5 percent) in fiscal year 2016, and 20,516 (41 percent) in fiscal year 2017 (U.S. State Department 2017; see also Wilson 2019).

35. Arthur 2014.
36. Model 2008.
37. Ibid., 12–17; Hamilton 2019, 22.
38. Hamilton 2019, 23.
39. Model 2008, 26.
40. Ibid., 20–25.
41. Hamilton 2019.
42. Kretsedemas 2012, 39–44.
43. Ibid., 40.
44. Ibid.
45. Gelatt 2018.
46. I analyzed the two NIS waves (2003 and 2007–2008) using the restricted data sets to get country-level data.
47. American Community Survey 2022.
48. Wilson 2019 makes clear that more than 50 percent of recent diversity immigrants will have at least a bachelor's degree because the United States has upskilled the DC Program since 2003, the year from which the 50 percent number was obtained from the first NIS wave.
49. Imoagene 2017a.
50. There is one other migration lottery in the world: New Zealand's Pacific Access Category (PAC) migration lottery. This lottery gives citizens of the islands of Tonga an opportunity to migrate to New Zealand. But it has an employment requirement: immigrants are given a period of time in which to find a job in New Zealand before their resettlement in the country is approved (Gibson et al. 2018).
51. I thank Allison Pugh for the comments she gave me when I presented some of my findings from this project at the University of Virginia.
52. Kuhn et al. 2011. A study of jackpot lottery winners in the Netherlands found that the majority end up well. Lottery winners spend some money on durable goods, such as cars and home improvements, and convert the rest to other goods and savings.
53. A recent change in the application rules for fiscal year 2021 that requires applicants to provide a number for a valid, unexpired, international passport is likely to stem the spontaneity of these applications. But once applicants obtain international passports, this posture will return. The rule change further

structures the population of those who can apply for the program, a point elaborated on in this book.
54. Piot and Batema 2019.
55. In actuality, the window is much shorter than twelve to eighteen months for many diversity immigrants, as lottery selectees are advised to act promptly to apply for the visa so they do not run the risk of visas becoming unavailable because either their country cap or the fifty thousand annual diversity visa cap has been reached. Thus, a winner could receive their visa a few months into the fiscal year and, because their visa expires in six months, have to emigrate before the end of the fiscal year.
56. Sometimes people who intend to emigrate acquire skills and certifications that will help them obtain jobs in their destination country. Diversity immigrants do not have the time to acquire skills that entail lengthy training given the limited time they have from when they are notified that they have been selected in the lottery or that they have received their immigrant visa.
57. Alba and Nee 2003.
58. Chiswick 1978.
59. Ibid., 919.
60. Ibid., 920.
61. Borjas 1985.
62. Duleep and Regets 1997.
63. Alba and Nee 2003, 237. When compared to White U.S.-born natives, most U.S. immigrants have not achieved economic parity.
64. Alba and Nee 2003; Borjas 1985, 1990; Bratsberg and Ragan 2002; Chiswick 1978, 1982; Friedberg 1992, 2000; Scheoni 1997; Smith and Edmonston 1997.
65. While some studies show that the returns from U.S. education are higher than the returns from foreign education when it comes to immigrants' wages (see Borjas 1985, 1990; Bratsberg and Ragan 2002; Scheoni 1997; Smith and Edmonston 1997), these studies report different degrees of magnitude in the returns. Rachel Friedberg (1992) found that, among immigrants, the returns from foreign education were lower than the returns from U.S. education; however, the differences were "economically small." Chiswick's (1978) findings were different. Running separate regressions within his samples of the foreign- and native-born, he found that an additional year of schooling for the foreign-born raised earnings by 5.7 percent, compared with 7.2 percent for the native-born. However, after disaggregating total years of education by source of education (in other words, premigration education and postmigration education), he found that the returns from premigration education were 5.8 percent, while the returns from postmigration education were 5 percent. The small difference of about one percentage point was in the margin of statistical significance at the 0.1 level. He argued that if years of post-school training in the United States is held constant, instead of the number of years

since migration, the difference between the coefficients of pre- and post-immigration schooling is even smaller and not significant. James Stewart and Thomas Hyclak (1984) found no significant differences in the returns from U.S. education or foreign education on immigrant wages. On the other hand, Brent Bratsberg and James Ragan (2002) reported that the returns from U.S. education are significantly higher than the returns from foreign education. Given these contradictory and inconclusive findings, it has not been unequivocally determined that the economic outcomes of comparable immigrants with some U.S. education are significantly better than the economic outcomes of immigrants with only foreign education. Such a finding would be significant because we could then make definite statements about the utility of this incorporation strategy to facilitate socioeconomic success.

66. Borjas 1985, 1990; Chiswick 1978; Dodoo 1991, 1997; Scheoni 1997.
67. Borjas 1985, 1990; Bratsberg and Ragan 2002; Chiswick 1978; Smith and Edmonston 1997.
68. Akresh 2006, 2008.
69. Portes and Rumbaut 2014.
70. Akresh 2006, 2008; Alba and Nee 2003; Portes and Rumbaut 2014; Smith and Edmonston 1997.
71. Akresh 2006.
72. Ibid.
73. Akresh 2008.
74. Alba and Nee 2003.
75. Akresh 2008, 437.
76. Ibid.
77. By defining "underemployment" in this way, Jeanne Batalova and Michael Fix (2021, 7) "exclude workers with four-year college degrees who are employed in middle-skilled jobs for which they are also overqualified. If these arguably overqualified workers were included in this report's estimates, they would increase the number of underemployed, highly skilled immigrants from 2 million to 3.5 million."
78. Batalova and Fix 2021.
79. Ibid.
80. Race and ethnicity matter: college-educated Black and Latinos, regardless of where they were born or whether they are immigrants, are more likely to be underemployed than their White counterparts (regardless of their birth location or immigrant status). Black immigrants are 54 percent more likely to be underemployed compared to their White counterparts, while Latinos are 40 percent more likely to be underemployed than their White counterparts. English proficiency matters too: college-educated immigrants who speak English well are less likely to be underemployed than college-educated immigrants with poor English fluency. And legal status matters: college-educated,

undocumented immigrants are more likely to be underemployed than most immigrants with legal status. The United States allows undocumented immigrants to go to school through university without questions being asked, but undocumented immigrants receive a rude awakening when they graduate and find that they cannot get hired for well-paying jobs in the primary labor market without papers (Gonzales 2016). There are also legal-status restrictions on obtaining professional licenses or credentials. The source of an immigrant's education also has an impact, if not on wages then on employment status: immigrants who received their education abroad are more likely to be underemployed (24 percent) than those educated in the United States (17 percent). In all but three U.S. states, immigrants with at least a bachelor's degree had higher underemployment rates than their U.S.-born peers (Batalova and Fix 2021, 12).

81. The first cohort was first surveyed from June 2003 to June 2004 (NIS-2003-1, referred to as time 1) and subsequently followed up with from June 2007 to December 2009 (NIS-2003-2, referred to as time 2).
82. The statistical analysis shows that we cannot rule out, at the 95 percent confidence interval, the null hypothesis that there is no statistical difference between the wages of immigrants from all four categories of admission at time 2.
83. Research tells us that the diversity immigrants in this study, as Black Nigerians and Ghanaians, would feel the effects of race and racial discrimination even as educated immigrants in the U.S. labor market. Participants mentioned several ways in which they had been impacted by race in the U.S. labor market that were consistent with what research on immigrants' socioeconomic attainment finds. They felt that their educational qualifications and work experience were less valued and less transferable in the U.S. labor market, even though they were from countries linguistically similar to the United States, as English is the official language of all three countries. They experienced an erasure of their linguistic capital, as their foreign accents were counted against them even when they spoke English well or even fluently. Race remained a factor explaining the differential outcomes of Black people, both immigrant and U.S.-born, compared to their White U.S.-born counterparts with similar educational levels, even when we control for key individual characteristics such as age, educational level, U.S. work experience, and English fluency. Many Black immigrants hit a glass ceiling (also called an "ebony ceiling") that prevented them from reaching the acme of their careers.
84. Portes and Rumbaut 2014.
85. Of course, it is somewhat ironic to posit the support that refugees obtain as significant (at least when compared to diversity immigrants), since many experts would argue that refugees in the United States receive inadequate support. And while it can be argued that the government's support fails to fully cover refugees' living costs and does not last long enough, it must be

acknowledged that refugees and asylees are the only immigrants allowed to receive federal welfare benefits.

Heba Gowayed, in her book *Refuge* (2022), compares the support given to refugees in the United States and Canada and finds that the U.S. refugee support is the most threadbare. In the United States, refugees have to pay the government for the cost of their flights to America and receive federal resettlement assistance for only ninety days, at which time they become eligible for Temporary Assistance for Needy Families (TANF), which grants $701 per month to a family of four. This assistance is in contrast to Canada, which provides refugees with a significant start-up sum and a stipend that covers their expenses in full for their first year. Subsequently, refugees have access to welfare benefits. Refugees can attend free English classes and classes for skill development, and those enrolled in English classes who have children receive free childcare from the Canadian government. Refugees receive the most generous financial support in Germany, which fully covers their needs and expenses (Gowayed 2022, 3–6).

86. It should be noted that some diversity immigrants from especially underrepresented nations are pioneers who are establishing beachheads in the United States for their coethnics. Their experiences are similar to what earlier pioneer immigrants faced. Also, their communities grow once the family members and other relatives they sponsor join them. But this takes years, often six years or more. For Nigerian and Ghanaian immigrants, wait times for sponsored relatives who are not close family members are over ten years. Until that time of family reunification, these immigrants are alone. It is not easy to be separated from a spouse for five to six years. These are the realities of many immigrants' lives that sometimes are overlooked.

87. A fourth finding (see table 1.1) suggests that the value added to postmigration human capital investment dissipates over time. This finding provides some support for the immigrant human capital investment (IHCI) model, which shows that the returns from U.S. schooling are higher than the returns from foreign education. But it also shows that human capital attained after gaining lawful permanent residency status does not make a statistically significant difference in earnings, suggesting that being a legal immigrant combines with the passage of time to give all legal immigrants a similar boost in the labor market.

CHAPTER 2: A CONTEXT OF DESPERATION: "WHY DOES EVERYONE WANT TO GO ABROAD?"

1. Adebayo 2021.
2. Pew Research Center 2017, 2018b.
3. Pew Research Center 2018b.

4. Pew Research Center 2017.
5. Of the three African countries included in the 2018 Pew survey, Nigeria had the highest percentage of citizens who planned to leave. Twenty-four percent of Tunisians said that they planned to move to another country in the next five years, while 19 percent of Kenyans answered in the affirmative to the same question.
6. Pew Center of Research 2018a, Q55, Q56a, Q56b, Q56c.
7. Pew Center of Research 2018a, Q57.
8. Afrobarometer 2017.
9. Pew Center of Research 2018a, Q58a, Q58b, Q58c, and Q58d.
10. Ibid., Q4, Q34a, Q34c, and Q34e.
11. Tamir 2019.
12. Piot 2010.
13. Kaba 2009; Lobo 2006; Konadu-Agyemang and Takyi 2006.
14. Logan and Thomas 2012.
15. According to the 2006 Nigerian census, Nigeria's total population was 142 million in that year. The 2021 population estimate is from the *CIA World Factbook* (https://www.cia.gov/the-world-factbook/).
16. *CIA World Factbook*, 2023 estimates.
17. Ethnologue 2022.
18. As defined in the 2006 Nigerian census, a literate person is someone who can read and write with understanding a short and simple statement about his or her daily life in any language (local or foreign). Nigeria counts its literate population from those over the age of six. According to the 2006 census, 113 million individuals were over the age of six, out of total population of 142 million. Of those 113 million people, 75.75 million were literate.
19. Core Welfare Indicators Questionnaire Survey 2006.
20. Ayittey 2005. These GDP figures are given in purchasing power parity figures to make it easier for country comparisons.
21. World Bank 2022a, 2022b.
22. As Peter Schraeder (2020, 69) describes it: "The most notable challenge associated with the creation of these artificial colonial states was the potential clash between highly diverse political cultures. In the case of Nigeria, the hierarchical political culture of the Hausa/Fulani clashed with the egalitarian political culture of the Igbo. The Hausa/Fulani political culture demanded deference of its subjects to the proclamation of the Emir (king), whereas the Igbo political culture considered it the citizen's duty to publicly challenge and criticize the errors of his or her leaders. A Hausa/Fulani subject was expected to bow facedown, his or her nose touching the ground, as a sign of deference. An Igbo would never bow. The political ramifications of these differences, especially when one multiplies them by the over 250 ethnic groups that comprise Nigeria were enormous, even under the best of circumstances."

23. Davidson 1992; Nugent 2012.
24. Arnold 2005; Nugent 2012.
25. Davidson 1992.
26. Ayittey 2005.
27. Ibid.; Nugent 2012.
28. Akintayo 2022.
29. Falola and Heaton 2008b, 220.
30. Ayittey 2005.
31. Elumoye and Addeh 2022. These figures were provided by Bismarck Rewane, a member of the current Nigerian president Muhammadu Buhari's Economic Advisory Council.
32. Elumoye and Addeh 2022.
33. Falola and Heaton 2008a, 111.
34. World Bank 2022a, 2022b.
35. Nigerian National Bureau of Statistics 2020.
36. Olurounbi 2021.
37. Ayomikun 2021.
38. World Bank 2022c.
39. Imoagene 1990; Lentz and Nugent 2016; Oyebamji and Adekoye 2019.
40. Falola and Heaton 2008a; Ketefe 2013; Lobo 2006; Logan and Thomas 2012; Rotimi 2005.
41. National Foreign Assessment Center 2022.
42. American Community Survey 2021.
43. American Community Survey 2021.
44. Chua and Rubenfeld 2014.
45. American Community Survey 2021.
46. Migration Policy Institute 2015b, RAD Diaspora Profile.
47. In the Bronx, Nigerians are found in low- to middle-income neighborhoods that are 40 to 50 percent Black or more. In Brooklyn, the largest concentration of Nigerians is in East New York, which is low-income and, as of 2010, was approximately 51 percent non-Hispanic Black, 37 percent Hispanic, 6.4 percent Asian, and 1.9 percent non-Hispanic White. In the 2013 *Newest New Yorkers* report, "census tracts with a median household income in twenty-fifth percentile or lower were labeled lower income, while those in the seventy-fifth percentile or higher were categorized as upper income. For New York City, this translated into a median household income under $35,800 for lower income neighborhoods, and above $69,500 for upper income neighborhoods" (NYC Planning 2013, 151).
48. Ethnologue 2022.
49. Ayittey 2005; Aryeetey and Kanbur 2017.
50. Available data from the Bank of Ghana suggests that gold, cocoa, and oil now account for over 80 percent of total exports. If steps are not taken to diversify

the economy, Ghana will become more vulnerable to price volatility in the commodities market and increasingly unable to continue to invest in health care, education, job training, and infrastructure.
51. Asare 2022.
52. Ibid.
53. American Community Survey 2021.
54. Migration Policy Institute 2015a.

CHAPTER 3: "COME, LET US PLAY THE LOTTERY!"

1. Guare 1990.
2. U.S. State Department 2020.
3. Rotimi was thirty-nine years old when I interviewed him. The ages of study participants reported here are their ages at the time I interviewed them—all in the United States, except in one case.
4. Borjas 1989.
5. Massey 1999.
6. Thomas 2011.
7. Olurounbi 2021.
8. O'Neill 2023; World Bank 2020.
9. A-levels are advanced-level school-leaving examinations taken by students between the ages of sixteen and nineteen (but usually eighteen). They are required for entering university.
10. I interviewed Adaobi in November 2016, when the currency exchange rate was N320 to 1 USD.
11. Kretsedemas 2012.
12. "An overstayer is a nonimmigrant who was lawfully admitted to the United States for an authorized period but stayed in the United States beyond his or her authorized admission period. Nonimmigrants admitted for 'duration of status,' who fail to maintain their status, can also be considered overstays. 'Duration of status' is a term used for foreign nationals who are admitted for the duration of a specific program or activity, which may be variable, instead of for a set timeframe. The authorized admission period ends when the foreign national has accomplished the purpose for which they were admitted, or is no longer engaged in authorized activities." U.S. Department of Homeland Security 2020, 7–8.
13. In 2019, the total overstay rate for non-immigrant Ghanaians admitted to the United States for business or pleasure was 5.97 percent, and it was 9.88 percent for Nigerians. For Ghanaians with foreign student or exchange visitor visas (F, M, and J), the total overstay rate was 12.74 percent; for Nigerians, it was 13.43 percent. The total overstay rate for all students and exchange visitors was 3.09 percent. In 2019, the average overstay rate for all persons who entered

the United States with non-immigrant visas was 1.21 percent. The U.S. government tells countries whose citizens have high rates of overstaying to educate their citizens about the severe consequences of not following U.S. immigration rules. Nigeria was one of the countries included in the Trump administration's immigration ban, which went into effect in 2016 but was rescinded by the Biden administration in 2021.
14. U.S. State Department 2021.
15. Even if they came to the United States with few to no social ties, the U.S. family preference system makes it possible for diversity immigrants to bring their family members over after a while. But until then, many experience loneliness, and married diversity immigrants who did not enter the United States with their spouse are separated for years.
16. Kamran, Liang, and Trines 2019.
17. Ibid.
18. Dennis Martine, interview with President Muhammadu Buhari, March 5, 2016, Al Jazeera, quoted in Kanu and Okonkwo 2019.
19. Koikkalainen and Kyle 2016, 767.
20. This suggests that a participant's stage in the life cycle does play a role in the decision-making process.
21. Pew Research Center 2017, Q14a.

CHAPTER 4: DIVERSITY VISA ENTREPRENEURS IN GHANA AND UNINTENDED CONSEQUENCES

1. Large-scale MI actors include huge, often transnational, companies that function globally and contract with nation-state governments to offer their immigration management services.
2. Hernández-León 2012, 155.
3. Ibid. In recent years, the migration industry has broadened to encompass "non-state actors who provide services that facilitate, constrain, or assist international migration" (rescue industry), such as nongovernmental organizations (NGOs) and humanitarian organizations that are involved in anti-trafficking efforts (Gammeltoft-Hansen and Nyberg Sorensen 2012, 6).
4. In one well-known example, the labor recruitment agencies in the Philippines and other Asian countries help recruit nurses. As scholarship shows, they help individuals get jobs and necessary documentation in foreign countries. In the Philippines, labor recruitment agencies working in conjunction with official government efforts have placed millions of Filipino workers in semiskilled and highly skilled occupations all over the world, from the United States (which is home to a large population of Filipino nurses) to the Middle East. See Choy 2003; De Parle 2019; Parrenas Salazar 2021.

5. There is a cottage industry of migration facilitators who help people enter the United States. Increased militarization and enforcement of the U.S.-Mexico border has increased the number of MI actors smuggling people across the southern border. In his study of contemporary Mexican migration to the United States, Rubén Hernández-León finds that MI actors (from coyotes, who transport undocumented immigrants for a fee across the U.S.-Mexico border, to currency exchange and shipping agents) help maintain high levels of Mexican migration to the United States even when the precipitating events that began the migration exodus have ended. In other countries, elite families seeking better opportunities for their children via U.S. educational degrees can take advantage of a U.S. immigration law that allows private secondary schools, but not public secondary schools, to issue student (F) visas to international students for a full four-year program and to grant them high school diplomas. That rule has created the conditions on the ground for the emergence of an educational consultant industry, one that helps foreign students gain admission into elite prep schools and tertiary institutions (see Tu 2020). This is yet another example of how U.S. immigration laws and policies, along with conditions in countries of origin, create an environment conducive to the proliferation of varied types of MI actors.
6. Andersson 2014; Carling 2007; Schapendonk 2018; Schapendonk and Steel 2014.
7. CNN 2017.
8. Amin and Thrift 2008.
9. Cranston 2018.
10. Secondary schools are the equivalent of high schools in the United States.
11. These are pseudonyms for both the individuals and their businesses.
12. Four-year institutions in Ghana and Nigeria that grant bachelor's degrees are known as universities, while they are called colleges in the United States. They are also called universities in England, which is why I used the term when discussing Nat. It must be noted that, as former British colonies, both Nigeria and Ghana are still influenced in some ways by that colonial history.
13. With the new requirement added in 2020 that registrants provide the number of a valid, unexpired international passport, the opportunity to apply on impulse now will be available only to those who already have a passport (and who have it on hand). But I expect that as more people obtain international passports in order to be ready to register for the program in the future, the number of applicants who impulsively register will increase again. I predict that this administrative change in the diversity visa application requirements will accomplish two things. First, it will create more MI actors who, for a fee, will act as middlemen between people and the passport-issuing offices to "help" people acquire international passports. Second, it will spur more migration overseas because, when more people have international

passports, even if they cannot get to the United States, they may travel to other countries in hopes of eventually ending up in the United States, Canada, or other economically advantaged countries in Europe. In other words, they may take a more circuitous route to the United States than that of the diversity visa. This could be another unintended consequence of changing U.S. immigration policy.

14. The lottery results are published in May of the year after registration. The longest the process can take is thus twenty-three months, if the lottery winner obtained their visa, which is valid for six months, on the last day of the fiscal year. But winners usually have less time than that because they are urged to act promptly to apply for the visa once the period for processing opens so as not to run the risk of visas for that year becoming unavailable.
15. "Internet World Stats: Africa," https://www.internetworldstats.com/africa.htm#ghr (accessed January 21, 2020); Statista, "Number of Internet Users in the United States from 2015 to 2023," https://www.statista.com/statistics/276445/number-of-internet-users-in-the-united-states/ (accessed January 21, 2020).
16. Ghana Statistical Service and National Communications Authority 2020.
17. Goodman 2019, 35–36.
18. U.S. Department of State, Bureau of Consular Affairs, "U.S. Visa: Photo Requirements," https://travel.state.gov/content/travel/en/us-visas/visa-information-resources/photos.html#DV (accessed January 17, 2020).
19. Bourdieu 1986, 243. Pierre Bourdieu sees cultural capital as existing in three forms: "in the embodied state, that is, in the form of long-lasting dispositions of the mind and body; in the objectified state, in the form of cultural goods such as pictures, books, dictionaries, and machines; and in the institutionalized state, a form of objectification such as through educational qualifications."
20. Swidler 1986, 284.
21. Ibid., 273.
22. Piot and Batema 2019.
23. Piot 2010.
24. Piot (2010; Piot and Batema 2019) found that a visa broker in Togo whose business was facilitating diversity visa marriages engaged in similar practices. These marriages are called "pop-up" marriages and are viewed suspiciously by U.S. consular officers. Piot details the contortions that both people in these fake marriages and U.S. embassy officials go through, either to prove that the marriages are real (lottery winners) or to prove that they are fake (embassy officials) (Piot and Batema 2019, 32–34).
25. Piot and Batema 2019.
26. Ibid., 31.
27. Piot 2020, 1–41.
28. Comaroff and Comaroff 2016. If anything, isn't "selling" a capitalist imperative and thus highly valued by the West?

29. Piot and Batema 2019, 86.
30. Ibid., 86–87.
31. Ibid., 87, 88.
32. See Piot and Batema 2019.
33. The "indifference threshold" is part of the threshold approach theorized by Martin Van der Velde and Ton van Naerssen (2011, 2015).

CHAPTER 5: DISRUPTED UNDERGRADUATES: A CREATED CATEGORY OF DIVERSITY IMMIGRANTS

1. Some immigrants who come into the United States with a college degree have similar employment experiences as Kofi, but they have more options to improve their social position than those who do not have a college degree.
2. Joubert 2020.
3. Markus and Nurius 1986, 954.
4. Ibid.
5. Koikkalainen and Kyle (2016, 767) define "cognitive migration" as "the phase of decision making in which the experimental, always-on, imagination actively, though not always consciously, negotiates one's future social worlds, and hence emotional states converging around a core destination. This mental time travel into a possible future in a different country constructs a narrative on how one's life is likely to proceed if one chooses to migrate, not in the abstract, but under specific conditions in specific destinations."
6. Here I use the word "university" when discussing these diversity immigrants in their home country context and the word "college" when discussing the U.S. context.
7. An associate's degree in nursing involves two years of study, at the end of which the student takes the NCLEX exam administered by the National Council of State Boards of Nursing (NCSBN). Those who pass the exam receive an ADN credential, which is not a bachelor's of science in nursing (BSN), which requires an additional year or two of study.
8. Cooper 2019.
9. Kalleberg 2011.
10. Seamster and Charron-Chenier 2017, 199–200. For example, White college graduates on average owe $28,000, while Black college graduates on average owe $53,000. There are several reasons for that disparity: Black students start off with fewer resources and less familial support than White students do and thus need more help, in the form of loans, to complete their degrees; and compared to White students, Black students are also overrepresented at for-profit colleges, which are more expensive than public universities, are associated with higher student-debt accumulation, and are more likely to use

private student loan companies. The racial disparities in student debt must be understood as a product of predatory lending practices that continue to produce racialized inequality for people of color in the United States. In the past, credit lines for Black and Hispanic people were scarce to nonexistent. Although access to credit has now been expanded to include minorities, the increased access has been accompanied by exploitative financial terms. Forms of credit from subprime mortgages to payday lenders to private student-debt financing offer unfavorable terms, including higher interest rates to people of color, which undermine the economic benefits and returns of such loans and widen the wealth gap between White people and minorities. Sociologists Louise Seamster and Charron-Chenier describe the seemingly good outcome of greater access to student loans for Black students as "predatory inclusion," by which they mean "a process whereby members of a marginalized group are provided with access to a good, service, or opportunity from which they have historically been excluded but under conditions that jeopardize the benefits of access. In the long term, however, predatory inclusion reproduces inequality and insecurity for some, while allowing already dominant social actors to derive significant profits." For these reasons, West African immigrants' difficulties in attaining degrees cannot be divorced from the larger structural forces that are creating a racial gap in student debt (particularly among the college-educated), reproducing the racial wealth gap between Whites and Blacks, and entangling new Black migrants in similar disparities.
11. Imoagene 2017b; Waldinger 2001.
12. Data from Houston Community College, "Nursing, Transition to Registered Nursing, AAS," https://catalog.hccs.edu/preview_program.php?catoid=14&poid=6788&returnto=1092.
13. Portes and Rumbaut 2014.
14. Model 2008; Waldinger 2001.
15. Alba and Nee 2003, 163.
16. Alba and Nee 2003; Foner 2001a, 2001b; Light 1972.
17. Alba and Nee 2003; Foner 2001a, 2001b; Model 2001.
18. Model 2008.
19. Showers 2022.
20. Halter 2010.
21. Showers 2022, 97.

CHAPTER 6: "WE ARE TALKING ABOUT AMERICAN CITIZENSHIP"

1. There are several reasons why African migrants are less willing to migrate to the United States as undocumented persons than Mexican and other Latin American migrants who choose to come illegally despite knowing full

well (and often even better than African immigrants) the challenges of being undocumented. First, migrating and living as an undocumented person in the United States is often less difficult for Hispanic and Latin American immigrants than it would be for an African immigrant because of the support that the former receive from long-established social networks of Mexican and Latin American immigrants in the United States. In his elaboration of cumulative causation theory, Douglas Massey (1999) posits that immigrants still migrate to the United States even if the precipitating event that began the migration flow has ended because having contacts and social networks in the United States lowers the cost of migrating. An immigrant's ethnic community can become a resource that facilitates settlement and incorporation: knowing people already in the United States helps new immigrants get jobs (through referrals at contacts' workplaces), access food and shelter for a time, obtain necessary documents, and learn the ways of the host country. African immigrants, arriving from countries thousands of miles away, might not have such robust networks to lean on. Additionally, the shared border between the United States and Mexico makes it possible for many Hispanic and Latin American immigrants to try crossing the border themselves or to pay fees to MI actors who can help them do so. Sub-Saharan African immigrants starting their journey from the African continent do not have the infrastructure in place to reduce the cost—financial, social, and emotional—of making such a decision. In the future, as economic hardships mount in several sub-Saharan African countries, it is possible that people who might have refused to come in as undocumented immigrants before will decide to risk it. Finally, the fact that Hispanic and Latin American immigrants have a better chance at repeated attempts to enter the country if they are stopped or caught makes them more willing to risk ejection, whereas African migrants would have a lot to overcome in order to make return trips.
2. Bourdieu 1986; Coleman 1988.
3. Bourdieu 1986.
4. Portes and Rumbaut 2014.
5. Arthur 2014.
6. Ibid.
7. Ibid.
8. Ibid.
9. To satisfy the physical presence requirement, a green card holder must be resident in the United States for at least thirty-six months within a five-year period before applying to become a U.S. citizen.
10. The United States allows both spouses and engaged persons to come via the fiancée visa.
11. Arthur 2014; Imoagene 2017a.
12. Imoagene 2017a.

CHAPTER 7: CONCLUSION: MAKING SENSE OF THE LUCKY WIN

1. Sauder 2020.
2. The probability given here is based on fifteen million entries. In years when more than twenty million entries are received, which has happened often, an individual's chances are, of course, lower.
3. See my discussion of possible selves in chapter 6.
4. There are cases of migrant workers being charged exorbitant fees to obtain employment-based green cards via the EB-5 program, which allows U.S. poultry processing plants to recruit foreign unskilled workers to fill jobs they report cannot be filled by workers already in the United States (see Grabell 2017).
5. My first book, *Beyond Expectations*, examined the nature of incorporation among the adult children (the second generation) of Nigerian immigrants in the United States and Britain. It described the highly selective nature of Nigerian populations in both countries and discussed how the Nigerian second generation is incorporating into the Black middle class. It identified an important social norm that promotes second-generation Nigerians' high educational attainment and upward mobility—the idea that it is un-Nigerian not to go to college. It explored intraracial ethnic relations between second-generation Nigerians and African Americans, discussing the tensions between the groups, the emergence of a middle-class Black coalition, and the need to build bridges that improve relations among the different Black groups in the United States.
6. Menjívar and Abrego 2012.
7. Doyle 2013.
8. Fahrenthold and Partlow 2019. Undocumented immigrants worked for Trump in several hotels and golf courses in New York, New Jersey, Virginia, and Florida as housekeepers, waiters, groundskeepers, and builders.
9. Zolberg 2006.
10. U.S. Census Bureau 2018.
11. Frey 2021.
12. Chishti, Gelatt, and Meissner 2021.
13. National Academies of Sciences, Engineering, and Medicine 2017, 5–7. Research shows that immigration reduces the number of hours worked by native-born teens, but not their employment rate.
14. The argument for the wage-boosting impact of skilled immigrants is that they complement native-born workers and increase productivity through their innovations. However, there is some evidence that highly skilled immigrants in "narrowly defined fields" can reduce the wages and productivity of U.S.

native-born workers in these fields (National Academies of Sciences, Engineering, and Medicine 2017, 6).
15. Ibid., 12.
16. Ibid.
17. Ibid.
18. Egbejule 2020.
19. Kazeem 2018.
20. Egbejule 2020.
21. *Daily Trust* 2021.
22. See Massey, Durand, and Malone 2003.
23. Kushnick 1993, 17.
24. Smith 2001.
25. The Biden administration wants to expand the presidential parole process used for Venezuelans to include citizens from Haiti, Nicaragua, and Cuba; each month allow thirty thousand citizens from these four countries who pass vetting and background checks and have a willing U.S. sponsor to apply for a two-year U.S. work authorization; and triple to twenty thousand the number of refugees admitted per year from the Caribbean and Latin America (White House Briefing Room 2023).
26. National Academies of Sciences, Engineering, and Medicine 2017.
27. Wilson (2019) argues that the 50 percent statistic obtained from the first wave of the New Immigrant Survey, which surveyed legal immigrants who received their green cards in 2003, would be much higher in subsequent years because, as discussed in the introduction and chapter 1, the United States has upskilled the DV Program.
28. Clemens 2007; Gibson and McKenzie 2012; McKenzie, Gibson, and Stillman 2007.
29. One way to minimize brain drain and increase avenues for green card migration to the United States and skilled migration to other economically advantaged countries would be for these net-emigration African countries to develop migration governance structures to train and prepare their sizable youth populations to get skilled jobs overseas. These countries should emulate the Philippines' migration governance model, which has made the Philippines one of the largest exporters of labor migrants in the world. Becoming a migrant labor–exporting country requires investing substantially in the education sector; building up education infrastructures, including numerous tertiary institutions with sufficient training facilities; hiring and retaining skilled faculty and administrative staff to run these institutions; and creating and staffing government agencies to oversee the process.

Once the educational infrastructure is established for tertiary and other skills credentialing institutions, West African governments can enter into bilateral labor agreements (BLAs) with other countries to place their citizens (who have been trained in these domestic educational institutions) in jobs in foreign countries. This aspect of their migration governance model would be similar to what is done in the Philippines. According to a World Bank report (Adhikari, Chaudhary, and Ekeator 2021), while Nigeria and the Philippines both signed their first BLA in 1960, the Philippines currently has over thirty BLAs to place Filipinos in jobs in foreign countries, while Nigeria still has only one. But citizens can be placed in jobs overseas even without BLAs. Private actors can handle the tasks of training, preparing, and placing people in overseas jobs, and in conjunction with educational institutions they can predict what new occupations will have openings overseas and react nimbly to address such expected labor demands (see Ortiga 2018a, 2018b).

To train their citizenry in the skills needed for the jobs available in foreign countries, these governments must provide the right business climate, financial support and tax incentives, and national guidance to encourage private-sector actors to establish tertiary educational institutions in their country. If these governments go a step further by establishing policies and committing funds to make these educational institutions affordable for their citizens, they can train their burgeoning youth populations and ensure that these educational institutions have the intended impact.

Supporting both foreign and domestic private institutions in setting up training academies in fields such as nursing and hospitality (the top areas in established labor-exporting countries such as the Philippines), plus newly emerging fields such as information technology, data science and security, and food production, would strengthen the educational systems in these countries and attract both domestic and international students (particularly from the African continent). It would prevent a worsening of "brain drain" by establishing a pipeline that, while training nationals for jobs overseas, would also train a sufficient number to take up jobs in the domestic labor market to support essential sectors, including health care and food production.

Developing a migration governance model founded on training African youths to fill needed jobs both domestically and globally would benefit all stakeholders by providing gainful employment for citizens; reducing the channels of irregular migration and trafficking of their citizens, which would help protect them; increase the amount of the remittances sent back to non-migrants because more of their citizens overseas would be employed in more skilled and thus better-paying jobs; and bolstering economic development in these African countries by developing education and other infrastructures, attracting domestic and foreign investment, and improving the knowledge base of their citizenries through rising educational levels, "brain gain" from hired faculty and returned migrants, and brain circulation (which is circular migration of skilled migrants from their country of origin to the host country).

These outcomes are in line with the stated objectives in the national migration policy documents of Nigeria and Ghana.

Unfortunately, I am pessimistic that such elaborate and beneficial plans would be enacted. In Africa, where many leaders have so far failed to improve their people's standards of living and provide adequate fixed and social amenities, would today's leaders be committed to this path? Based on their track records since independence from European colonial powers, it is doubtful. But if they were, African countries, with their rapidly growing populations, most of them under the age of thirty, have the enviable resource of being people-rich—compared to many economically advanced countries in Europe whose populations are declining. (Also, as noted in this conclusion, the U.S. White population declined for the very first time according to the 2020 census.) Whereas certain Asian countries, including Singapore, Hong Kong, and the Philippines, boast of being education hubs that train a global labor force, and the Philippines, one of the largest migrant labor exporters in the world, trades in its knowhow in preparing migrants, African countries can trade in a reservoir of young people that economically advanced countries in the world increasingly need to power their economies. And these are people ready to pursue better jobs to support their families and attain upward social mobility overseas. What they lack is more and better opportunities.

References

Adebayo, Sakiru. 2021. "The Nigerian Dream Is to Leave Nigeria." *Africa Is a Country*, March 1.

Adhikari, Samik, Sarang Chaudhary, and Nkechi Linda Ekeator. 2021. "Of Roads Less Travelled: Assessing the Potential of Economic Migration to Provide Overseas Jobs for Nigeria's Youth." Washington, D.C.: World Bank.

Afrobarometer. 2017. "Findings from the Afrobarometer Round 7 Survey in Ghana." https://www.afrobarometer.org/wp-content/uploads/2022/02/gha_r7_presentation_2811017.pdf.

Akintayo, OpeOluwani. 2022. "Oil Exports Account for 80% of Total Revenue." *Punch*, September 15. https://punchng.com/oil-exports-account-for-80-total-national-revenue/#:~:text=The%20oil%20and%20gas%20sector,oil%20theft%2C%20OPEOLUWANI%20AKINTAYO%20writes.

Akresh, Ilana Redstone. 2006. "Occupational Mobility among Legal Immigrants in the United States." *International Migration Review* 40(4): 854–84.

———. 2008. "Occupational Trajectories of Legal U.S. Immigrants: Downgrading and Recovery." *Population and Development Review* 34(3): 435–56.

Alba, Richard D., and Victor Nee. 2003. *Remaking the American Mainstream: Assimilation and Contemporary Immigration*. Cambridge, Mass.: Harvard University Press.

American Community Survey. 2021. "S0201: Selected Population Profile in the United States: Nigerians." https://data.census.gov/table?q=nigerians&tid=ACSSPP1Y2021.S0201 (accessed December 14, 2022).

———. 2022. "Table DP02: Selected Social Characteristics in the United States." https://data.census.gov/table?tid=ACSDP1Y2021.DP02 (accessed December 20, 2022).

Amin, Ash, and Nigel Thrift, eds. 2008. *The Blackwell Cultural Economy Reader*. London: Blackwell Publishing.

Andersson, Ruben. 2014. *Illegality Inc.: Clandestine Migration and the Business of Bordering Europe*. Berkeley: University of California Press.

Arnold, Guy. 2005. *Africa: A Modern History*. London: Atlantic Books.

Arthur, John A. 2014. *Class Formations and Inequality Structures in Contemporary African Migration.* Lanham, Md.: Lexington Books.

Aryeetey, Ernest, and Ravi Kanbur, eds. 2017. *The Economy of Ghana Sixty Years after Independence.* Oxford: Oxford University Press.

Asare, Kingsley. 2022. "Ghana Records 13.9 Percent Unemployment Rate in 2nd Qtr. of 2022—GSS Report." *Ghanaian Times*, September 2. https://www.ghanaiantimes.com.gh/ghana-records-13-9-unemployment-rate-in-2nd-qtr-of-2022-gss-report/.

Ayittey, George B. N. 2005. *Africa Unchained: The Blueprint for Africa's Future.* New York: Palgrave Macmillan.

Ayomikun, Aladeselu Margaret. 2021. "Nigeria's Failing University System." *Assembly*, February 17. https://assembly.malala.org/apple-news/nigerias-failing-university-system.

Batalova, Jeanne, and Michael Fix. 2021. "Leaving Money on the Table: The Persistence of Brain Waste among College-Educated Immigrants." Washington, D.C.: Migration Policy Institute (June). https://www.migrationpolicy.org/research/brain-waste-college-educated-immigrants.

Berntsen, Dorthe, and David C. Rubin. 2002. "Emotionally Charged Autobiographical Memories across the Life Span: The Recall of Happy, Sad, Traumatic, and Involuntary Memories." *Psychology and Aging* 17(4): 636–52.

Bierman, Noah. 2018. "Trump Concedes Using 'Tough' Language at Meeting on Immigrants but Implies He Didn't Say 'Shithole Countries.'" *Los Angeles Times*, January 12. https://www.latimes.com/la-na-app-essential-washington-updates-trump-20180112-story.html.

Borjas, George. 1985. "Assimilation, Changes in Cohort Quality, and the Earnings of Immigrants." *Journal of Labor Economics* 3(4): 463–89.

———. 1989. "Economic Theory and International Migration." *International Migration Review* 23(3): 4574–85.

———. 1990. *Friends or Strangers: The Impact of Immigrants on the U.S. Economy.* New York: Basic Books.

Bourdieu, Pierre. 1986. "Forms of Capital." In *Handbook of Theory and Research for the Sociology of Education*, edited by John Richardson. New York: Greenwood Press.

Bratsberg, Brent, and James F. Ragan. 2002. "The Impact of Host Country Schooling on Earnings: A Study of Male Immigrants in the United States." *Journal of Human Economics* 37(1): 63–105.

Brückner, Erika. 1990. "Die retrospektive Erhebung von Lebensverlaufen." *Kolner Zeitschrift für Soziologie und Sozialpsychologie* 31: 374–403.

Carling, Jorgen. 2007. "Migration Control and Migrant Fatalities at the Spanish-African Border." *International Migration Review* 41(2): 316–43.

Chavez, Leo R. 2013. *Shadowed Lives: Undocumented Immigrants in American Society.* Belmont, Calif.: Wadsworth.

Chishti, Muzaffar, Julia Gelatt, and Doris Meissner. 2021. "Rethinking the U.S. Legal Immigration System: A Policy Road Map." Washington, D.C.: Migration

Policy Institute (May). https://www.migrationpolicy.org/research/rethinking-us-legal-immigration-road-map.

Chiswick, Barry R. 1978. "The Effect of Americanization on Earnings of Foreign-Born Men." *Journal of Political Economy* 86(5): 897–921.

———. 1982. "Immigrants in the U. S. Labor Market." *Annals of the American Academy of Political and Social Science* 460: 64–72.

Choy, Catherine Ceniza. 2003. *Empire of Care: Nursing and Migration in Filipino American History*. Raleigh, N.C.: Duke University Press.

Chua, Amy, and Jed Rubenfeld. 2014. *The Triple Package: How Three Unlikely Traits Explain the Rise and Fall of Cultural Groups in America*. New York: Penguin Press.

Clemens, Michael A. 2007. "Do Visas Kill? Health Effects of African Health Professional Emigration." Working Paper 114. Washington, D.C.: Center for Global Development (March). https://www.cgdev.org/sites/default/files/13123_file_Clemens_Do_visas_kill_3_.pdf.

CNN. 2017. "Migrants Being Sold as Slaves." November 13. https://www.cnn.com/videos/world/2017/11/13/libya-migrant-slave-auction-lon-orig-md-ejk.cnn.

Coleman, James. 1988. "Social Capital in the Creation of Human Capital." *American Journal of Sociology* 9(4): 95–120.

Comaroff, Jean, and John Comaroff. 2016. *The Truth about Crime: Sovereignty, Knowledge, Social Order*. Chicago: University of Chicago Press.

Cooper, Preston. 2019. "How Many College Dropouts Go Back to School?" *Forbes*, November 11.

Core Welfare Indicators Questionnaire Survey. 2006. Federal Government of Nigeria, Bureau of National Statistics. Available at International Household Survey Network: https://catalog.ihsn.org/index.php/catalog/3905.

Cranston, Sophie. 2018. "Calculating the Migration Industries: Knowing the Successful Expatriate in the Global Mobility Industry." *Journal of Ethnic and Migration Studies* 44(4): 626–43.

Daily Trust. 2021. "Doctors in Mass Exodus amidst NARD Strike." *Daily Trust*, August 23. https://dailytrust.com/doctors-in-mass-exodus-amidst-nard-strike (accessed September 17, 2021).

Davidson, Basil. 1992. *The Black Man's Burden: Africa and the Curse of the Nation-State*. New York: Times Books.

Dawsey, Josh. 2018. "Trump Derides Protections for Immigrants from 'Shithole' Countries." *Washington Post*, January 12. https://www.washingtonpost.com/politics/trump-attacks-protections-for-immigrants-from-shithole-countries-in-oval-office-meeting/2018/01/11/bfc0725c-f711-11e7-91af-31ac729add94_story.html.

De Parle, Jason. 2019. *A Good Provider Is One Who Leaves: One Family and Migration in the 21st Century*. New York: Viking.

Dodoo, Frank Nii-Amoo. 1991. "Earnings Differences among Blacks in America." *Social Science Research* 20(2): 93–108.

———. 1997. "Assimilation Differences among Africans in America." *Social Forces* 76(2): 527–46.

Doyle, Michael. 2013. "Farmers Want Obama to Back Off Immigration Workplace Enforcement." *McClatchy DC*, September 30. https://www.mcclatchydc.com/news/politics-government/congress/article24755269.html (accessed July 11, 2021).

Duleep, Harriet O., and Mark C. Regets. 1997. "The Decline in Immigrant Entry Earnings: Less Transferable Skills or Lower Ability?" *Quarterly Review of Economics and Finance* 37 (special issue on immigration): 189–208.

Dwyer, Colin. 2018. "'Racist' and 'Shameful': How Other Countries Are Responding to Trump's Slur." *The Two-Way*, NPR, January 12. https://www.npr.org/sections/thetwo-way/2018/01/12/577599691/racist-and-shameful-how-other-countries-are-responding-to-trumps-slur.

Egbejule, Eromo. 2020. "The Migration Driven by Developed Countries." *Atlantic*, January 18. https://www.theatlantic.com/international/archive/2020/01/nigeria-canada-skilled-workers-immigration-trudeau/604894/.

Elumoye, Deji, and Emmanuel Addeh. 2022. "Report: Nigeria's $15.7bn 2022 Fuel Subsidy Projection to Exceed All 36 States' Budget." *ThisDay*, September 23. https://www.thisdaylive.com/index.php/2022/09/12/report-nigerias-15-7bn-2022-fuel-subsidy-projection-to-exceed-all-36-states-budget/#.

Ethnologue. 2022. "Nigeria." https://www.ethnologue.com/country/NG (accessed December 12, 2022).

Ette, Ezekiel Umo. 2012. *Nigerian Immigrants in the United States: Race, Identity, and Acculturation*. Lanham, Md.: Lexington Books.

Fahrenthold, David A., and Joshua Partlow. 2019. "5 Questions about President's Trump's Use of Undocumented Workers." *Washington Post*, December 4. https://www.washingtonpost.com/politics/5-questions-about-president-trumps-use-of-undocumented-workers/2019/12/04/29439928-16a2-11ea-a659-7d69641c6ff7_story.html.

Falola, Toyin, and Matthew M. Heaton. 2008a. "Civil Society and Democratic Transition, 1984–2007." In Falola and Heaton, *A History of Nigeria*. Cambridge: Cambridge University Press.

———. 2008b. "Concluding Remarks: Corruption, Anti-Corruption, and the 2007 Elections." In Falola and Heaton, *A History of Nigeria*. Cambridge: Cambridge University Press.

Fitzgerald, David, and David Cook-Martin. 2014. *Culling the Masses: The Democratic Origins of Racist Immigration Policy in the Americas*. Cambridge, Mass.: Harvard University Press.

Foner, Nancy. 2001a. *Islands in the City: West Indian Migration to New York*. Berkeley: University of California Press.

———, ed. 2001b. *New Immigrants in New York*. New York: Columbia University Press.

Frey, William, H. 2021. "What the 2020 Census Will Reveal about America: Stagnating Growth, an Aging Population, and Youthful Diversity." Washington, D.C.: Brookings Institution (January 11). https://www.brookings.edu/research/what-the-2020-census-will-reveal-about-america-stagnating-growth-an-aging-population-and-youthful-diversity/.

Friedberg, Rachel M. 1992. "The Labor Market Assimilation of Immigrants in the United States Labor Market: The Role of Age at Arrival." Providence, R.I.: Brown University (December). https://www.brown.edu/Departments/Economics/Faculty/Rachel_Friedberg/Links/Friedberg%20Age%20at%20Arrival.pdf.

———. 2000. "You Can't Take It with You? Immigrant Assimilation and the Portability of Human Capital." *Journal of Labor Economics* 18(2): 221–51.

Gammeltoft-Hansen, Thomas, and Ninna Nyberg Sorensen, eds. 2012. *The Migration Industry and the Commercialization of International Migration*. Abingdon, U.K.: Routledge.

Gelatt, Jeanne. 2018. "The Diversity Visa Program Holds Lessons for Future Legal Immigration Reform." Washington, D.C.: Migration Policy Institute (February). https://www.migrationpolicy.org/news/diversity-visa-program-holds-lessons-future-legal-immigration-reform.

Ghana Statistical Service and National Communications Authority. 2020. "Household Survey on ICT in Ghana: Abridged Report." March. https://statsghana.gov.gh/gssmain/fileUpload/pressrelease/Household%20Survey%20on%20ICT%20in%20Ghana%20(Abridged)%20new%20(1).pdf.

Gibson, John, and David McKenzie. 2012. "The Economic Consequences of 'Brain Drain' of the Best and Brightest: Microeconomic Evidence from Five Countries." *Economic Journal* 122(560, May): 339–75.

Gibson, John, David McKenzie, Halahingano Rohorua, and Steven Stillman. 2018. "The Long-Term Impacts of International Migration: Evidence from a Lottery." *World Bank Economic Review* 32(1). https://doi.org/10.1093/wber/lhx003.

Glick Schiller, Nina, Linda Basch, and Cristina Blanc-Szanton. 1995. "From Immigrant to Transmigrant: Theorizing Transnational Migration." *Anthropological Quarterly* 68(1): 48–63.

Gonzales, Roberto. 2016. *Lives in Limbo: Undocumented and Coming of Age in America*. Berkeley: University of California Press.

Goodman, Carly Beth. 2016. "Global Game of Chance: The U.S. Diversity Visa Lottery, Transnational Migration, and Cultural Diplomacy in Africa, 1990–2016." PhD diss., Department of Sociology, Temple University.

———. 2019. "Selling Ghana Greener Pastures: Green Card Entrepreneurs, Visa Lottery, and Mobility." *Journal of Social History* 53(1): 27–52.

Gowayed, Heba. 2022. *Refuge: How the State Shapes Human Potential*. Princeton, N.J.: Princeton University Press.

Grabell, Michael. 2017. "Who Would Pay $26,000 to Work in a Chicken Plant?" *ProPublica*, December 28. https://www.propublica.org/article/who-would-pay-26000-to-work-in-a-chicken-plant.

Green, Nancy L., and Roger Waldinger, eds. 2016. *A Century of Transnationalism: Immigrants and Their Homeland Connections*. Urbana: University of Illinois Press.

Guare, John. 1990. *Six Degrees of Separation: A Play*. New York: Random House.

Hagan, Jacqueline. 2008. *Migration Miracle: Faith, Hope, and Meaning on the Undocumented Journey*. Cambridge, Mass.: Harvard University Press.

Hailu, Tekleab Elos, Bernadette M. Mendoza, Maria K. E. Lahman, and Veronica M. Richards. 2012. "Lived Experiences of Diversity Visa Lottery Immigrants in the United States." *The Qualitative Report* 17(article 102): 1–17.

Halter, Marilyn, with Violet M. Showers Johnson. 2010. "Young, Gifted, and West African: Transnational Migrants Growing Up in America." In *Helping Young Refugees and Immigrants Succeed*, edited by Gerald Holton and Gerhard Sonnert. New York: Palgrave Macmillan.

Hamilton, Tod G. 2019. *Immigration and the Remaking of Black America*. New York: Russell Sage Foundation.

Hernández-León, Rubén. 2008. *Metropolitan Migrants: The Migration of Urban Mexicans to the United States*. Berkeley: University of California Press.

———. 2012. "Conceptualizing the Migration Industry." In *The Migration Industry and the Commercialization of International Migration*, edited by Thomas Gammeltoft-Hansen and Ninna Nyberg Sorensen. Abingdon, U.K.: Routledge.

Holtzman, Jon D. 2000. *Nuer Lives, Nuer Journeys: Sudanese Refugees in Minnesota*. Boston: Allyn & Bacon.

Hsin, Amy, and Sofya Aptekar. 2022. "The Violence of Asylum: The Case of Undocumented Chinese Migration to the United States." *Social Forces* 1(3): 1195–1217.

Imoagene, Onoso. 2006. "Do Immigrants with 'Some U.S. Education' Enjoy a Wage Advantage over Immigrants with 'Foreign Education Only'? Revisiting the Question: A Study of Legal, Highly Educated, Male Immigrants in the United States." Master's thesis, Harvard University.

———. 2017a. *Beyond Expectations: Second-Generation Nigerians in the United States and Britain*. Berkeley: University of California Press.

———. 2017b. "Affecting Lives: How Winning the U.S. Diversity Visa Impacts DV Migrants Pre-and Post-Migration." *International Migration* 55(6): 170–83.

Imoagene, Oshomha. 1990. Know Your Country Series (Books 1–6). Ibadan, Nigeria: New-Era Publishers.

Jasso, Guillermina. 2011. "Migration and Stratification." *Social Science Research* 40(5): 1292–1336.

Joubert, Shayna. 2020. "10 Benefits of Having a College Degree." Northeastern University, January 9. Bachelors-completion.northeastern.edu/is-a-bachelors-degree-worth-it/.

Kaba, Amadu Jacky. 2009. "Africa's Migration Brain Drain: Factors Contributing to the Mass Emigration of Africa's Elite to the West." In *The New African Diaspora*, edited by Isidore Okpewho and Nkiru Nzegwu. Bloomington: Indiana University Press.

Kalleberg, Arne L. 2011. *Good Jobs, Bad Jobs: The Rise of Polarized and Precarious Employment Systems in the United States, 1970s to 2000s*. New York: Russell Sage Foundation.

Kamran, Mehwish, Yigu Liang, and Stefan Trines. 2019. "Education in Ghana." *World Education News + Review*, April 16. https://wenr.wes.org/2019/04/education-in-ghana.

Kanu, Daniel, and Henry Okonkwo. 2019. "Nigeria's Education System Suffers as Rich Send Children, Wards Abroad." *Sun*, August 19.

Kazeem, Yomi. 2018. "Nigeria's Stressed-Out Middle-Class Is Trying to Leave in Droves and the Destination Is Canada." *Quartz Africa*, May 11. https://qz.com/africa/1271591/nigerias-stressed-out-middle-class-is-trying-to-leave-in-droves-and-the-destination-is-canada/.

Kessler, Glen. 2018. "President Trump's Consistent Misrepresentation of How the Diversity Visa Lottery Works." *Washington Post*, February 26. https://www.washingtonpost.com/news/fact-checker/wp/2018/02/26/president-trumps-consistent-misrepresentation-of-how-the-diversity-visa-lottery-works/.

Ketefe, Kayode. 2013. "U.S. Visa Lottery Is Brain Drain, Modern Slavery." *National Mirror*, November 17.

Koikkalainen, Saara, and David Kyle. 2016. "Imagining Mobility: The Prospective Cognition Question in Migration Research." *Journal of Ethnic and Migration Studies* 42(5): 759–76.

Konadu-Agyemang, Kwadwo, and Baffour K. Takyi. 2006. "An Overview of African Immigration to the U.S. and Canada." In *The New African Diaspora in North America, Trends, Community Building, and Adaptation*, edited by Kwadwo Konadu-Agyemang, Baffour K. Takyi, and John A. Arthur. Lanham, MD: Lexington Books.

Kremer, Michael. 2011. "The Diversity Visa Lottery: A Study Linking Immigration Politics to Immigrant Characteristics and Experiences." Senior thesis, Department of International Relations, Tufts University.

———. 2014. "The Golden Ticket: Adjustment of African Diversity Visa Lottery Winners in the America." In *Engaging the Diaspora: Migration and African Families*, edited by Pauline Ada Uwakweh, Jerono P. Rotich, and Comfort O. Okpala. Lanham, Md.: Lexington Books.

Kretsedemas, Philip. 2012. *The Immigration Crucible: Transforming Race, Nation, and the Limits of the Law*. New York: Columbia University Press.

Kuhn, Peter, Peter Kooreman, Adriaan R. Stoetevent, and Arie Kapteyn. 2011. "The Effects of Lottery Prizes on Winners and Their Neighbors: Evidence from the Dutch Postcode Lottery." *American Economic Review* 101(5, August): 2226–47.

Kushnick, Louis. 1993. "'We're Here Because You Were There': Britain's Black Population." *Trotter Review* 7(2), 17–19.

Law, Anna O. 2002. "The Diversity Visa Lottery: A Cycle of Unintended Consequences in United States Immigration Policy." *Journal of American Ethnic History* 21(4): 3–29.

Lentz, Carola, and Paul Nugent, eds. 2016. *Ethnicity in Ghana: The Limits of Invention.* New York: Palgrave Macmillan.

Light, Ivan H. 1972. *Ethnic Enterprise in America: Business and Welfare among Chinese, Japanese, and Blacks.* Berkeley: University of California Press.

Lobo, Arun. 2006. "Unintended Consequences: Liberalized U.S. Immigration Law and the African Brain Drain." In *The New African Diaspora in North America: Trends, Community Building, and Adaptation,* edited by Kwodwo Konadu-Agyemang, Baffour K. Takyi, and John A. Arthur. Lanham, Md.: Lexington Books.

Logan, B. Ikubolajeh, and Kevin J. A. Thomas. 2012. "The U.S. Diversity Visa Programme and the Transfer of Skills from Africa." *International Migration* 50(2): 1–19.

Lorenzi, Jane, and Jeanne Batalova. 2019. "Sub-Saharan African Immigrants in the United States." Washington, D.C.: Migration Policy Institute (May 11). https://www.migrationpolicy.org/article/sub-saharan-african-immigrants-united-states.

Ludwig, Bernadette. 2013. "'Wiping the Refugee Dust from My Feet': Advantages and Burdens of Refugee Status and the Refugee Label." *International Migration* 54(1): 5–18.

Markus, Hazel, and Paula Nurius. 1986. "Possible Selves." *American Psychologist* 41(9): 954–69.

Massey, Douglas. 1999. "Why Does Immigration Occur? A Theoretical Synthesis." In *The Handbook of International Migration: The American Experience,* edited by Charles Hirschman, Philip Kasinitz, and Josh DeWind. New York: Russell Sage Foundation.

———. 2007. *Categorically Unequal: The American Stratification System.* New York: Russell Sage Foundation.

Massey, Douglas S., and Katherine Bartley. 2005. "The Changing Legal Status Distribution of Immigrants: A Caution." *International Migration Review* 39(2): 469–84.

Massey, Douglas, Jorge Durand, and Nolan J. Malone. 2003. *Beyond Smoke and Mirrors: Mexican Immigration in an Era of Economic Integration.* New York: Russell Sage Foundation.

McKenzie, David, John Gibson, and Steven Stillman. 2007. "Moving to Opportunity, Leaving Behind What? Evaluating the Initial Effects of a Migration Policy on Incomes and Poverty in Source Areas." *New Zealand Economic Papers* 41(2): 197–224.

Menjívar, Cecilia. 2006. "Liminal Legality: Salvadoran and Guatemalan Immigrants' Lives in the United States." *American Journal of Sociology* 111(4): 999–1037.

Menjívar, Cecilia, and Luisa J. Abrego. 2012. "Legal Violence: Immigration Law and the Lives of Central American Immigrants." *American Journal of Sociology* 117(5): 1380–1421.

Migration Policy Institute. 2015a. "The Ghanaian Diaspora in the United States." Prepared for the Rockefeller Foundation–Aspen Institute Diaspora Program (RAD). Revised May 2015. https://www.migrationpolicy.org/sites/default/files/publications/RAD-Ghana.pdf.

———. 2015b. "The Nigerian Diaspora in the United States." Prepared for the Rockefeller Foundation–Aspen Institute Diaspora Program (RAD). Revised June 2015. https://www.migrationpolicy.org/sites/default/files/publications/RAD-Nigeria.pdf.

Model, Suzanne. 2001. "Where New York's West Indians Work." In *Islands in the City: West Indian Migration to New York*, edited by Nancy Foner. Berkeley: University of California.

Model, Suzanne. 2008. *West Indian Immigrants: A Black Success Story?* New York: Russell Sage Foundation.

Muggenburg, Hannah. 2021. "Beyond the Limits of Memory? The Reliability of Retrospective Data in Travel Research." *Transportation Research Part A: Policy and Practice* 145(March): 302–18.

National Academies of Sciences, Engineering, and Medicine. 2017. *The Economic and Fiscal Consequences of Immigration*. Washington, D.C.: National Academies Press.

National Foreign Assessment Center, United States, and United States Central Intelligence Agency. 2022. *The World Factbook*. Washington, D.C.: Central Intelligence Agency.

Newton, Andowah. 2005. "Injecting Diversity into U.S. Immigration Policy: The Diversity Visa Programme and the Missing Discourse on Its Impact on African Immigration to the United States." *Cornell International Law Journal* 38(5): 1049–82.

New York City Department of City Planning. 2013. "Newest New Yorkers: Characteristics of the City's Foreign-born Population." NYC Planning. https://www.nyc.gov/assets/planning/download/pdf/planning-level/nyc-population/nny2013/nny_2013.pdf.

Nigerian National Bureau of Statistics. 2020. "2019 Poverty and Inequality in Nigeria: Executive Summary." National Bureau of Statistics. https://nigerianstat.gov.ng/elibrary/read/1092#:~:text=In%20Nigeria%2040.1%20percent%20of,considered%20poor%20by%20national%20standards.

Nugent, Paul. 2012. *Africa since Independence: A Comparative History*, 2nd ed. New York: Palgrave Macmillan.

O'Neill, Aaron. 2023. "Ghana: Unemployment Rate from 1999 to 2022." Statista, June 1. https://www.statista.com/statistics/808481/unemployment-rate-in-ghana/.

Oberauer, Klaus, Ulrich Mayr, and Rainer Kluwe. 2006. "Gedächtnis und Wissen." In *Lehrbuch Allgemeine Psychologie*, edited by Hans Spada. Bern: Hans Huber.

Olurounbi, Ruth. 2021. "Nigeria Unemployment Rate Rises to 33%, Second Highest on Global List." *Bloomberg*, March 15. https://www.bloomberg.com

/news/articles/2021-03-15/nigeria-unemployment-rate-rises-to-second-highest-on-global-list.

Ortiga, Yasmin. 2018a. "Constructing a Global Education Hub: The Unlikely Case of Manila." *Discourse: Studies in the Cultural Politics of Education* 39(5): 767–81.

———. 2018b. *Emigration, Employability, and Higher Education in the Philippines*. Oxford: Routledge.

Oyebamji, Sunday I., and Abimbola Adekoye. 2019. "Nigerians' Migration to the United States of America." *Journal of African Foreign Affairs* 6(1): 165–80.

Painter, Gary, Stuart Gabriel, and Dowell Myers. 2001. "Race, Immigrant Status, and Housing Tenure Choice." *Journal of Urban Economics* 49: 150–67.

Parrenas Salazar, Rhacel. 2021. *Unfree: Migrant Domestic Work in Arab States*. Stanford, Calif.: Stanford University Press.

Pew Research Center. 2017. "Spring 2017 Global Attitudes Survey." https://www.pewresearch.org/global/dataset/spring-2017-survey-data/.

———. 2018a. "Spring 2018 Global Attitudes Survey." https://www.pewresearch.org/global/dataset/september-2018-u-s-survey-data/.

———. 2018b. "At Least a Million Sub-Saharan Africans Moved to Europe since 2010." Washington, D.C.: Pew Research Center (March 22). https://www.pewresearch.org/global/2018/03/22/at-least-a-million-sub-saharan-africans-moved-to-europe-since-2010/.

Piot, Charles. 2010. *Nostalgia for the Future: West Africa after the Cold War*. Chicago: University of Chicago Press.

Piot, Charles, with Kodjo Nicolas Batema. 2019. *The Fixer: Visa Lottery Chronicles*. Durham, N.C.: Duke University Press.

Portes, Alejandro, and Rubén Rumbaut. 2014. *Immigrant America: A Portrait*. Berkeley: University of California Press.

Rotimi, Sankore. 2005. "Africa: Killing Us Softly." *New African* 445: 8–12.

Sauder, Michael. 2020. "A Sociology of Luck." *Sociological Theory* 38(3): https://doi.org/10.1177/0735275120941178.

Schapendonk, Joris. 2018. "Navigating the Migration Industry: Migrants Moving through an African-European Web of Facilitation/Control." *Journal of Ethnic and Migration Studies* 44(4): 663–79.

Schapendonk, Joris, and Griet Steel. 2014. "Following Migrant Trajectories: The Im/mobility of Sub-Saharan Africans en Route to the European Union." *Annals of the Association of American Geographers* 104(2): 262–70.

Scheoni, Robert F. 1997. "New Evidence of the Economic Progress of Foreign-Born Men in the 1970s and 1980s." *Journal of Human Resources* 32(4): 683–740.

Schraeder, Peter J. 2020. *Understanding Contemporary Africa*. Boulder, Colo.: Lynne Reinner Publishers.

Seamster, Louise, and Raphael Charron-Chenier. 2017. "Predatory Inclusion and Education Debt: Rethinking the Racial Wealth Gap." *Social Currents* 4(3): 199–207.

Showers, Fumilayo. 2020. "'Nursing Was the Talk around Town': West African Immigrant Communities, Labor Recruitment, and the Crises of Care in Advanced Economies." In *Liberal Arts Perspectives on Globalization and Transnationalism: Within the Knot*, edited by Hyun Wu Lee and Mark van de Logt. Newcastle upon Tyne, U.K.: Cambridge Scholars Publishing.

Smith, Robert C. 2001. "Mexicans: Economic, Political, and Educational Problems and Prospects." In *New Immigrants in New York*, edited by Nancy Foner. New York: Columbia University Press.

Smith, James P., and Barry Edmonston. 1997. *The New Americans: Economic, Demographic and Fiscal Effects of Immigration*. Washington, D.C.: National Academy Press.

Spada, Hans, ed. 2006. *Lehrbuch Allgemeine Psychologie*. Bern: Hans Huber.

Stewart, James B., and Thomas Hyclak. 1984. "An Analysis of the Earnings Profiles of Immigrants." *Review of Economics and Statistics* 66(2): 292–96.

Sudman, Seymour, Adam Finn, and Linda Lannom. 1984. "The Use of Bounded Recall Procedures in Single Interviews." *Public Opinion Quarterly* 48(2): 520–24.

Swidler, Ann. 1986. "Culture in Action: Symbols and Strategies." *American Sociological Review* 51(2): 273–86. https://www.doi.org/10.2307/2095521.

Talarico, Jennifer M., Kevin S. Labar, and David S. Rubin. 2004. "Emotional Intensity Predicts Autobiographical Memory Experience." *Memory and Cognition* 32(7): 1118–32.

Tamir, Christine. 2019. "As Elections Near, Nigerians View Their Country's Economy and Political System Negatively." Washington, D.C.: Pew Research Center (February 12). https://www.pewresearch.org/fact-tank/2019/02/12/as-elections-near-nigerians-view-their-countrys-economy-and-political-system-negatively/.

Tatum, Sophie. 2017. "Trump to End Protected Status for Haiti." *CNN Politics*, CNN, November 21. https://www.cnn.com/2017/11/20/politics/dhs-temporary-protected-status-haiti/index.html.

Teke, John, and Waleed Navarro. 2016. "DHS Factsheet: Nonimmigrant Admissions and Estimated Nonimmigrant Individuals: 2016." Washington: U.S. Department of Homeland Security, Office of Immigration Statistics (January). https://www.dhs.gov/sites/default/files/publications/Nonimmigrant%20Admissions%20and%20Estimated%20Nonimmigrant%20Individuals%20Fact%20Sheet%202016_0.pdf.

Thomas, Kevin J. A. 2011. "What Explains the Increasing Trend in African Emigration to the U.S.?" *International Migration Review* 45(1): 3–28.

Thompson, Charles P., John J. Skowronski, Steen F. Larsen, and Andrew L. Betz. 1996. *Autobiographical Memory: Remembering What and Remembering When*. Abingdon, U.K.: Routledge.

Tu, Siqi. 2020. "Destination Diploma: How Chinese Upper-Middle-Class Families 'Outsource' Secondary Education to the United States." PhD diss., Graduate Center, City University of New York.

U.S. Census Bureau. 2018. "Older People Projected to Outnumber Children for First Time in U.S. History." Press release CB18-41, March 13. https://www.census.gov/newsroom/press-releases/2018/cb18-41-population-projections.html.

U.S. Department of Homeland Security. 2020. "Fiscal Year 2019: Entry/Exit Overstay Report." March 30, 2020. https://www.dhs.gov/sites/default/files/publications/20_0513_fy19-entry-and-exit-overstay-report.pdf.

———. 2017. "Year Book of Immigration Statistics 2008–2017." https://www.dhs.gov/immigration-statistics/yearbook.

U.S. State Department, Bureau of Consular Affairs. 2017. "Number of Selected Entrants for Recent DV Programs 2009-2017." https://travel.state.gov/content/travel/en/us-visas/immigrate/diversity-visa-program-entry/diversity-visa-program-statistics.html.

———. 2020. "Diversity Visa Program Statistics." https://travel.state.gov/content/travel/en/us-visas/immigrate/diversity-visa-program-entry/diversity-visa-program-statistics.html.

———. 2021. "Adjusted Refusal Rates, B-Visas Only, by Nationality Fiscal Years 2006–2020." https://travel.state.gov/content/travel/en/legal/visa-law0/visa-statistics/nonimmigrant-visa-statistics.html.

Van der Vaart, Wander, and Tina Glasner. 2010. "Personal Landmarks as Recall Aids in Survey Interviews." *Field Methods* 23(1): 37–56.

Van der Velde, Martin, and Ton van Naerssen. 2011. "People, Borders, Trajectories: An Approach to Cross-Border Mobility and Immobility in and to the European Union." *Area* 43(2): 218–24.

———. 2015. *Mobility and Migration Choices: Thresholds to Crossing Borders*. Abingdon, U.K.: Routledge.

Waldinger, Roger, ed. 2001. *Strangers at the Gates: New Immigrants in Urban America*. Berkeley: University of California Press.

Walter, Nicholas, Philippe Bourgois, and H. Margarita Loinaz. 2004. "Masculinity and Undocumented Labor Migration: Injured Latino Day Laborers in San Francisco." *Social Science and Medicine* 59(6): 1159–68.

Watkins, Eli, and Abby Phillip. 2018. "Trump Decries Immigrants from 'Shithole Countries' Coming to U.S." *CNN Politics*, CNN, January 12. https://www.cnn.com/2018/01/11/politics/immigrants-shithole-countries-trump/index.html.

White House Briefing Room. 2023. "Fact Sheet: Biden-Harris Administration Announces New Border Enforcement Actions." Washington: The White House (January 5). https://www.whitehouse.gov/briefing-room/statements-releases/2023/01/05/fact-sheet-biden-harris-administration-announces-new-border-enforcement-actions/.

Wilson, Jill H. 2019. "The Diversity Immigrant Program." Washington: Congressional Report Service.

World Bank. 2020. "Addressing Youth Unemployment in Ghana Needs Urgent Action, Calls New World Bank Report." September 29. https://www.worldbank

.org/en/news/press-release/2020/09/29/addressing-youth-unemployment-in-ghana-needs-urgent-action.

———. 2022a. "GDP per Capita (Current US$)—Nigeria." https://data.worldbank.org/indicator/NY.GDP.PCAP.CD?locations=NG.

———. 2022b. "GDP per Capita, PPP (Current International $)—Nigeria." https://data.worldbank.org/indicator/NY.GDP.PCAP.PP.CD?locations=NG.

———. 2022c. "The World Bank Indicator." https://data.worldbank.org/indicator/NY.GDP.PCAP.CD?locations=NG.

Zolberg, Aristide. 2006. *A Nation by Design: Immigration Policy in the Fashioning of America.* New York: Russell Sage Foundation.

Index

Tables and figures are listed in **boldface**.

ACS (American Community Survey), 48–49, 52
Adebayo, Sakiru, 38
affective Americans, 7, 142, 160
African Americans: African immigrants compared, 49, 53; Congressional Black Caucus, 17, 23; ethnic employment niche of, 138; relations with African immigrants, 64, 204n5
African immigrants: African Americans, experiences with, 64, 204n5; African Americans compared, 49, 53; brain waste and underemployment of, 192–93n80; education levels of, 1, 22, 147; goals and dreams of, 152–56; history of migration, 19–22, 189–90nn33–34; impactful experiences of study respondents, **181**; increase in, 2; IRCA adjustment of status for, 147; migration difficulties of, 66, 197–98n13; motivations for emigration, 4, 37–40, 54, 55, 117, 165, 170–71; sharing experiences and information on DV Program, 4, 56, 58–61, 63, 65, 69; stereotypes of, 164, 204n5; stratified population in United States, 146–48; studies on, 1–2, 183–84n2. *See also* disrupted undergraduates; Diversity Immigrant Visa Program
African Union, 17
Afrobarometer survey, 39
aging U.S. population, 166, 207n29
agricultural labor, 165–66
Akresh, Ilana Restone, 31–33, 183n2, 186n25
Alba, Richard, 13, 137
American Community Survey (ACS), 48–49, 52
Asian immigrants: DV Program and, 18–19, 22; employment outcomes for, **178–80**; ethnic niches in employment, 137, 139, 198n4; history of migration, 14–15; occupational downgrading of, 32; Visa Waiver Program and, 164
assimilation: employment and, 29–36, **36**, 183n2, 186n1; of human capital immigrants, 13–14; migrapolicy interventions and, 5–6; reception of immigrants in host country and, 31, 38; support networks and, 172

Basch, Linda, 185*n*23
Batalova, Jeanne, 192*n*77
Batema, Kodjo Nicolas, 102, 107
Benson, Sean, 15, 188*n*13
Berman, Howard, 15–16
Berman visa program, 15–16
Beyond Expectations (Imoagene), 54, 64, 204*n*5
Biden, Joe, 22, 173, 175, 205*n*25
bilateral labor agreements (BLAs), 205–6*n*29
Blanc-Szanton, Cristina, 185*n*23
Boehner, John, 22
Boko Haram, 46
Borjas, George, 30
Bourdieu, Pierre, 98, 145, 200*n*19
brain drain: benefits to sending country through remittances, 175; Ghana and, 54, 111; minimizing, 91, 205–6*n*29; Nigeria and, 48, 54; resulting from DV Program, 3–4, 159, 184–85*n*18
brain gain, 175, 184*n*18, 206*n*29
brain waste and occupational downgrading, 14, 32–33, 169, 173–74, 192*n*77, 192–93*n*80
Bratsberg, Brent, 192*n*65
Buhari, Muhammadu, 42, 48, 71

Canadian immigration policy, 168, 172
capitalism, 40, 166, 168
Caribbean immigrants. *See* Latin American and Caribbean immigrants
chain migration. *See* family reunification migration policy
Charron-Chenier, Raphael, 202*n*10
children of immigrants: economic benefits to United States, 167; education and, 70–71, 120, 204*n*5; ethnic niches in employment, rejection of, 139; immigrant bargain, 120, 173; increased opportunities for, 155–56; migrating with parents, 150–51; undocumented status of parents and, 173
Chiswick, Barry, 29, 191–92*n*65
Citizenship Act (2021), 22
cognitive migration, 73, 117, 122, 201*n*5
Coleman, James, 145
colonialism: Caribbean immigrants in United Kingdom, 21, 169; cultural clashes created by, 41–42, 195*n*22; legacy in Africa, 41–42, 45, 47, 50, 52, 54, 147, 199*n*12
Comaroff, Jean and John, 108
cultural capital, 98, 200*n*19
cultural economy, 77–78
cultures of migration, 7

demographic changes, 19, 166, 207*n*29
discrimination: Black people in the United States and, 63–64; employment outcomes and, 31, 193*n*83; ethnic niches in employment and, 137; immigration policy and, 20–21
disrupted undergraduates, 116–40; continuing education in United States, 117–18, 121–30, **124–26**; decisions to leave college, 120–21; disrupted undergraduates as subgroup, 139–40; economic and ethnic employment niches, 118, 132–39; employment outcomes for immigrants, 29, 123, **124–26**, 127–29; as negative migrapolicy intervention, 6, 88, 118–19, 139–40, 162, 169; possible selves and cognitive migration, 121–23, 136, 140, 160–61; recommendations for improvements to DV Program, 174–75, 205–6*n*29; social support, lack of, 130–32; visa entrepreneurs

marketing to secondary school and university students, 84–88, 119, 162
Diversity Immigrant Visa Program (DV Program): African and Caribbean migration, 19–22, 189–90*nn*33–34; application steps in, 24–29, **26–27**, 96, 191*nn*55–56, 200*n*14; benefits of, 5–7, **8–9**, 12, 142–46, 160, 184–85*n*18; chances of selection, 158, 204*n*2; costs associated with, 28, 29, 79, 100, 108–10, 121, 150–52; defined, 1, 183*n*1; documentation and passport requirements of, 18–19, 57–58, 91–95, 163–64, 189*n*30, 190–91*n*53, 199–200*n*13; educational attainment levels of immigrants, 1, 22; educational or work experience requirements of, 13, 17, 22–23, 81, 85, 186–87*n*2, 190*n*48; employment outcomes for, 29–36, **36**, 117–19, 123, **124–26**, 128–29, 172–73, **178–80**, 191–92*n*65; families, benefits for, 6–7, 61, 67–72; global migration patterns, effect on, 163–65; history of, 14–17, 187*n*7; implementation and administration of, 4–5, 108; importance of, 2–4; increase in visas through, 22; interviews and ethnographic observation on, 7, 10, 185–86*n*25; language used to market, 23–24, 87, 119, 127, 159; lawful immigration status obtained through, 66–67; learning about, 56–57; limits of, 16, 25, 188*n*20; motivations for applying, 4, 55, 58–72, 117, 165; political debate about, 17–19, 22, 166, 175; recommendations for improvements to, 12, 169–76, 205–6*n*29; stages of decision making in, 57–58; suboptimization of immigrants' potential, 5, 14, 127, 159–61, 164, 169, 173–74; time limit to emigrate, 58, 96, 191*n*55, 200*n*14; unintended consequences of, 3–4, 5–6, 12, 90. *See also* disrupted undergraduates; fraud; visa entrepreneurs
Donnelly, Brian, 15, 187–88*n*13
Donnelly visa program, 15–16, 187–88*n*13

EB-5 visa program, 204*n*4
education: of African immigrants, 1, 22, 147; brain waste of immigrants and, 14, 32–33, 169, 173–74, 192*n*77, 192–93*n*80; cultural capital and, 98; discontinuing, 123; of DV Program immigrants, 1, 22; DV Program requirements for, 13, 17, 22–23, 81, 85, 186–87*n*2, 190*n*48; educational consultant industry for elite families, 199*n*5; employment outcomes and, 62–65, 119, 183–84*n*2, 194*n*87; in Ghana, 52, 69–71, 120, 129–30; of Ghanaians in United States, 53; migrant labor–exporting countries and investments in, 205–7*n*29; in Nigeria, 22, 23, 47–48, 69–71, 120; of Nigerians in United States, 48; social mobility and, 119, 155, 204*n*5; student debt and, 118, 119, 127, 129–30, 201–2*n*10; from United States vs. other countries, 30–31, 69, 71, 119–20, 123, 169, 191–92*n*65. *See also* disrupted undergraduates; human capital
employer-sponsored immigrants, 32–36, **36**
employment outcomes: brain waste and occupational downgrading of immigrants, 14, 32–33, 169, 173–74, 192*n*77, 192–93*n*80; for DV Program immigrants, 29–36, **36**, 117–19, 123, **124–26**, 128–29, 172–73, **178–80**,

191–92*n*65; education and, 62–65, 119, 183–84*n*2, 194*n*87; education challenges and, 127–29; ethnic niches and, 118, 132–39, 164, 186*n*1; human capital immigrants and, 14; job competition with native-born citizens, 167, 204–5*nn*13–14; labor demand in United States and, 12, 165–66, 171, 204*n*4; migrant labor–exporting countries and, 205–7*n*29; for Nigerians in United States, 49; transferable skills and, 30; for undocumented immigrants, 164, 173, 186*n*1
ethnic communities, 35–36, 194*n*86
ethnic niches in employment, 118, 132–39, 164, 186*n*1
European immigrants: DV Program and, 18–22, 189–90*nn*33–34; employment outcomes for, 29, **178–80**; history of migration, 14–16; occupational downgrading of, 32; Visa Waiver Program and, 67, 164
exchange rates, 43–44, 71, 169
exploitation: brain waste and occupational downgrading of immigrants, 14, 32–33, 169, 173–74, 192*n*77, 192–93*n*80; colonialism and, 169; in ethnic employment niches, 137–38; of undocumented immigrants, 173, 186*n*1; visa entrepreneurs and, 99–115, 162–63

Falola, Toyin, 45
families: DV Program and separation of, 28–29, 103, 148–52, 198*n*15; DV Program benefits for, 6–7, 61, 67–72; financing DV Program costs, 101–2, 121, 162–63; remittances to, 71–72, 128, 131–32, 152–55, 175, 184*n*18
family reunification migration policy: abuse of, 146, 148–49; criticism of, 17–18, 171; earnings outcomes for immigrants, 35–36, **36**; Hart-Celler Act preference system, 14, 187*n*7; Immigration Reform and Control Act facilitating, 15; occupational downgrading and, 32–33; pioneer family member starting, 68, 194*n*86; rate of migration through, 2, 143–44; for spouses, 149–50; wait times for, 194*n*86, 198*n*15
farmworkers, 165–66
Feinstein, Dianne, 165–66
fiancée visas, 149–50
fictive kinship ties, 6, 102–9, 146, 148–49, 165, 200*n*24
Filipino immigrants: ethnic niches in employment, 137–38, 198*n*4, 206*n*29; Philippines migration governance model and, 111, 138, 198*n*4, 205–7*n*29
Fix, Michael, 192*n*77
The Fixer: Visa Lottery Chronicles (Piot), 107
fraud: DNA testing requirements and, 148–49; fictive kinship ties, 6, 102–9, 146, 148–49, 165, 200*n*24; prevention efforts, 18–19, 57, 90, 107–9, 149; visa entrepreneurs identifying, 112–14
Friedberg, Rachel, 191*n*65

gender: employment and skills requirements for visa, 21; occupational downgrading of immigrants, 33
German immigration policy, 168
Ghana: country history and overview, 49–52, 196–97*n*50; currency exchange rates, 71; education in, 22, 69–71, 120, 129–30; employment in, 51–52, 61–64; internet use in, 89; migrant population in United States, 52–53; motivations for emigration from, 37–40, 54; number of

applications for DV Program from, 3, 189n33; number of DV Program immigrants from, 3, 184n17; policy improvements necessary for, 53–54; prevention of emigration from, 91, 170–71; reduction in DV Program applicants, 188n23; visa entrepreneurs and government relations, 110–12; visa refusal rates for, 66
Global Attitudes Survey (Pew Research Center), 39, 40, 74, 140, 195n5
Goodman, Carly, 90–91, 185n24, 188n13
Gowayed, Heba, 194n85
Gowon, Yakubu, 37
Great Recession (2008), 45

Haiti: refugees from, 21; TPS designation for, 17, 188n23
Hart-Celler Act (1965), 14, 20, 187n7
Heaton, Matthew, 45
Hernández-León, Rubén, 199n5
Hispanic immigrants. *See* Latin American and Caribbean immigrants
H-1B visas, 32–36, **36**
human capital: defined, 185n22; human capital immigrants, 13–14, 186n1; immigrant human capital investment model, 194n87; remittances facilitating increase in, 175. *See also* disrupted undergraduates
human trafficking, 76, 199n5
Hyclak, Thomas, 192n65

IMF (International Monetary Fund), 37, 43, 51, 165
immigrant bargain, 120, 173. *See also* children of immigrants
immigrant human capital investment (IHCI) model, 194n87

Immigration Act (1924), 20, 21
Immigration and Nationality Act (1965), 14, 20, 187n7
Immigration Reform and Control Act (IRCA, 1986), 15–16, 20–21, 147, 175
imperialism, 165, 169–70
infant mortality rates, 48
International Monetary Fund (IMF), 37, 43, 51, 165
internet access and computer use: cultural capital and, 98; DV Program online application, 57, 75; in Ghana, 89; in Nigeria, 89; sharing DV Program application through, 56–57; visa entrepreneurs and, 75, 80–81, 89–90, 92, 99
Irish Immigration Reform Movement (IIRM), 15–16, 188n13

"Japa syndrome", 38
Johnson-Reed Act (1924), 20, 21

Koikkalainen, Saara, 73
Kremer, Michael, 183n2
Kyle, David, 73

labor immigrants, 127, 165–66, 186n1
Latin American and Caribbean immigrants: DV Program and, 20–22, 189–90nn33–34; employment outcomes for, 29, **178–80**; ethnic niches in employment, 137, 186n1; history of migration, 14–16; human trafficking of, 199n5; legal migration pathways for, 173; occupational downgrading of, 32, 192–93n80; refugees from, 21, 173, 205n25; TPS program and, 17, 188n23; undocumented status and, 144, 202–3n1; in United Kingdom, colonialism and, 169
lawful permanent resident (LPR) status: benefits for children of

immigrants, 155–56; benefits of, 3, 6–7, 13, 79, 187n5; of DV Program immigrants, 66–67; negative consequences of, 148–50; pathways to, 146; as positive migrapolicy intervention, 6, 139, 142–45, 162; separation of families to obtain, 150–52, 162; social stratification of immigrants, 146–48; support of families in home countries through, 152–55

legal violence against immigrants, 3, 34, 164

life expectancy rates, 48

literacy rates, 93, 195n18

lottery. *See* Diversity Immigrant Visa Program

Markus, Hazel, 121–22

Massey, Douglas, 203n1

migrant categories, 186n1

migrant labor–exporting countries, 205–7n29

migrapolicy interventions: defined, 5; disrupted education, 6, 88, 118–19, 139–40, 162, 169; families, outcomes for, 6–7, 162; lawful permanent residency, 6, 139, 142–45, 162; overview, 5–6, **8–9**; visa entrepreneurs, negative consequences created by, 6, 99–115, **112–13**, 162–63

migration governance model, 111, 138, 198n4, 205–7n29

migration industry (MI): advertising DV Program information, 57; human trafficking, 76, 199n5; interviews of employees, 10; market creation of, 6, 185n24; non-state actors involved in, 75–76, 198n1, 198–99nn3–5. *See also* visa entrepreneurs

migration rates, 19, 21–22, 144, 189n32

Minihane, Sean, 15

Morrison, Bruce, 16

National Association of Credential Evaluation Services (NACES), 127

National Student Clearing House, 123

Navarro, Waleed, 189n32

Nee, Victor, 13, 137

New Immigrant Survey (NIS), 22, 31–36, **36**, 171–72, 183n2, 205n27

Nigeria: Canada, Nigerians migrating to, 168; country history and overview, 40–48, 195n18, 195n22; currency exchange rates, 71; DV Program status in, 3; education in, 22, 23, 47–48, 69–71, 120; employment in, 46, 61–64; internet use in, 89; migrant population in United States, 48–49, 196n47; migration governance model and, 206n29; motivations for emigration from, 37–40, 54; number of applications for DV Program from, 3; number of DV Program immigrants from, 3, 184n17; policy improvements necessary for, 53–54; prevention of emigration from, 91, 170–71; visa entrepreneurs and government relations, 111–12; visa refusal rates for, 66

Nurius, Paula, 121–22

Obama, Barack, 45, 165

occupational downgrading and brain waste, 14, 32–33, 169, 173–74, 192n77, 192–93n80

Pew Research Center Global Attitudes Survey, 39, 40, 74, 140, 195n5

Philippines migration governance model, 111, 138, 198n4, 205–7n29

Piot, Charles, 40, 102, 107–9, 185n24, 200n24

Pirro, Jeanine, 18
presidential parole power, 14–15

race and ethnicity: brain waste and underemployment of immigrants, 192–93n80; criticisms of DV Program based on, 17; DV Program and, 19; economic outcomes for immigrants, 29–31; employment outcomes for immigrants, 193n83; immigration policy and, 20; student debt and, 130, 201–2n10; U.S. demographics and immigration policy, 19, 166; White immigrant outcomes, 31. *See also* discrimination
Ragan, James, 192n65
Reagan, Ronald, 175
Refuge (Gowayed), 194n85
Refugee Act (1980), 20
refugees: during Cold War, 14; earnings outcomes for, 35, **36**; government support for, 35, 145, 172, 193–94n85; increase in, 20–21, 205n25; occupational downgrading of, 32–33; social capital of, 145
remittances, 71–72, 128, 131–32, 152–55, 175, 184n18

Saudi Arabian immigration policy, 168
Schiller, Nina Glick, 185n23
Schraeder, Peter, 195n22
Seamster, Louise, 202n10
social capital. *See* support networks and social capital
social mobility: benefits of DV Program visas, 5, 159–60; education and, 119, 155, 204n5; ethnic niches and, 138; legal status and, 173; migration to achieve, 146; remittances facilitating, 154–55
social stratification: college education and, 140; of DV Program applicants, 80–81, 101, 163–64; internet access and, 89; internet and computer use, 98; lawful permanent resident status and, 146–48; undocumented immigrants and, 3, 173
sponsors of immigrants: DV Program requirements for, 28, 58; employers as, 32–36, **36**; lack of support from, 144–45. *See also* family reunification migration policy
Stewart, James, 192n65
student visas, 67, 144, 197–98n13, 199n5
support networks and social capital: disrupted undergraduates and lack of, 130–32; DV Program immigrants and, 35–36, 69; failure of, 144–45; governments boosting, 145; pioneer immigrants creating, 194n86; reception of immigrant groups and, 31; of refugees, 32, 34, 35, 145; successful immigrant outcomes and, 172; of undocumented immigrants, 203n1
Swidler, Ann, 98

Teke, John, 189n32
Temporary Protected Status (TPS) program, 20, 147, 188n23
terrorist groups, 46
Tinubu, Bola, 44
Togo, fictive kinship ties to obtain visas in, 102, 107, 109, 200n24
Trump, Donald, 1, 17–19, 166, 175, 204n8

underemployment, 33, 192n77, 192–93n80
undocumented immigrants: attempts to reduce migration of, 173; brain waste and underemployment of, 192–93n80; employed by Donald Trump, 166, 204n8; employment

challenges for, 164, 173, 186*n*1; human trafficking of, 76, 199*n*5; IRCA adjustment of status for, 21, 147; Irish lobby for immigration policy reform, 15, 187–88*n*13; labor demand and necessity of, 165–66; legal violence against, 3, 34, 164; overstaying visas, 143–44, 197–98*nn*12–13; regularizing status, 146; social stratification and, 3, 173; undesirable outcomes for, 142–43, 202–3*n*1
unemployment: in Ghana, 51–52, 61; in Nigeria, 46, 61
United Kingdom immigration policy, 21, 168–69. *See also* colonialism
U.S. Census Bureau, 29–30, 166
U.S. immigration policy: application fees, 28, 100, 108–9; benefits provided by immigrants, 127, 165–67; discrimination and, 20–21; EB-5 visa program, 204*n*4; fiancée visas, 149–50; fraud prevention efforts, 18–19, 57, 90, 107–9, 148–49; history of, 20–21; H-1B visas, 32–36, **36**; increase in Diversity Visas, 22; recommendations for improvements to, 12, 169–76, 205–6*n*29; student visas, 67, 144, 197–98*n*13, 199*n*5; unattainable requirements of, 89, 91–92; visa entrepreneurs, creating market for, 6, 77–78, 90–92, 115, 185*n*24; visa refusal rates, 66; Visa Waiver Program, 67, 144, 164. *See also* Diversity Immigrant Visa Program; family reunification migration policy; migrapolicy interventions; undocumented immigrants

Van der Velde, Martin, 114
van Naerssen, Ton, 114
visa entrepreneurs, 75–115; defined, 75; expertise and services of, 75–76, 89–93; fees charged by, 77, 81, 88, 95, 97, 99–102, 162–63; fictive kinship ties encouraged by, 102–7, 200*n*24; government relations, 110–14, **112–13**; intrepid vs. doubting customers of, 97–99; locating winners, 88, 96–97; market creation of, 6, 77–78, 90, 92, 108, 115, 162, 185*n*24; as negative migrapolicy intervention, 6, 99–115, **112–13**, 162–63; record keeping of, 88, 93–95, 99–100; secondary school and university students, marketing to, 84–88, 119, 162 (*see also* disrupted undergraduates); street tents and outreach of, 78–81, **82–84**
visa lottery. *See* Diversity Immigrant Visa Program
visa refusal rates, 66
Visa Waiver Program (VWP), 67, 144, 164

Wilson, Jill, 205*n*27
World Bank, 43, 51, 165, 206*n*29
world systems theory, 40